4L

My Sister a  **W9-AKS-304**

i

By J.R.Ackerley

The Prisoners of War

Poems by Four Authors (with Archibald Y. Campbell,
Edward Davison and Frank Kendon)

Hindoo Holiday

Escapers All

My Dog Tulip

We Think the World of You

My Father and Myself

E.M. Forster: A Portrait

Micheldever & Other Poems

My Sister and Myself

THE DIARIES OF
J.R. ACKERLEY

Edited and introduced by
Francis King

OXFORD UNIVERSITY PRESS
1990

Oxford University Press, Walton Street, Oxford OX2 6DP

Oxford New York Toronto
Delhi Bombay Calcutta Madras Karachi
Petaling Jaya Singapore Hong Kong Tokyo
Nairobi Dar es Salaam Cape Town
Melbourne Auckland

and associated companies in
Berlin Ibadan

Oxford is a trade mark of Oxford University Press

First published 1982 by Hutchinson & Co. Ltd, an imprint of the
Hutchinson Publishing Group
First issued as an Oxford University Press paperback 1990

British Library Cataloguing in Publication Data
Ackerley, J. R. (Joe Randolph), 1896–1967
My sister and myself: the diaries of J. R. Ackerley.
1. English literature. Ackerley, J. R. (Joe Randolph) 1896–1967
I. Title II. King, Francis, 1923–
828.91209
ISBN 0–19–282732–4

Printed in Great Britain by
Clays Ltd.
Bungay, Suffolk

Illustrations

'The beautiful Nancy Ackerley' — with her brother in Richmond,
  c. 1920
  (Reproduced by permission of Richard Shone)
Ackerley and E. M. Forster on holiday in Dover in the late 1930s
  (Reproduced by permission of Richard Shone)
Ackerley with Jack (Sebastian) Sprott and his sister Velda
  (Reproduced by permission of Richard Shone)
Ackerley with an Athenian kitten
  (Reproduced by permission of Francis King)
Ackerley with two Japanese students
  (Reproduced by permission of Francis King)
Ackerley with his dog Queenie (Tulip in *My Dog Tulip*)
  (Reproduced by permission of Francis King)
Ackerley and his sister Nancy (portraits by Don Bachardy)
  (Reproduced by permission of the artist)
Siegfried Sassoon in 1915
  (Reproduced by permission of the Hulton-Deutsch Collection)
Siegfried Sassoon as an old man
  (Reproduced by permission of Times Newspapers Limited)
James Kirkup
  (Reproduced by permission of James Kirkup. Photograph: Tamaki)

Introduction

I was in my house in Brighton on the morning of 4 June 1967 when Joe Ackerley's sister, Nancy West, telephoned to tell me that she had found him dead in his bed. She was both composed, as she recounted the circumstances, and commanding, as she went on, 'You're his executor, aren't you, dear? I think you'd better come up as soon as you can manage'; and since I had rarely known her to be the first of these things and had never known her to be the second, I remember that, mixed with my shock and grief at the news, there was also amazement.

By the time that I had reached the dilapidated top-floor flat, 17 Star and Garter Mansions, above a cavernous pub overlooking the Putney towpath, both Sonia Orwell, who had hurried round to be with Nancy, and the doctor had gone. Nancy, as calm as she had been on the telephone, put out her cheek for me to kiss. Then, as though she had not already told me the story, she repeated it in even greater detail. 'When I got up this morning and heard no sound from his room, I thought he must be lying in. He went for a long walk last night and, on his return, he told me how tired he was feeling. But as the morning went on, I thought I'd better take a peep. The first time I did that, he just seemed to be asleep. But the second time . . . '

We were standing in the hall, used by Joe and Nancy as their communal sitting room and the dining area. At the end of it, french windows led out on to a magnificent terrace the size of the whole flat.

'Would you like to see him?'

Once, in similar circumstances, I had mortally offended a Greek woman friend by saying, 'No, not really,' when asked if I should like to view her dead husband; and so reluctantly I now nodded.

On either side of the hall, two doors faced each other, the one to

Nancy's bedroom above the noise of the Lower Richmond Road, the other to Joe's bedroom above the quiet sweep of the river. Nancy went to Joe's door and, from habit, raised a hand to knock at it, as she would always do to announce her presence. Then she lowered the hand and hesitantly grasped the handle. As hesitantly, she turned it. 'There he is. Poor darling.'

I went slowly forward; she remained by the door. He lay on his side, sheet and blanket drawn up over his shoulder – but whether by him the previous night or by Nancy or the doctor that morning, I could not know. There was no sign of struggle or distress on his face; but I did notice that the lips had a bluish tinge to them, as had the nose. It was easy to see how, going into the curtained room in the morning, Nancy had supposed him to be asleep. Beside his bed, there was a half-drunk glass of whisky on a table. (When he stayed with me, he would always take a glass of whisky to bed with him; and, the next morning, I would often find it with an inch or so still in it.) Nancy pointed to his desk, many of its drawers now open. 'I found his will there. You'll want to see that.'

At no time were there any of the paroxysms of grief that I had so much dreaded. We went through the will together – she had already read it before my coming – and, as we did so, in that gloomy hall that served as sitting room and dining area, we sipped at strong Indian tea and nibbled at wholemeal biscuits (Nancy was a great one for roughage) from the dented, rectangular tin between us. We then talked of Joe's past, as, strangely, we had never done before; and went on to talk of Nancy's future, as, no less strangely, we had also never done before. A close friend of Joe's, John Morris, had remarked brutally to me, when I had told him that I had agreed to be Joe's executor, 'All you'll get for your pains will be Nancy.' As she now put innumerable questions and requests to me, I remembered that ominous warning. Joe had often said resignedly, 'I'll never be free of Nancy until one of us dies.' Would I now find myself in the same position?

When I at long last got up to leave, promising that I would return the next morning to help her, Nancy said, 'Oh, I found this addressed to you.' She crossed over to one of the canvas chairs beside the front door and took off it a large parcel, wrapped in brown paper. 'It was in his desk.' The parcel had my name and address written on it in Joe's handwriting and, above that, 'The private property of Francis King – Personal and Confidential.' The last three words were underlined. I took the parcel from her. 'What do you think it is?' she asked.

'Oh, I expect it's all my letters to him. He always said he'd let me have them back.'

Except that some intuition prompted me, I do not know how I came to lie so glibly, on the spur of the moment. Joe rarely kept any letters other than those written to him by E. M. Forster, and I had never supposed that he would have broken this rule in the case of mine.

Nancy accepted the lie; and she never subsequently said to me, as I dreaded that she might, 'Do tell me – what *was* in that parcel? Was it your letters, as you thought?' Joe had so often railed against her *feminine* (a pejorative in his vocabulary) inquisitiveness. She would, he declared, read anything that he left on his desk or even in it, and, nitwit that she was, she did not even have the sense to put things back where she had found them. Yet this inquisitiveness was never applied to the parcel. Had she perhaps opened it and already seen what it contained?

That evening on the Brighton Belle, I put the parcel on the table before me, unpicked the string and unwrapped the paper. Inside, there were seventeen small notebooks, each numbered, with entries in both pen and pencil. There were also five notebooks of larger size, covering periods both before and after that of the seventeen. It is from the smaller notebooks that this selection has been made. It represents about a quarter of their bulk.

The entries that I have omitted are, for the most part, either about Joe's Alsatian bitch Queenie (the Tulip of 'My Dog Tulip' and the Evie of his only novel *We Think the World of You*) or about things and people that he had noticed in his walks on Putney Heath or on his travels around London. There are also summaries of passages that had interested him in newspapers or books, often about animals. There is little about his friends, many of them famous, or about his work as literary editor of the *Listener*. Perhaps, eventually, the excised passages will also be published. Joe could not write badly and most of them, even when dealing with trivialities, are beautifully written.

What I have concentrated on in this selection is the extraordinary relationship between Joe and what he would call, in the tones of a sultan speaking of his often refractory harem, 'my women': meaning by that not merely Nancy and his ancient, twice-married Aunt Bunny, but also the Alsatian bitch. By the beginning (1948) of the period covered by the diaries, all the most important events of Joe's life, with the exception of his visit to Japan and Nancy's recurrent breakdowns and suicide attempts, already lay behind him; and by the end of that period (1956), all the most important of his writings, with the exception of *Hindoo Holiday* (1932), still lay ahead.

'I was born in 1896 and my parents were married in 1919,' is the characteristic opening of *My Father and Myself*; and he later records, no less characteristically, that his brother, Peter, older by a year, had been 'an accident' – ' "Your father happened to have run out of french letters that day," remarked my Aunt Bunny with her Saloon Bar laugh.' Nancy, born in 1899, was the baby – a role that, for the rest of her life, she was always reluctant to relinquish. Both sons volunteered at the outbreak of the First World War; but Peter, always weakly – the result, Joe inferred, of his mother's attempts at an abortion – had to have an operation to repair a long-standing hernia before he was passed as fit. Both served in the trenches of the Western Front. Peter was killed by a whizz-bang shortly before the Armistice; Joe, captured, became first a prisoner-of-war in Germany and then an internee in Switzerland.

In 1919 Joe went up to Cambridge, already having published some poems and drafted his play, one of the first ever to be written in English with an overtly homosexual theme, *The Prisoners of War* (first produced in 1925). His father, known as 'the banana-king' because of the fortune that he had made from importing that fruit, was indulgent and generous when Joe switched from reading law to reading English and announced that his career was to be that of a writer. It was E. M. Forster, met in 1922, who procured for Ackerley the job of companion secretary to the Maharajah of Chhatarpur; and subsequently Forster was to become the most consistently loved and the most deeply respected of all Joe's friends.

In 1935 Joe took up his appointment as literary editor of the *Listener* – where he was to remain until 1959. During the Second World War, he had the passionate, dangerous relationship with the East End charmer whom he described, half-heartedly presented as fiction, in that unflinchingly truthful book *We Think the World of You* (1960). The soldier, called 'Johnny' in the 'novel', was the source not merely of its inspiration but of the Alsatian dog, Queenie, who is so important a figure in these diaries.

When *My Father and Myself* was published posthumously, Forster wrote to Duncan Grant: 'It seems to be so ill-tempered and such a reproach to his friends', and John Morris remarked to me, 'Fancy devoting so much time and artistry to the task of demonstrating to the world that one's father certainly had syphilis and was probably at one time a male tart!' Each judgement has some truth in it; and yet each is wholly inadequate for what has now come to be acknowledged, not merely in England but abroad, as a minor masterpiece. The story of how the former guardsman had used his two protectors to buy his discharge from the army, of how he became a highly successful businessman, and of how he then kept two separate families, only a few miles from each other, is not merely told in this book but taken up in one no less absorbing, *The Secret Orchard of Roger Ackerley*, by Joe's half-sister, Diana Petre. It was only on his father's death that Joe learned of the second ménage of a mistress and three daughters at Barnes.

Two of the questions posed and left unanswered by *My Father and Myself* are, firstly, why Joe's father should have waited more than twenty years before marrying Joe's mother, and secondly, how he decided which set of children to legitimize. My own answer, perhaps overly romantic, to the first of these questions is that, until approximately 1919, there may already have been an Ackerley wife, of whom we know nothing. I once put this to Joe; but no doubt because it did not fit into the artistic scheme, as formal as that of a novel, of the book that he was perpetually gestating up to the time of his death, he showed little interest.

All three of Joe's women – Aunt Bunny, Nancy, Queenie – were jealous of each other; but Bunny, admirable old woman that she was, with her jaunty, slightly raffish air but her unwavering dignity and decency, differed from the other two in rarely expressing her jealousy. As the diaries will show, Joe was far fonder of the bitch than of the two humans. All Joe's friends, even those who were dog-lovers like myself, hated Queenie. 'Beastly animal,' Forster once muttered to me, when Joe had left us alone together in his room and the dog, squatting on its haunches on his bed, its ears laid back, had begun to set up a continuous low growl. 'Joe has ruined her – no discipline,' was the verdict of John Morris, a believer in discipline, both for himself and for others. Yet Joe would freely give to this hysterical, capricious animal all the love that he grudged his hysterical, capricious sister. The dog would always follow him into his room; but the sister, having knocked, as she had all but knocked when taking me to view the body, would often be told, 'Sorry, old dear, we're busy,' when all that was keeping Joe busy with some friend like myself was a bottle of wine and gossip.

11

Because of this exclusion, it was a long time after I had met Joe and after I had been invited to his flat (these two events were separated by half a dozen years) that I got to know Nancy as more than a tall, beautiful woman, with jerky movements and unsettlingly desperate eyes (so well caught in her portrait by Don Bachardy, American friend of Christopher Isherwood), with whom I would exchange a few words before Joe, impatient beside me, would usher me into his room, firmly closing the door behind us.

Later in our friendship, the three of us would eat dinner in the hall or would drink together out on the darkening terrace, while the boat crews skimmed up and down the river to the hoarse cries of their coaches and, in a gymn in the building opposite (how Joe would love to gaze into it), young athletes sweated at the parallel bars or weights. But even then there would come a moment when Joe would say, 'Let's go inside, it's getting chilly,' and we would leave Nancy alone out on the terrace, fidgeting with her knitting. (She was forever knitting pullovers for Joe, until he once protested to her in my presence, 'I have far too many pullovers, darling,' and suggested that she should instead knit one for James Kirkup or myself. Perhaps she did eventually knit one for Kirkup, since she adored him. She never knitted one for me.)

Joe was fond of good food, often entertaining his contributors at the expense of the *Listener* to excellent meals at such restaurants as Chez Victor or Le Jardin des Gourmets; and, though he often declared that he did not care a damn what he drank, he was also fond of good wine, if the *Listener* was going to pay for it. But at Star and Garter Mansions it was usually a joint and two veg that Nancy provided, and the wine would be Algerian in the early years of our friendship and Spanish in the later. As the evening progressed, with Joe consuming glass after glass, the only indication of drunkenness was an increasing irritation with Nancy; but this was expressed not so much in what he said to her as in what he did not say to her. It was this irritation that would eventually drive him into his own room with his guest and the dog, while Nancy would remain excluded.

'Tiresome woman,' Joe would often say of her; and he would go on to relate how, when he was putting together his pages of the *Listener* on the day she knew they went to press, she would ring him up either with some trivial, fatuous question (How long should she roast the shoulder of pork? Where had he put those stamps he had bought for her? Should she buy a 40-watt or a 60-watt bulb to replace the one that had failed in the lavatory?) or with some trivial, fatuous request (Would he be sure to get a cauliflower? He wouldn't forget her *Woman's Own*, would he? Could he please see if he could find the telephone number of the dentist in the book?). Together, they were more like a married couple than a brother and sister; but like a married couple who have decided that, on balance, they had better stick together, even though everyone else knows that a divorce would be best for them.

Clearly, Nancy loved Joe; and, when I once said that to E. M. Forster, he gently corrected me, 'Nancy is in love with Joe.' No less clearly, Joe loved Nancy, and was perhaps, in some measure, also in love with her; but since that love and that being in love both frightened him, they were transformed, in the years when first I knew him, into what often seemed to be cruelly near to hatred.

When, in 1960, his fare paid by E. M. Forster, Joe came out to Japan to stay alternately with me in Kyoto and James Kirkup in Sendai for several months on end, he told me that he thought that, once Queenie was dead, he might settle in the country forever.

'But what about Bunny and Nancy?'

'Oh, let them stew together in the flat! Anyway, Bunny can't have long to go.'

But he never, in fact, came back to Japan, preferring to spend the money again provided by Forster on drink instead. But his relationship with Nancy seemed to slacken and mellow. When one now asked after her, he did not so often answer with 'Tiresome woman!' or, even more shocking, 'Dreadful woman!'; and, when I visited the flat, he was less apt to lead me off into his bedroom to finish our second bottle of wine, Nancy excluded.

Not long before Joe's death, the designer John Drummond, then a lecturer at the Royal College of Art, lent him for a fortnight his beautiful house, almost opposite mine, in Montpelier Road, Brighton. Joe brought Nancy with him. When I said, 'Come to lunch tomorrow,' Joe would accept and then add, even when Nancy was also present, 'But what about Nancy? Do you want Nancy?'

'Of course,' I'd reply. It would, after all, have been extremely rude and hurtful to ask him without her.

'Are you sure, dear?' he would then say. 'She doesn't *have* to come.'

By then, Nancy and I had become fond of each other and I had begun to see her through my own eyes and through the shrewd and sympathetic ones of my mother, and not merely through those of Joe and his often misogynistic friends.

Joe had now long ceased to be literary editor of the *Listener* and, frequently idle and bored, had taken to drinking heavily. Nancy, who had always shown a pathetic eagerness to share in all his activities, shared in this too. Almost every morning of that holiday in Brighton, they would make their way down to our local, the Temple Bar, just before it opened; and, just after it had closed, one would see them dragging their way slowly up the hill again, back to the once spotless house that Nancy rarely cleaned.

Once, as they were making this slow progress home, the novelist Clifford Kitchin, then an old man dying of heart disease, was standing in the bow window of my first-floor sitting room, an after-luncheon cup of coffee in one hand. He looked down and saw Joe, whom he did not like, and Nancy, whom he did. 'Charles and·Mary Lamb,' he murmured. Joe was leading her, as though she was reluctant to follow, walking one step ahead of her, while his left hand grasped hers and his right hand a wine bottle.

There was a terrible pathos about them at that moment. Both had once been so beautiful and so high-spirited; and now they looked so shabby and so dejected. In 1965, Joe had had a return of one month to the *Listener*, in a brief interregnum between one editor, Anthony Thwaite, and his successor, Derwent May. The recall had had an astonishingly vivifying effect on him; but when he was once again back, as he put it, 'in the junk-yard', his spirits seemed to sink even lower than before it. Sadly, he was too proud to ask literary editors for work; so that when, after his death, I remarked to one of them that I wished that he had been able to get more reviewing during his retirement, the editor replied, 'Oh, but if only I'd known that he *wanted* to review! I never realized!'

Because of the increasing depression of his last years and because of the suddenness of his death, there were rumours that Joe had committed suicide. A friend of James Kirkup, a woman now dead, wrote to him in Japan to tell him that Joe had been found 'with syringes scattered around him' and Kirkup, believing the tale, then repeated it in the *London Magazine*. If Joe did, indeed, die in that fashion, then the doctor who signed the death certificate must have been singularly remiss in reaching his diagnosis and Nancy un-characteristically quick-witted and resourceful in clearing up the evidence before the doctor, Sonia Orwell or I came on the scene. Joe had certainly experimented, like many other people, with pot;

but, having lived with him at close quarters for weeks on end, I can say categorically that the gossip that he was a drug addict is totally nonsensical. In his last years, he had an addiction; but it was an addiction to drink.

However, though Joe did not decide to die, he certainly decided that he was going to die. Perhaps the chest pains from which he had been suffering had acted as a warning; and perhaps the meticulousness of Clifford Kitchin in leaving all his affairs in perfect order (as his literary executor, I had commented to Joe on his foresight) had acted as an example. Joe spoke to me more than once about his wishes: in particular about the completed manuscript of *My Father and Myself* and about the negotiations with the well-known firm of Bertram Rota to sell, without their author learning of it, the many letters that Forster had written to him over a long period. *My Father and Myself* was to be published posthumously; but it was only to be published if his sister and his two surviving half-sisters, Diana and Sally, gave their assent. I was to complete the sale of the Forster letters and was then to persuade Nancy to invest the money, £6000, as otherwise 'the silly old dear' would only fritter it all away.

In the event, none of the three women objected to the publication of *My Father and Myself*, which had a success greater than that of any of Joe's other books. The money received for the Forster letters enabled Nancy to live after Joe's death at least as comfortably as the two of them had lived before it. Joe, of course, predeceased Forster, when each of them might have supposed that it would be the other way around. Since other people might also have supposed that it would be the other way around, Kenneth Clark, a friend of both men, came to believe that it had been, telling me on one occasion, 'Poor old Joe was in such a bad way when he came to stay with us after Morgan's death. Nothing would console him.' Lord Clark also made the same observation in his autobiography. An interesting example of what might be called creative memory – a common phenomenon.

Nervous about how much he had betrayed of his secret life and the secret lives of others, Forster had made some half-hearted attempts to recover his letters; but Joe had foiled him. As always in such cases, a moral problem was involved: the letters contained things that the writer wished to conceal from posterity and that the recipient felt that posterity should learn. There was also, understandably but less creditably, the question of the financial value of the letters to a man subsisting on a niggardly pension and worried about his sister, if (as he clearly expected) he were to predecease her.

Ackerley put his decision in its most favourable light when he wrote:

How good he is. He would have felt safer, even in his death, to have had his letters returned, he thinks he is not a good letter-writer and betrays himself and others. It may be that he *is* not a good letter-writer, but whether he is or not, his letters, and his friendship, have been the major influence in my life from Cambridge onwards; and if I gave up his letters I should give up one of the foundations of my life. I expect he knows that, he knows everything; he tried it on out of nervousness, and has easily let it go.

Joe put it in its least favourable light when he wrote to Sonia Orwell:

I am interested . . . in securing for them [the letters] a sum of money which will enable Nancy and me to drink ourselves carelessly into our graves.

The irony here is that Forster, who disapproved of alcoholism in general and Joe's alcoholism in particular, would have hated to think that the sale of his letters might enable anyone to drink himself carelessly into his grave.

Whether Forster ever found out about the sale of the letters is, in the view of his biographer, P. N. Furbank, uncertain. In moments of morbid guilt, Joe was sure that he had; and he would then seek from his friends some assurance that he had done the right thing, not merely by himself and Nancy, but by Forster and posterity. Certainly it is odd that in his will, made before Joe's death, Forster should have left this once beloved friend only £500 out of a large estate. (The bequest was, of course, invalid – as I had to point out to a disappointed Nancy when, by mistake, the solicitors forwarded a cheque.) But Forster may well have decided to show so little generosity because he had already shown so much – responding to Joe's ill-judged request that the older and richer man should settle an income on him by giving him £1000, and financing not merely trips to Japan and Greece, of which he approved, but also a lot of drinking, of which he did not.

For a brief time, my fears that Nancy would now make the same demands on me that she had once made on Joe were amply realized; and I began to appreciate that strange mixture of irritability, forbearance and remorse with which he would respond to them. The telephone would summon me from my typewriter. She wondered if David Higham, Joe's incorruptible agent, might not being trying to 'diddle' her – a preposterous suspicion. The ceiling of the hall was leaking badly (a constant problem throughout the years when I visited the flat) and, since the landlords would pay more attention to a man than a woman, would I please be an angel and give them a ring? She had a peculiar nagging pain under her right ribs and wondered if I thought she ought to see a doctor.

Then, miraculously, the calls that had come almost daily began to average first one a week, then one a month. Having kept afloat for years by all but strangling the brother around whose neck she had flung her arms in convulsive panic, she had now learned, if not to swim, at least to tread water on her own.

In this process of achieving independence, she was greatly helped by Sonia Orwell, best of foul-weather friends. Sonia, always quick to perceive methods of helping people more effective than merely writing another cheque, arranged for an interior decorator friend to supervise, at her expense, the total rehabilitation of a flat that had for so long gathered dust and grime. This renewal of her home seemed to become for Nancy a personal renewal; so that her pride, as of a young bride, in showing the home off to her friends was also a pride in showing off her rehabilitated self.

Immediately after Joe's death, my mother, ten years senior to Nancy and, unlike me at that period, living in London, made a point of keeping in regular touch with her. She would telephone; more frequently, since she belonged to a generation more used to letter-writing than telephoning, she would write letters. The two women would meet for luncheon or tea. But then, gradually, my mother sensed that Nancy wanted to distance herself. She was less effusive on the telephone, less quick to reply to a letter; and when my mother suggested a meeting, she would come up with some pretext for postponement – it was too cold or too hot, Christmas was so near, there was a talk of a bus strike.

What had happened was that Nancy had made friends with a precociously clever boy, still in his teens. He was precisely the sort of protégé, not lover, that Joe had found in such people as David Sylvester, James Kirkup, Henry Reed, Simon Raven and myself; and now it was she, not Joe, who opened the door to him, instead of having the door shut on her, as Joe and he disappeared into the other room, leaving her behind. I tried to explain this to my mother; but, a woman of another time and another world, she found it hard to understand.

When the young man passed on to Cambridge and gradually out

of her life, Nancy was content with a few other friends: neighbours in the block of flats or the immediate vicinity; Harry Daley (Joe's 'intellectual policeman', who had been instrumental in bringing E. M. Forster and Bob Buckingham, then also a policeman, together); Daley's brother, David, and David Daley's friend; the bookseller Ian McKelvie; her half-sister, Diana. There were also the people, primarily interested not in her but in Joe, whose friendships exhausted themselves as soon as her stocks of photographs, papers and information were exhausted. With her sweet, childlike unworldliness, she would often muse, 'I wonder why I never see X or hear from him now? Do you think I did something to upset him?'

With her cat for company, increasingly she seemed neither to want nor to need people much. It was Diana Petre who, with her usual insight, gave me the key to much that Joe and others found unsatisfactory in Nancy, when she said, 'Of course, the poor dear suffers from agoraphobia. Joe never realized that.' Nancy did not mind being with familiars in a familiar place; but she had a terror of being with strangers in a strange environment. When I used to try to coax her to spend a weekend in my Brighton house or, after I had moved from there, to have a meal in my London one, she would always counter, 'Oh, but darling, you don't want all that trouble. You're far too busy. Come to me instead. That's far better.' Once I persuaded her to meet me for lunch in a Kensington restaurant. The bus went door to door and I promised to wait for her at the stop in High Street Kensington. She arrived tremulous and sweating, as though she had not been sitting on the upper deck of a bus but had run all the way. 'I must have a drink,' she gasped even as the waiter was drawing back her chair. With the years, this agoraphobia got worse and worse, so that only if she were fetched back and forth by car (I do not drive) would she venture far. Yet, after all the torments, tantrums and tears, so vividly and often so pitilessly recorded in this diary, I think that she was happy.

'What does she do with herself all day? What does she do?' Joe would often ask, as he came home with a guest to find that the potatoes had not been peeled, the dog had not been exercised, and the table had not been laid. But Nancy was one of those people who do not wish to live under the pressure of having to do things. She did things when she felt like doing them; and for the rest of the time she mooned and pottered, in a spirit of 'Sometimes I sits and thinks. And sometimes I just sits.'

Her son, resident in the States, paid her a visit. She was overjoyed at the prospect of his arrival; but she was also secretly fearful. At first, all went well, but then the responsibility of having someone else in the flat to feed and talk to and guide about London proved too burdensome for her. Like her, he had had his psychological problems. She was relieved when he went back to New York; and when I visited her after his departure, she shook her head sadly. 'It didn't work out. It didn't do. Two neurotic people. I'm hopeless, I'm afraid. I couldn't cope.'

To the end, she retained a childlike sweetness that would make it difficult to believe the portrait that Joe draws of her in these diaries, did one not know him to have been the most scrupulously truthful of writers. It was with the pleasure of a child that she would respond to some trivial act of friendship or even notice; and it was with the caprice of a child that she would sometimes favour some stranger or someone hardly known to her over a faithful intimate. She liked to give, rather than to receive; so that, if one made some present to her, the obscure sense that she was somehow unworthy of it would soon drive her to attempt a return. 'Oh, darling, you mustn't!' It was with genuine anguish that she would cry that out when one handed over to her some such small offering as a box of after-dinner mints or a bottle of cheap wine.

Joe often said of her, 'I just don't understand her'; and these diaries may perhaps best be regarded as his tormented, perpetually frustrated attempt to understand both her and his relationship with her. But in the years after his death, when I really came to know her, she did not seem difficult to understand. She was an essentially good-hearted woman who, by some freak, had never fully come to maturity. When she indulged in those rages of which Joe has left so painful a record and even when she lapsed into her 'madness', it was merely the equivalent of the spoiled child that holds its breath until blue in the face, in order to force its terrified parents to give it what it wants.

Joe, on the other hand, I still try to understand in all his complexity, despite the fact that he wrote and talked so much and so freely about himself. The extraordinary kindness was balanced by a no less extraordinary ruthlessness; and the people whom he loved the most seemed often to fill him with the most irritation. ('He's becoming such a *silly* old man!' he once cried out to me in exasperation, as Forster toddled off from us; and yet there was no one for whom he cared more deeply or whom he respected more.) One key to his character was that he was, from his buoyant early years to his depressed later ones, a charmer. Blessed are the charmers, for theirs is the kingdom of heaven; but also cursed are the charmers, for insincerity becomes their hell. Joe had at first been used to charming people with his looks; then, as he aged and the looks ceased to be irresistible, he was increasingly obliged to find some other weapon of conquest. This was to flatter people by making them feel that, of all the inhabitants of the world, they were of the greatest importance to him.

Joe never pretended to any view that he did not genuinely hold; indeed, he would often give offence by blithely coming out with views that were anathema to his hearers. But he often exaggerated his emotions of pleasure, sympathy, interest or love, and muted or wholly masked his emotions of contempt, boredom, indifference or dislike.

Those who believed all that he wrote to them or said to them were often later doomed to experience bitterness and disenchantment, when they learned what he had been writing or saying about them to others. But the abrasive criticism no more represented his true feelings than the honeyed flattery, from which it was merely a reaction. I myself experienced many amusing examples of this variation of response. For example, at almost the precise moment when he was saying to me, during his visit to Japan, 'Oh, I do love staying here with you! I think this must be one of the happiest times of my life!' he was writing to a mutual friend (I quote from memory, since the letter has been lost), 'I really don't know how long I can bear to hang on here, Francis is so fussy. I have only to drop the pages of *The Times*, one by one, to the floor, for him to stoop, pick them up, and reassemble them. I have only to stub out a cigarette for him to get up to empty the ashtray. . . .'

In this book I have included some excerpts in which he writes both of his working-class lover, Freddie, and of the working classes in general. Like many other homosexuals of his generation, Joe combined a sexual passion for the male working classes with a thorough-going contempt for them, male and female. They were lazy, dishonest, incompetent, selfish, money-grubbing. . . . Yet, when he wished, he could always charm them, as he could charm anyone.

At the close of his life, all his love seemed to be concentrated on his irascible, possessive bitch; and when, after agonizing far too long, he realized that the time had come when he must have her destroyed, the blow was mortal to him. From that time, there began a slow but inexorable deterioration both in his spirits and in his health.

Joe left me no instructions about whether these diaries should be published or not; but since he wrote with such frankness about himself and his family, revealing not merely the facts of his father's 'secret orchard' but also of his syphilis, I guess – though I may well be wrong – that he would have approved of publication, once his sister was dead. He was consumed by an urge both himself to know everything about himself and his antecedents, and to enable the public to know it. So intense was this hunger for truth-telling that even considerations of libel would not persuade him to make the kind of alterations deemed expedient by lawyers. That was how it happened; and that was how it must be recorded as having happened. If the truth must be fudged or blurred, then he would prefer to delay publication.

In his self-absorption, he was extraordinarily like Siegfried Sassoon; and since Joe himself saw the parallel, there is a relevance in the long passage, here included, that describes a visit to the poet at his country home. The difference between the two men was that Joe could listen to others, giving them the impression that anything, however trite or silly, that passed their lips was of enormous interest to him, while Sassoon could not, at least in his later years. But, like many people who rarely listen, Sassoon seemed to have developed a faculty to take in information by osmosis.

Nancy died on 14 November 1979. She had once confessed to my mother that she lived in terror of 'crumbling to pieces' with the syphilis from which her jolly father had died. This terror had been created in her mind when she had succumbed to a mysterious illness that had caused her to lose her balance. At the hospital, Joe had said to the baffled specialist, 'Would it help you to reach a diagnosis if I told you that our father had died of syphilis?' and the specialist replied, according to Joe, 'Yes, it would.' Joe, inadvisedly, passed this on to Nancy. But what killed her was not the hereditary syphilis that she feared might be at work in her, but a slow cancer. She died in a hospice in Clapham, reduced (in her own words) 'to a rag and a bone and a hank of hair' and yet splendidly serene. She who had been so demanding was the least demanding of patients. At her cremation at Putney Vale Crematorium – where Joe had been cremated twelve years before – there were only ten mourners.

It is in many ways a sad and terrible story that is told in these pages; and Joe concentrates on it with such intensity that it is sometimes difficult to believe that, while this domestic drama was raging, he continued with his job as literary editor of the *Listener* (his indulgent editor, Alan Thomas, prescribed no fixed times of attendance at the office for him), went to theatres, cinemas and art exhibitions, and entertained and was entertained by his contributors and friends (the two were often synonymous).

At the time covered by these diaries, Joe's and Nancy's symbiosis was a ghastly caricature of the kind of marriage, devoid of sex, that is held together merely by feelings of obligation, pity and guilt. But, as in many such marriages, the two participants, exhausted by their conflicts, eventually reached an undemanding and even mutually helpful *modus vivendi*.

Joe's friends, many of them women-haters, would often say that Nancy had ruined his life; but it could be said with no more injustice that, kind only to be cruel, he had subtly ruined hers.

I should like to express my gratitude to the Phoenix Trust for assistance with the expense of secretarial help in having the diaries deciphered and typed.

Francis King

My Sister
and Myself

20 August 1948

I was thinking of my mother. I suppose that her human relationships were unsatisfactory. She had always had a feeling for dogs and relied upon them for love up to almost the end. My father was dead, she and my sister never got on together, I abandoned her; she ended her sensible life with a housekeeper and a succession of Sealyham dogs. Upon them in the end she lavished all her love and care. I see that I have reached the same conclusion. Indeed, I find myself using the same peculiar phrases – they spring to my lips – that she herself would use, in her anxiety and reproofs, to my dog. I see that, in this much, I have returned to her. Owing to some psychological failure in us, we were both unable to manage a human relationship and turned instead to dogs. Dogs captivate the inadequate and unloved, and my mother's last Sealyham, Barbarita, like my Queenie with me, became the nearest thing to her heart. My conscience directs me to this sad thought. I failed my mother. She would have liked me to live with her, though she was too self-effacing and good to press such claims; she was a darling but a tiresome, talkative one. I would have been unkind, I would have gone mad, in her society; how can the young and the old be expected to live together?

Her life was drawing to its end, mine beginning; I resisted her slight pressures and set up house on my own, leaving her to a housekeeper and her dog. But I saw her regularly nevertheless once or twice a week until she died. Yes, we were fond of each other, but in the way that exists between people who have no intelligent understanding of each other's hearts. Her love for me, I know, contained a lot of awe: her tall, handsome, dear – ah all-too-dear – son. She herself was not clever. She was childish, gay, sentimental, romantic, and my love for her was as for a prattling, kittenish, sweet and tiring child. 'Do you luff me?' she would say. 'Love' would have

25

been too serious and embarrassing a word, but it was what she meant. I did not take her seriously enough. Now I wish I had.

It was when she began to fade away and lose her faculties, when I saw that I should lose her, that I gave her, the sweet creature, in full measure, the love that she had always wanted and was now too dim to understand. Ah, how I would lavish upon her my demonstrative, kissing love and remorse, which I had not lavished upon her before although I had always loved her! But she no longer had the awareness to enjoy it. Barbarita had taken my place, as Queenie has now taken in my life the feelings of all the humans I have failed to attach and keep. My mother and myself. Like Queenie on mine, Barbarita slept on her bed and, in course of the night, growled as she moved. My mother did not mind, nor did she mind being nipped by the disturbed dog. My mother and myself; if Queenie gets as crotchety as that, *I* shall not mind either. I have gone the same way myself. She talked a lot to her dog, I talk endlessly to mine; sometimes I notice people looking strangely at me in the street and realize that I have been chattering to Queenie without thinking what I was doing. My mother and myself.

30 September 1948

Today Queenie bit my hand. I do believe she was horrified as soon as the accident occurred. She grovelled on the pavement before I had rebuked her; no doubt she both tasted and smelt the blood that was dripping from my hand. I was angry and upset and gave her a number of cuts from the lead. Then I took her back to the flat so that I could bathe and bandage the wound. She went straight down the passage into my dark bedroom and stayed there, not coming out again for some time, which she would ordinarily have done, hearing me moving about (in search of bandages, scissors, etc.) outside. It was only when I had finished attending to my wound and, feeling slightly faint, sat down for a moment on the stool in the bathroom to rest, that she came in, looking very unhappy, and, gently putting her front paws on my lap, rose up, smelt my face and then licked it. I petted her and said it didn't matter. I felt awfully sorry I'd hit her. After that I took her down the towing path a short way, so that she could do her shits. There were dogs about so I put her on the lead, but they followed us back to my front door, Queenie barking at them and then looking up into my face as though to say, 'That's what you want, isn't it?' Indeed, she loves me so much, it must have been dreadful for her to have hurt me.

4 October 1948

A very high tide tonight. The water flooded over the road high up the buildings on the other side and the swans floated with it on to the roadway through the riverside railings. So odd to see them floating and swimming about in the road beneath the low walls of people's front gardens. When the tide ebbed many of them were left high and dry in the road or pavements, but trailing along in file they eventually managed to find the openings that led, by wooden steps, back to the water.

9 October 1948

Kingsmere was befogged this morning. The world ended at the belt of trees on the farther side, finely pencilled as in a Japanese print against whiteness. But the sun was rising, its light giving an incandescent effect to the mist, and in this luminous silvery haze the white swans were just visible as part almost of the mist, delicately sketched onto the shimmering veil that was sky and water. Enchanting the woods beyond, light grey tunnels of smoke with the sun striking shining spears into them, casting the shadows of the trees across the misted glades and touching with glitter the golden leaves, shed now by the trees.

12 October 1948

She caught a squirrel on Wimbledon Common this morning. A short burst of barking, then silence. I turned off the track to see. She was standing beneath some large trees, chestnut, beech, on a carpet of fallen leaves, lemon, gold, red, the first hues of arboreal death. The grey squirrel lay dead at her feet. Bright spots of blood gleamed like rubies upon the fallen richness. A lovely day, an enchanted glade, death beautiful in its midst. Beautiful the fallen leaves, beautiful the dead squirrel, its little childlike hands still opening and shutting, beautiful the bright red rubies of its blood, and beautiful my Alsatian bitch, black and ivory against the green and golden bracken.

She carried the dead squirrel after us for a moment, then laid it upon the ground and left it. Wanton killing – ah yes, wanton killing.

15 October 1948

I took my old aunt (aged eighty) who lives with me to Bertorelli's this evening to dinner. I was wearing an open-neck shirt, an ancient pair of corduroys and sandals; perfectly suitable to the scruffy little place we were making for; my aunt, as usual, was dressed up to the nines, a black Dresden shepherdess hat, her hair neatly netted in a white net, long kid gloves made in the reign of Edward VII, the fingers of each took a minute or so to coax on, and a minute or so to coax off, a fur tippet (although it was a warm night), smart black coat and skirt with a fine white stripe, and at her throat a lace cravat which she spends much time in washing and ironing. I took Queenie along with us, and her inquisitiveness soon brought me into conversation with the proprietress, a dark handsome Italian woman of about forty years old. She had only just arrived from Italy, her first visit to England, and I felt interested to know more about her, about post-war Italy and what the woman thought of London. We were not in the restaurant much more than forty-five minutes and were the only customers in it; during that time my aunt managed to put the proprietress in possession of most of the facts of her life. The word 'Italy' started her off about the opera and gave her an easy opportunity (she would have done without opportunity if she had not been given it) to boast about her youthful prowess as a vocalist; it also reminded her of Mrs Ferrini with whom she and her husband used to lodge, and of Quadruccio's, the wine merchant at Carshalton, where she lived with and looked after my mother: we had therefore a good dose of these two periods in her past; it then led her on to the Spanish language – so like Italian – which she had managed to teach herself, and the Spanish language led on to South America, so that we were treated to all her reminiscences of her visit there: the eighties and nineties, her experiences in 'the wilds', and the tears that came into the eyes of the lumberjacks when she sang to them. Since there was little else to eat but fish and chips, we had that, which reminded my aunt both of her successes with a rod and line and her skill as a punter and rower.

She ended up by referring to her age – 'I am eighty years old' – and was delighted with the response of surprise she had been angling for: 'Well fancy that, you don't look it! Did you hear that?' (to the waitress) 'This lady says she's eighty years old.'

Well, I had brought the old lady out in order to please her, so the evening, which I cut short when I thought that pleasure enough had been gained, must be accounted a great success. I got none of the information I wanted. Shall I be like that when I get old, talk endlessly about myself and such successes as I have had in life, my books, my good looks when young, my successes in love? I can't believe it. Indeed I think it is female vice. Women are naturally vain and self-centred, interested only in themselves or what other people think of them; boasting in old age is what they are all too liable to come to. My mother was the same; her theatrical notices, which she had once treasured, then lost, how she went on about them! My sister at least will not be able to do it; she has had no successes of any sort, only failures. She may finish up as a complainer; she will scarcely be able to boast.

18 October 1948

I took Queenie to Barnes Common by train this evening. I had never taken her to the common that way before, and it transforms the walk from prose to poetry. It sets one down in the middle of the common. One emerges through a stone entrance, like the entrance to a castle or a church, into the midst of great beeches and chestnuts: one emerges into the country. It is wonderfully romantic, and pleasure is given even before one leaves the station, for a single tree, a plane tree, grows out of the centre of the middle platform. It is only one station from Putney, five minutes, and I have often thought how much I would like it to be my station, in summer to emerge into such cool green shade, in autumn, as now, to be greeted by the delicious smells from the thick carpet of fallen leaves. It was to this station that my father used clandestinely to come from time to time, on a Saturday or Sunday afternoon, from Richmond where we lived until he died in 1929. He came there because he had a second family, of which we knew nothing, a mistress and three daughters, and had housed them in Sheen, on the border of the common. When he felt he could do so without arousing suspicion he would 'take the dogs for a walk'; the walk he took them was to Richmond station, thence by train to Barnes, a few stops farther on. No one noticed. No one knew. He would emerge at this station, this tall distinguished-looking man, and walk through the trees to the house where his mistress and three young daughters lived. They did not know he was their father. They never did know it while he was alive. They knew him as an uncle, Uncle Bodger. His name was Roger. He was a strange man. I loved, and slightly feared, him; I wish I had known him better. He bought the children presents, they were in their early teens, they were lonely and adored him; no doubt they sat about in summer on the benches or the grass; the children dressed his hat with flowers, stuck in the band, and saw him off when he left; off he would go with the flowers in his hat, and had to take them out and throw them away before he returned and rejoined us for dinner, for how could he come back to us looking so festive? Us? Most of this happened, I suppose, between 1914 and 1918 when my brother and I were at school or at the war. At any rate he kept this other family going, in Sheen and later in Castelnau, Barnes, until he died, and none of us ever suspected it, while he lay dying in Southsea. He was so clever about it. He seemed to live quite by routine, the routine we were used to, and always to be where he was expected to be when he was expected. Yet he lived this double life and, excepting for his colleagues in his office, and later for his chauffeur, when he became heavy and inactive and had to be driven to Castelnau on his way home, none of us ever knew of it. Why did he think fit to conceal it? We had been intelligently brought up. We all loved him. Everyone loved him. None of his true family – mine – would have minded; my mother, I am convinced, would not have minded in the least.

21 October 1948

What should I do if I came upon a murder, I sometimes ask myself as Queenie and I push our way through the vast tangles of bracken where few other people walk? The common is a likely place for murder, as it is for suicide – the angry lustful man who finds he is not, after all, to be granted the sexual relief that his pick-up has led him to expect. What should I do, I ask myself, if I suddenly smelt something nasty – as I often do – and pushing along came upon a strangled woman? I wouldn't do anything, unless I covered it up with leaves to give the murderer a better chance of escape. I certainly wouldn't report it. I have harboured thoughts of murder myself in my life; I could never help to denounce or catch anyone else.

22–26 October 1948

I am down in Worthing with Queenie, paying a four- or five-day visit to my sister Nancy. She found a lodging for us with some difficulty (6s.6d., bed and morning tea) – the Alsatian dog in particular is unpopular with landladies – and met us at the station. We had managed to travel first class on third class tickets: a nice, empty, untroubled train.

She launched at once into a detailed recital of a row she's just had with her landlady, Mrs Young. Nancy rows with everyone in course of time; her path through life is strewn with the wreckage of love and friendship. Close on fifty, and she has no friends at all. But not one! Acquaintances, friendships, are occasionally begun: they never last long. She does or says something in time which no one can forgive.

Still the holiday was pleasant enough. I took care to say nothing that would set it wrong. We had a bottle of wine with our dinner – in Nancy's room – the first evening, although alcohol is not good for Nancy (I think she has an inkling of this herself and goes without it for long periods) and makes her more temperamental. It had no worse effect this evening however than to bring me a lecture on training a dog. Queenie got onto her bed, and Nancy chose to make a business of this, not because it was her bed, it was the principle, if dogs were allowed to get on beds and chairs at home they would get on the beds and chairs in other people's houses, who would naturally resent it. Well-brought-up dogs did not do such things, etc., etc. This sudden concern for the feelings of others rather amused me, though of course I said nothing; nor did I say that there was something extremely impertinent in lecturing me about my dog, though I thought that too. I knew the whole rigmarole was caused by jealousy. She herself would have liked to live with me and look after the dog. But my aunt was with me instead, and my flat was too small to contain even a second person. But I had all too good reasons to know that Nancy resented my aunt living with me, and the lecture, which went on and on, was caused by that. I

31

was weak and indulgent with the dog. I spoilt her, she should be corrected and disciplined.

I got bored at last and merely remarked that no doubt she was quite right, but it had been going on now for so long that the mistake was beyond correction.

The lecture then stopped, we passed to other matters, all infinitely distasteful, stale and boring. Her own financial position to start with. Her husband has stopped sending her alimony, she has not received a penny for the last two months, and I am providing her keep myself to the tune of £30 a month, gradually selling out my small capital to do it. I pushed aside this sickening subject, over which I have kindly attempted to help her (dutifully attempted to help her, *she* would say, her view being that it is a brother's place to help his sister) and devised lawyer's letters for God knows how many years, and so we reached the last subject of her repertoire. She must get a job. This ghastly, time-wasting theme, over which one is expected to knit one's brows, comes up every time I see her, has come up ever since I can remember. For the last twenty years she has been talking about getting a job – with no intention of getting one! If people want jobs they go off and get them without talking endlessly about it to relatives. The moment Nancy gets anywhere near a job she has a nervous breakdown. There is not a job that has ever been invented that would suit her – or a person who would be tempted to employ her. Nor any job that I know of that a woman so uneducated, uninterested, vain, self-centred, hypochondriac, idle-minded, irresponsible, left-handed, ignorant and untalented could hold for a week. Even if she baby-minded or took another dog for a walk, she would fail her appointment if she had a headache, or her bowels hadn't acted, or she saw that she would miss her afternoon tea. I listened politely and said as little as possible; the only thing I did say, misguidedly, as it turned out, was that a number of women, unqualified women, seemed able to earn quite a sum of money nowadays in purely automatic jobs that anyone could do, such as sorting letters in a post office. The talk of jobs petered out, as it always does, and we got onto the next inevitable, alternative and abhorrent subject of putting the lawyers back onto Paul's tracks to force him to pay his alimony. This, it might be thought, was a job in itself, and so it was, as I know to my past cost, but a job not for her, but for me. She claims to be helpless even over that.

Next evening – another bottle of wine – and I was attacked for my post office suggestion: it had upset and displeased her very much. Fancy suggesting that she should do the sort of work that skivvies, prostitutes and little brainless girls did. It was insulting. She wouldn't dream of doing such a thing; in any case she was too old for a routine job. How difficult she is! It doesn't seem to occur to her that she has less brains, less enterprise, less gumption and energy than the skivvies, prostitutes and little brainless girls she derides, that they are infinitely more useful than, superior to, herself. Alas! Alas! But I said nothing. I did not wish to add fuel to the row she was working up to. Her notion was that she should work as a tomato-grower in a conservatory. I nodded. Why not? She then grew calmer and mentioned other employments suited to her 'organizing' talents and looks: a receptionist, for instance, in a hotel, looking after the engagement book of some professional man, or running some flatlets. 'Excellent!' I said to everything, trying to picture the fate of any hotel, professional man or block of flatlets that Nancy, with her ignorance, laziness and lack of tact, had the managing of. Or, said she, she could be a private taxi-driver if I bought her a taxi. What a notion for a person who has not the slightest sense of direction and cannot do the smallest sum in arithmetic. However, I only nodded. I knew perfectly well that she didn't want a taxi, wouldn't drive it if she had one, and had in fact no intention of getting work of any kind. At any rate, she concluded, those were the sort of things she felt she could do, but no routine jobs, no sitting-down jobs (her health would go), and no such jobs as companion to old women, she would never be able to keep her patience with them.

We got through all this without further dispute and for the rest of the short holiday she behaved very nicely. Jolly walks over Cissbury Hill and Chanctonbury Ring – though not as interesting to Queenie as Wimbledon Common where 'game' is more plentiful.

On the last day, however – job now forgotten – we came back, as I expected we should, to the pursuit of her husband. 'How shall we get at him?' We! Extraordinary woman! She does not even say, 'Would you mind helping me?' – it is simply taken for granted that I will spend my time consulting lawyers and writing letters for her. But I won't. 'You wreck things with your good-natured handling of my affairs.' That was my thanks last time, after years of worry and work, because I reached a friendly agreement with him, accepted on her behalf a reduced allowance, and disposed of the lawyers. Besides I am sorry for him, much sorrier than I am for her. Poor fellow! Though his latter-day behaviour has not been good, I liked him once very much, and he me; she ruined his life for him, no doubt of that. And no wonder he has got bored paying her ever since – twenty years or so – a monthly sum of £30, then £20, he himself being far from rich. What a law to make a man support a discarded wife for ever! A specified number of years would be the juster thing, time for the woman to find another man or get some occupation. Years ago I urged her to protect herself against his insecurity – the money was often late, sometimes didn't arrive at all – by doing one or other of these things. But she wouldn't. Though she picked up other men, they were always the wrong sort – unreliable, already married, even working-class – and in any case she always ended by rowing with them and putting them off. As for jobs – that subject has long been a joke, though not apparently to her. She has no objective interest in life or people. For twenty years she has lived a life of instability, dependent upon a grudged alimony, a life of unpunctual cheques, financial crises, lawyers' letters, cables, ill-temper and threats. Deplorable. When the war came and there was so much fear about, she renewed personal correspondence with her husband (whom she believes herself still to 'love'), sent her only son over to him so as to get the boy out of England, and dropped the lawyers. This new arrangement went all right for some years. Now the money has stopped again.

I am sorry for her too. Once she had youth, beauty, money, husband, child, a home of her own; now, a woman nearing fifty, she lives quite alone, absolutely friendless, in poky bedsitting rooms at 35s. a week, cooking on a hotplate and washing up her dishes in her bedroom in a tin basin. Once she had the world at her feet. Now she has nothing and no one, only me. And to me she is devoted; I get, when she is calm, the best of her nature; yet how terrible she is – 'You are killing your dog', 'How shall we get at him?'

27 October 1948

Bunny told me some long story tonight, recollected from her youth, about some performing dogs she had once seen acting a play. The husband (a terrier) goes off on a shooting trip, wearing a deerstalker hat, his gun on his shoulder; no sooner has he gone than his wife (another terrier) throws open her casement, to be serenaded by her lover (another dog). She invites him up, he clambers up the ivy, slips and she hauls him up to her balcony in her teeth. All are absurdly dressed. Bunny laughed as she recounted this until tears rolled down her cheeks, and I suppose I ought to have pretended to be amused too, but I couldn't, so she was disappointed and put out by my cold and I daresay priggish reception of her funny story. But I really hate such things. I even dislike seeing a dog 'begging', like the porter's dog, sitting up and working its arms up and down, or a dog 'offering its paw'.

I remember going to a variety show with my old friend General Charlton. I think it was at the Richmond Theatre and we hoped to be amused by clowns and jugglers, etc. But one of the turns was a display by performing lions. I forget now what they performed; at any rate they were made to look silly in some way or other, and Charlton rose indignantly in his seat and exclaiming in a loud voice, 'The King of Beasts! The King of Beasts!' stalked out of the theatre. People stared at him in amazement and annoyance. Dear Leo Charlton – yourself a lion – now old and gouty – wherever you now are, my old love and admiration surges towards you as I remember that.

1 November 1948

Freddie came in the evening. I was not really expecting him, for it had gone 8 p.m. and he usually comes just before eight at latest. Also it had been raining hard all day, and was still spitting. Also I must have disappointed him over money lately. He used to get £1 each visit, but recently, owing partly to my immense overdraft and now Nancy's financial collapse, owing also to the fact that my sexual life with Freddie is not always satisfactory, I have regarded him as, after cigarettes, a thing I must cut down or even altogether abolish, so on his last visit but one I gave him nothing at all, and on the next visit only 5s. Nothing had taken place between us on either occasion, and I asked myself, not for the first time, why I should stuff £1 into the pocket of a chap who was earning £6.10s., came for a social evening and ate one's dinner and got stood drinks and did not go out of his way – not being really interested himself – to offer to do anything for one. So I thought I had better reduce, or even stop, and last weekend I was away with Nancy till Tuesday, as I wrote and told him. I said I would be glad to see him next Monday – today – Monday is his night – but all things taken into consideration didn't really expect to. Nevertheless I had bought three halibut cutlets in case (4s.1d.), and Bunny had buttered some paper and put them ready to steam; but then at 7.15 she was taken rather queer and said she thought she had better lie in, and after looking after her, I decided that Freddie wasn't coming, and I didn't mind, and was too uninterested to cook the fish, so I settled down to a meal of bread and cheese and a bottle of Algerian wine.

At 8.10 when I was part way thro' it, Freddie rang and Queenie gave him her usual lovely greeting. She is awfully fond of him. He looked very well, and as soon as he appeared I knew I was jolly pleased to see him. Silly boring stories about himself, of course – how the working classes do love to describe and repeat their physical reactions to events. 'I felt the sweat come on me forehead. I felt it there. It was just like somethin' crawlin' on me face – *just like somethin' crawlin*' ', or (a skid) 'It was just like as if it *floated* over the road; just the least little turn of the wheel and – d'ya know what I mean. The 'ole van went sideways – and it was *just* as if it floated over the road.' These kind of sensational anecdotes with their literary flavour are liable to be told, spun out and repeated, over and over again, as though one couldn't be expected to take them in first time.

He was charming – no, not charming, for he has no charm, but sweet and, as almost always, good-humoured. When he realized that no food was prepared for him, he said it didn't matter, but I could see he was hungry and grilled the halibut steaks and he ate the two largest with relish. I ate the other.

'Is it nice?'

'Smashin'. What sort of fish is it? I don't think I've ever 'ad it before.'

'Halibut.'

'Don't know 'as I've ever 'ad it. It's smashin'. Oh, that's whot you get the oil from, isn't it?' He drank half the bottle of Algerian.

Queenie is tremendously fond of him, I don't quite know why, unless it is that she has still some childish memory of him or senses his fondness for her, and after eating we went into my bedroom, where Queenie began to make a fuss of him and he of her. He began to tickle her tits and the base of her little vulva, saying 'Is that what you like? Is this what you like?' Queenie reacted most touchingly and extraordinarily, exactly as if she were human. She took it mostly sitting up, facing away from him towards – at – me, sometimes looking round and down when he left her tits for her cunt. Her ears were back, her eyes simply liquid, welling with softness, happiness and pleasure. Indeed, it was almost disconcerting the way her eyes, looking up or round at him, registered a sort of slave-like devotion and pleasure in the devotion, and intimacy in her devotion. She looked extremely beautiful, and most human.

I said, 'Oh Queenie, isn't he nice. He gives one such pleasure. Now it's your turn. Next it will be mine.'

She sat with an expression of such love on her face, worship even, while he kept saying, 'Is this it, gal? Is this what you like? Is this it, Queen? Do you like this?' and she would turn her face, with its look of somnolent devotion and, as she does with me, with her old eyes blinking (almost as if they had tears in them) looking down, would press her forehead against his.

Freddie smiled and went on tickling and whispering to her, caressing and tickling her tits with his large gentle fingers with their grubby nails. 'This is where women like it, I know,' he said, moving his finger to the base of her cunt. And old Queenie sat there, quite united with us, putting out something human and intelligible though speechless thro' her eyes, an immense and humble happiness. Every now and then she would give a little muted whinny, a sighing noise, a whimper, which she found she could not control, and which dissolved into a short bout of hysterical barking, not very loud, and an access of playfulness.

'Give us a kiss,' Freddie was saying, and almost with a cry she would turn and lick his face. 'Now another,' he would whisper. 'There's a good girl,' and in ecstasy she would turn round and embrace him, pawing at his face (which he lets her do, only closing his eyes) with her great hands, licking him, emitting her cries.

'Dear Queenie. You *are* happy, aren't you? What a lovely time he gives one, doesn't he?'

After Queenie's turn it was mine. When he took off his shoes I asked if his shoes weren't damp, they looked it. He said they had been but had dried. It had been a very wet day and he had been out in it all morning. His shoes were quite wet still, and I said so.

'Well, my socks are dry,' he said. 'Feel.'

I felt them. They were wet.

'Is it wet?' he asked. 'I don't think it is. This one isn't anyway.'

I felt it. It was wet.

'Oh well, they're dry enough,' he said.

Dear Freddie, you can't really live on £6 a week if you have a wife and three children. The kind of life you have is one in which there are degrees of wetness in socks – mere dampness doesn't matter. He was in his working trousers, a good suit not so long ago, the turn-ups of the trousers safety-pinned to the main article. Very dilapidated they looked. I asked why he didn't buy cheap dungarees or overalls to work in – but he pulled a face and said he liked to go out looking respectable. Dear Freddie. Then he pleasured me as he had pleasured Queenie, thinking up all sorts of squeezes and tickles and doing his best to please. Succeeding too. Freddie was in one of his best moods, feeling well, pleased to be with us, glad of his food and drink. Though he does not even share actually in my pleasure, he puts himself out giving one enjoyment.

It was the sweetest evening for both Queenie and me, and after we had had a couple of pints at the Bricklayers, Freddie went off. He asked nothing from me, and I had meant to give him no more than 10s., but I slipped £1 into his pocket instead. 'A'right, Joe,' he always says, and I hope that pleased him as much as he had pleased us.

In the pub he stood the first two drinks himself. Queenie came with us. Her daughter Trixie was in the bar, six months old now, and gave us a joyous welcome. Poor Queenie did not care much for this, and having withstood one or two love assaults from her daughter manifested a desire not to enter the bar. I brought her in tho', and Yaxley controlled his little bitch. A pretty little bitch, an obvious mongrel, but charming, lively, large and pretty, very like Queenie in face and paws – Queenie has stamped herself on all the babies I have seen. Dear Queenie. She sat beside us on the seat, so good-looking, so charming and so mild – I heard customers saying how beautiful she was. I thought of what she had been at Trixie's age, and how that woman had said, 'Shoot her, it's the only thing,' and how much she had learned with her intelligence and how good she had become. The man on the other side of her started to stroke her, and she did not mind. Dear Queenie, and here was your child, six months old, and, you were three and a half, and in a week I should be fifty-two, and here was old Freddie, shabby and careworn old Freddie, so different, he too, from the bright handsome strutting irresponsible guardsman I had met five or six years earlier. An old friend. And he had pleasured us both.

10 November 1948

Siegfried Sassoon, prostrate in Park Royal Hospital with an incipient duodenal ulcer, invited Queenie and me to Heytesbury. At least he invited me, and I said I could not come without my dog, that she was to me what George [his son] is to him. He accepted her with alacrity. His duodenal is said to be caused by conflict with his wife Hester, whom I have never met. He was obviously very wrought up over her emotional persecution of him, and described at much length her jealous rows, resentments, emotional blackmail, etc. He was describing Nancy. Every now and then he would say, 'And why should one have to put up with all this? I want nothing in this world, only peace, just to be left alone.' He was quoting me. Morgan [Forster] disapproves of his conduct, I know, and thinks he treats Hester badly. It was rather worrying. Siegfried is said to be a little like me in appearance, the same lean look, the same high imperious nose. And there he was lying in bed in an old dressing gown, with a little pipe on the table beside him, dissecting my sister and voicing my opinions as his own. And Morgan thought him a highly unsatisfactory character. It was quite disturbing. It had the rather melancholy interest one might get out of finding that one was visiting oneself in hospital by mistake.

13 November 1948

A return to mild weather. The leaves were simply raining down on Wimbledon Common today, a perpetual shower. Oak leaves, beech leaves – I wish I were not so ignorant and could identify trees and their leaves. What is the pale yellow one that spreads such a fine lemon carpet on the ground? Alas, I know nothing of trees and flowers, and cannot identify even the commonest bird by its note. Yet I have a favourite tree on the common, a huge silver-barked tree – a birch? – that it is always a pleasure to me to find. At first I came upon it chancily – now I know the way, and usually take it. I expect it is some psychological thing that attracts me to it, for it is one of those divided trees, like the one on the towing path, that allows one passage between its stems. This Wimbledon one rises in the midst of one of the tracks; the track runs right through it between its two great forks. There is a slight step over between the two front boles, mossily greened at their base, bright silver in their tall extent above, like the huge long legs of some giant, buried head downwards in the ground. One stands on, one steps over, his crutch, passing through between his great legs. I love this tree, and when I come upon it chancily, I am superstitious about it, I regard it as a good omen. I pass between his legs as though it were a ritual, and tell myself that Queenie will come to no harm today.

The bracken is all subsiding back into the ground. Only here and there where the trees have sheltered it is it still green; elsewhere, as far as the eye can reach, it is a beautiful buff brown, dead and going back into the soil. Beautiful, beautiful death, how can one mind you? I think as I walk of all my dear dead – Goldie, Enrico, my mother and father, little Demetrios and many people I have known and liked, and I think of them as going back into the earth like this lovely bracken, and think of death as 'in the end is my beginning'. Queenie will sink back too, I think, dear happy Queenie with her diamond on her forehead, and I too, I shall sink back like the bracken, and it is all a song.

We walked on amid the fallen leaves and came upon a little bit of magic. After a puff of breeze had drifted down quite a shower of them from a tree I was passing under, I saw to my surprise that one leaf remained, suspended in midair. It looked so odd, as though it had simply stopped. It was suspended by a spider's thread, of course, I realized that immediately, but the thread was invisible, and extremely long. A leaf hung motionless in midair six foot at least below the nearest branch.

14 November 1948

It was a warm morning. We bussed to the Green Man and walked up towards Wimbledon. I was in the mood to see my tree, and passed between the silver pillars of its gigantic legs. The moss on the great gnarled thighs is the colour of verdigris. The subsiding bracken has uncovered a good deal of glass, and I collected all I saw, horrible bottle butts, sunk in the earth, their sharp splinter-points sticking upwards, enough to lame a dog for the rest of its life. I came on a handsome red toadstool, a magnificent brick colour, Walt Disneyish, and picked it to take home. Wonderful the delicate perfect fluting underneath, and the small cape hanging on the stem, no doubt to prevent insects crawling up. I thought it might be a pretty decoration in a glass in my flat, like a flower, but the stem broke off in my knapsack.

We found a small group of boy scouts crouching in a hollow on the way back, and as we passed them, their leader joined them and began to direct them in some mysterious campaign. He wore the tightest pair of light khaki shorts I ever saw. However he managed to get them on was a mystery. They fitted tightly around his legs, and into the cleft of his bottom; they also exposed in front the outline of a precarious sex. An interesting psychological study and only about fifteen; one could not help wondering what he was like to have exhibited himself like that. He was smart too, the shorts were clean and good. An odd face, pale, chin rather jutting, and that blue look round the eyes that suggests that boys have reached the age of discovery. Young guardsman's legs, straight and pink and close together – the kind of legs my father used to mean, I imagine, when he asserted that a well-formed guardsman should be able to hold three threepenny pieces between his legs when he stood to attention, one between the thighs, one between the knees and one between the calves. The boy took no notice of me and Queenie at all, though his troop goggled at her; he was obviously rather self-important and authoritarian, directing them about, stopping them talking – not a very nice child was my impression.

Bunny: 'Well, my definition of a gentleman is someone who is considerate to everyone, but especially to women.'

'A rather partial, female point of view,' I said irritably.

'Naturally,' said Bunny huffily, 'since I am a female. You don't agree?' she added.

'Of course not,' I said. 'And nor do you really. Why should women have special consideration? They are mostly far from giving it, as you well know.'

We wrangled a bit. She is awfully silly sometimes, quite the old school tie, and a fervent feminist. She imagines, I expect, that my own contrary and ungentlemanly opinions on such matters are due to the fact that I am a pervert. No matter. And it's useless to argue with her, for she soon leaves off listening in order to pursue some line of thought of her own. Doesn't Kenneth Walker in his *Physiology of Sex* say that women are much stronger and tougher than men? More considerate indeed! Shades of Siegfried Sassoon.

Bunny (again, with regard to some case of seduction in the *News of the World*): 'Well, in my opinion any white girl who goes off with a coloured man deserves all she gets.'

I was shocked enough to say, 'I call that a pretty disgraceful opinion.'

'It's not fair on the children,' said Bunny, who had meant nothing of the sort, on the retreat.

'Only because people hold opinions like you,' I retorted.

'I only mean the absolute buck nigger, of course,' said Bunny.

Strange that a really quite intelligent woman should hold such views. I doubt really if she holds them at all, but simply repeats, without thinking, the opinions of that frightful husband of hers to whom she was so devoted. Though dead this many a year, he still, alas, lives on.

27 November 1948

Bunny said this evening, 'I don't suppose Nancy has ever spared a sad thought for little Mummy.' Alas, I suppose not.

29 November 1948

Degrees of affection: I said to Bunny – perhaps thoughtlessly – the other day when I was preparing Queenie's meal, 'Thank God for this weather, it keeps Queenie's meat for me.'

'It's certainly an ill-wind,' coughed Bunny: the cold and fog get on her chest. 'However, so long as the dog's all right, that's the great thing.'

I suppose she was in a bad mood, poor old girl, for it is rare for her to make sarcastic remarks like this. Silly, too – for it is true. I am much fonder of the dog than of her. Degrees of affection, yes. I remember Nancy saying to me, 'I believe you'd sacrifice us any time to the dog.' I said, 'Yes, of course.' Being a woman, so vain, I suppose she thought I didn't mean it, but I did. I love my dog far more dearly than her. Some days later she remarked something about 'Joe puts his dog before people' – but there, of course, she was wrong. Only certain people. Only her, in that particular context.

1 December 1948

Poor Bunny had bought a young rabbit for our supper yesterday, and spent a lot of time cooking it, but I was so worried about

Queenie that I gave my portion to her. Bunny is very good really about such disappointments – she wore an aggrieved look, but said little to admonish me and eventually even picked bits out of the pot for me herself.

But women won't do, of course. Although I have said that Bunny was good about the sacrifice of her rabbit concoction, I mean that she was only comparatively good – compared with other women and with her behaviour on similar occasions. The trouble is they have this awful maternal instinct – a mother's heart (Nancy said to me once, 'Of course you can't be expected to understand a mother's heart.' 'I don't in the least want to,' I replied). Although she allowed me to do what I liked with my rabbit, Bunny resented it and showed it, and indulged herself enough to remark, 'I see I'm no good as a caterer. I suppose I'm too old.' Silly woman, angling for praise and apology. I did not feel inclined to apologize. It was an emergency occasion. The dog was unwell – or appeared to be – it was a moment for a change of plan. I don't care how much trouble she had taken with the rabbit, how much she had been looking forward to me enjoying it – it was an emergency occasion and, though she did not make too much fuss, she allowed her disapproval to be felt. The kind of woman I should love and approve would be the woman who said at once, 'Why don't you give the dog your rabbit and have some bread and cheese? She may be needing a change after her endless diet of horsemeat.' That would have accorded entirely with my own feelings, and I would love a woman who had the detachment and understanding to behave like that. But, alas, one never finds such women, and has always to defend oneself against the mother's heart, the voluble concern for one's 'welfare' – such a bore.

My mother – I don't think she had a mother's heart, the kind I am speaking of, the possessive, fussy, concerned sort. She scarcely missed us as children and did not play with us – entertain us – as much as my aunt did. But this is not to say she was not devoted to us, for she was. But she was, in character, too much of a child herself, a Peter Pan, gay, lively, dancing, singing, cracking jokes – living an eternal child's fantasy life to the end of her days. She was a nervous woman tho' – a chemist's delight – a puss in Boots – and was concerned about our health mostly because she was afraid of life and concerned about her own. 'Mind the bones': that was not so much a mother's heart as a general cautionary warning – extended to visitors or dogs – against the dangers of life. I don't think she would in the least have minded my giving my dinner to the dog; it was too much the sort of thing she did herself.

I often think, as I walk about with my dog, of my mother. I do not consciously put my mind to her, but suddenly some little gay remark or quip which she used to be fond of repeating enters my head, and I see her again and nod to her with a smile across the grass. 'I'll give you a snopper on the nose', 'What ho, my bully rook!', 'Uncontrolled enfranchisement' – these were some of the things she would say to her dogs – Sealyhams mostly – and though at the time I paid little attention to such silliness, or her preoccupation with her succession of animals on whom she doted, I see now how right she was about her dogs and how she entered into their minds; I smile and nod to her across the grass, for I see that I am so very like her, and that our characters were much the same. 'Desist, refrain and cease', 'Steeped in guile', 'A man who smokes and reads *The Times* is capable of *any* crimes.' Sweet silly little lady, with her quips and quotations; I loved you very much.

4 December 1948

Who would have believed that dear William [Plomer] has had a telephone for the last six months at least, and does not want anyone to know or have the number, not even his closest friends? He has always been a problem to us, for he has been difficult to communicate with, and we have often thought we would like to pay him a surprise visit or ask him down for a walk or drink, but he has always been out of reach. Of course we have all known that he wished to be out of reach; we knew he did not care for the chance caller, and had strong views about phones and people ringing him up when he did not wish it. One sympathized too, one has occasionally wished one did not have a phone oneself, when wrong numbers tease one, or irresponsible people like Henry Reed phone one at midnight; but who would have thought he would go to such lengths as to get a phone secretly, conceal it in his bedroom and never talk to anyone about it! It was only discovered by accident, by John Morris, who followed him into the bedroom one day and noticed the phone before William had time to perceive his mistake and throw a handkerchief over it! John told me. What eccentricity indeed – a wrong turning surely, a hypersensitiveness to what doesn't matter, an insensitiveness to what does. Poor old William.

He gave himself away to me later, for he and I are organizing a seventieth birthday dinner to Morgan and have been making plans for it together. With Jack's help I drew up a provisional list of the people we thought Morgan would most wish to have with him, the handful of intimate friends he loved, and some days ago I took this list up to William. He at once saw it did not contain the name – we don't even *know* his name, except his first one, Charles – of the German or Austrian baker with whom William lives, a good enough creature no doubt, but of no significance whatever in Morgan's life. William said he must be included. Personally I did not mind, and did not gainsay him – William is not a man easy to gainsay. But Morgan himself, staying with Jack, and discussing his party, asked if this C. was to come, and was quite put out to hear that he was. He was *too* put out over it – both he and Jack agreed on this later – but still he had been so upset at the time that Jack felt the party would be a pleasanter one for M. if such inappropriate people were excluded and suggested I should try to tackle W. tactfully about it. So I did: I wrote to say that Jack had sensed that M. would be pleased to be asked if outside people like C. would be welcome, since he had vetoed a friend of Jack's and was obviously taking a deep interest in his party and its constituents. Also, as we all know, M. has a deep feeling about such matters, an almost mystical feeling, different and more emotional than anything that any of us feel. I pointed all this out to W. in my letter, and a day or two later he rang me up. Needless to say he dismissed my letter gaily as nonsense; *we* were throwing the party, not Morgan, and it was not for him but for us to choose the guests, so let us invite whomsoever we liked, and as for 'a certain person – you know to whom I refer', he would be most upset and disappointed if he were excluded, and so . . . William always gets his way; the party's object supposedly was to please M. but no matter, and, it only occurred to me later, why refer to C. as 'a certain person' instead of as C.? Of course, W. was not phoning me, as he used to do, from a public call box, but from his own bedroom, with C. in earshot. Silly fellow, how can he hope to keep the thing secret? It is sure to ring one day when one is having tea or lunch there – not that one often is. But then, alas, when it is confessed, William will have taught us the lesson he wishes us to learn, and we shall not want his number nor even dare to ring him up.

8 December 1948

There is much to be said for living with an old woman: two things anyway. First, Bunny hardly ever listens to what one says, so there is really hardly any need to speak to her. One can see that she is not attending; she is pursuing some interesting train of thought of her own – quite right too, one's own thoughts are mostly far more interesting and less fatiguing than other people's. If I get irritated and say, 'But I see you're not listening,' Bunny will at once say, 'Of course I am,' and repeat exactly what one has said. But this does not mean she was listening, of course. What one has just said remains for a time on the air in the ear, so that one can accurately repeat it if brought back to consciousness, but one has not been attending nevertheless. I do it myself, so I know.

Second, she cannot accompany me on my walks with Queenie. I go off on my own. How awful it will be if Nancy ever comes to live here, as I fear she may, for she will deeply resent being left behind. And my lovely walks with Queenie on Wimbledon Common will be endlessly distracted with dreary discussions about alimony.

11 December 1948

En route for Nottingham.

A long walk with Queenie this morning – her third Wimbledon Common walk in three days – to enable her to put up with an idle Sunday while I am away. I do hate leaving her, even like this for a mere forty-eight hours. Yet I know that is silly, and saw that Freddie, who advised me to go, had sense upon his side. He pointed out that it didn't really matter if Queenie went without any exercise for a couple of days. True really. There are times when we all have to stay in – on bad rainy days, for instance. Besides, think of the life she used to lead – confined to his mother's house for months on end. A day or two – almost the first in about two and a half years – except when she has cut her pads – wouldn't matter at all. Yet I didn't like it much. I noticed that he didn't offer to come over on Sunday to take her out for me himself! He goes to bed on Sunday afternoons; he would never willingly forfeit his siesta. Lazy fellow. 'A working chap 'as to 'ave his kip,' I suppose he would say. I bet he doesn't work anything like as hard as I do, even tho' I'm what's called leisured class. If he had my life for a week it would flatten him, I'm sure of that; I couldn't do it myself if I hadn't my huge resources of nervous energy, combined with my constructive and planning mind. I look towards almost everything I do as a series of ordered movements to achieve my object as quickly and unexhaustingly as possible. Returning from a walk with Queenie, for instance, on a weekday afternoon, my mind thinks out the steps ahead; put on a pan of water for her vegetables, the first move, and turn on the bath, if I need one. While these two long-term things are happening, dry Queenie before she gets all wet and muddy on my bed. Then scrape a carrot or two for her, ready to put in the water when it boils. Begin then to cut up her meat and mix her gravy. If time, prepare our own dinner – the parts Bunny can't do, such as peeling potatoes. When carrot water is boiling, pop them in. Finish Queenie's meat cutting. Or dash round to off-licence if I have to, for a bottle of booze for ourselves. Bath ready by then – have it. By the time I've done so, the carrots will be cooked and I can mix and give Q. her meal. Then I can sit down and relax with no more fidgets and enjoy my cocktail and book. It is only by seeing my life always as a sequence of arranged steps or moves that I am able to get through the quantity of things I have to do.

Freddie could never do that. One can't imagine him hurrying – such a thing as 'running' would be out of the question. He is a victim of conventionality and self-consciousness. When I first knew him, I remember, when he had far more spirit than he has now, there were various simple things he would not do, such as carry a parcel, go out in the street in his shirtsleeves. To this day he will not enter a shop, if he can help it, to buy anything.

His hair is a typical example of working-class vanity and ineptitude and propriety. He has a lot of hair, and in fact it is rather nice hair, or would be if he left it alone, for it is naturally wavy and suits him very well when it is dry and tumbled about. If he used a small amount of oil on it and nothing else, people would notice what nice hair it is. But he does not want to be noticed at all – in any sort of way. Instead of that, he grows it very long, down to the nape of his neck, and plasters it down with water, so that his head is always as hard and round as a nut – not a hair out of place. But that is not quite true. He does not like it quite straight back, he likes a little quiff, a puff or ridge of hair in front, and immense care is taken to achieve this result. It is quite extraordinary to watch him doing his hair – in his shirtsleeves, with a towel draped round his neck to keep the water from running down his neck, trying to effect his quiff to his satisfaction. It is a matter of combing that lock straight backward first, puffing it up a little with the side of his hand and the back of the comb, and then combing other strands of his wet hair over the end of it to keep it in place. But it must be to his satisfaction, and I have seen him do and redo it a dozen or twenty times before he gets it right.

The other day we had only fifteen minutes to get over the road to our pub before closing time, but I could not get Freddie away from the mirror. Cursing and swearing, he tried to raise this little brown mound on his forehead, but could not get it exactly as he wanted it. I said at last, 'Does it really matter, Freddie? Why not just comb your hair straight back for once. We shall miss our drink otherwise. It's dark out, so no one will notice that your hair isn't done as usual.'

He said, 'I should feel strange without it.'

We just reached the pub as the 'last orders' call was raised.

How irritating and unsatisfactory the so-called working classes are seen to be, with their irrationalities, and superstitions, and opinion-atedness, and stubbornness, and food foibles, and laziness, and selfishness, the more one knows of them. Think of them – for one example – with their dogs! If I were a dog, God shield me from a working-class master, like Freddie or anyone else. We know what sort of a life poor Queenie had with his mother and then with him. They had no real feeling for or understanding of her at all. No sympathy. A dog to them is something between a slave, a plaything and a protector. Its character – what it may need to develop that character – never occurs to them. All dogs are the same, big or small. Their diet has nothing to do with what vets recommend – what working-class man would bother to go to a vet to ask advice? – or what the dog would seem to fancy – but is conditioned by various superstitions and scraps of folklore picked up in pubs, and ignorant opinions of all sorts. 'What's good enough for me is good enough for my dog.' 'Never give a dog raw meat, it makes them savage.' 'A Bob Martin a day keeps the vet away.' 'Cigarette ends are good for worms.' 'Every dog needs worming once a month.'. . . and so on. Poor blessed dogs – entirely at the mercy of these ignorant people who think they know everything.

15 December 1948

Nancy once told me that Bunny 'hated' Freddie. Well, what difference does that make to me? It is nothing to me whether she likes him or not. And as for me, I thought her own choice, her husband, Doc Fowler, the most odious man I had ever met. But I have never told her so, and she herself is too well bred to be anything but polite to Freddie. I don't expect other people to like Freddie, and see many reasons why they should fail to do so – there are many points of criticism – but I have loved him, and have still for him that affection which comes from understanding and habit and compassion, and it is no more to me what other people think than it would have been to Bunny what other people thought of her appalling husband. Do I covet William's friend? Morgan's friend? Nancy's interests? Certainly not. I regard many of them with polite surprise, finding it hard to see the attraction; but then I think of Freddie, and how these people, who have other choices, unsuitable to my own taste, regard him too with amused or disgusted surprise: what could be sillier than denying or questioning other people's love affairs? I regard Queenie, too, as exquisitely beautiful and fascinating in her behaviour, but I don't expect others to feel the same.

I took Queenie to London last Sunday, intending to take her along to Lilian Bowes-Lyon if she were well enough to receive us, but – I spoke to her from my office on the phone – she was expecting her doctors, so I walked Queenie off towards Hyde Park instead, and, happening to pass down Hinde Street where Rose Macaulay lives, I thought I could call on the old girl. She was dusting out her flat but was delighted to be visited. What a dear she is. Queenie did not behave very well, too restless, but Rose did not mind. I chatted with her for quarter of an hour. She admired my new brown knee-length 28s. lumberjacket, and said I looked like Richard Jefferies.

17th December 1948

Nancy. When I went down to stay with her in the late summer, I told her that I was hoping to get out of London for Christmas, perhaps to stay with the Sprotts and she did not seem to mind this desertion of Bunny or herself. However, I arranged nothing, but got into a wrangle with her instead about her alimony, which has ceased for months to arrive, and which she seemed to think it was my duty as a brother to go to lawyers about again. She began to write letters to me about my 'spineless' and 'unfraternal' behaviour towards her son and husband and said my opinions were 'hot air' – she can be the most offensive woman in the world – and this naturally got my back up. Letters on her side stopped, and I don't like this to happen, because I then feel I shall have to go down to Worthing to see her and effect one of those frequent reconciliations. She had moved in Worthing from the Youngs to another and better room I had never seen, and appeared to be satisfied with it. 'I think I shall like my little room,' she wrote. Easy to forget people, especially tiresome ones, when there seems nothing to worry about, so I troubled myself with little thought of her until I went to Jack Sprott in Notts. for the weekend I have mentioned, and in the train the nearness of Christmas burst upon me and I wondered whether I shouldn't do something about N. since I now saw that I should be staying that season in Putney.

So I wrote to ask whether she would come up and join us if I got her a room in the hotel next door. I said how nice it would be, while regarding the prospect of further conflict between her and Bunny in my flat with horror, but I did not for a moment suppose she would accept, and in fact she didn't answer the letter. I then sent another soothing letter to say how much I wanted to see her and would trot down one day soon with Queenie. I added however that I was awfully tired, which I was. I couldn't organize anything elaborate such as hoicking horsemeat about and staying nights. Meanwhile Bob Buckingham phoned to say he and May had a turkey which they and Morgan had bought, to eat at one on Christmas day, and would I and Queenie join them. I adore turkey but never get it. I temporized. Could I leave Bunny, I wondered, who has a Christmas mind and was purchasing chicken? I didn't see why I shouldn't eat turkey at Bob's and return to eat chicken with Bunny in the evening, and said so. Not that I wanted to hurry back – and May had said, 'You won't have to run away quickly, will you?' Bunny seemed a bit hipped, but always behaves in such matters with excellent good manners and correctness.

Then I had a brainwave: why shouldn't she invite Ann from Merstham for a day or two? This suited her fine; Ann was phoned to and accepted with alacrity; there was now no reason why I should not spend all day at Bob's. Poor Nancy, however, still remained out of it, and I thought I had better do something, so phoned her to ask myself down on the Saturday before Christmas for the day. I told her I was Christmas-daying at Bob's. She sounded flat and lifeless on the phone, but accepted the suggestion: 'If you like.' But alas, it had slipped my memory that on the previous Monday I had written to Joan Evershed, whom I like very much, and to whom I owe hospitality, to ask her to dine with me Friday or Saturday. I had said I would keep the evenings free. Her husband, Raymond, was in hospital having an operation for fistula, and this seemed a fine moment for taking the girl out. Unfortunately – she was in Norfolk when I wrote to the Albany – she didn't reply until Friday afternoon after I had engaged myself to N. Then she phoned and asked for Saturday. I couldn't and didn't want to put her off, so I wired N. that I would come Sunday instead. But alas again, a small cold I had caught, rapidly developed, and on Saturday night, when I went to Joan, I felt very poorly and knew I should not be fit to get Queenie down to Worthing next day. So I sent Nancy another wire Sunday night to postpone her again, and phoned her next morning. She seemed all right, sad, but concerned about my cold, and said I was quite right not to come. I said I was worried we weren't meeting for Christmas, but that I'd sent her some candies. But I felt sorry for the old girl Christmasing alone, and decided I must see her somehow and phoned again later in the week to suggest a plan by which we could meet halfway at Haywards Heath on the Sunday after Christmas for a drink and walk. She didn't seem to take to this – 'What for?' – but I persuaded her – 'Oh well, if you like' – and she was to phone me again when she found out what train she would get which would land her in Haywards Heath at about 11.30 a.m. She phoned and we fixed it. I didn't at all want to leave my armchair, but after all it was Christmas time. Bunny had told her on the phone that I was spending Christmas Day elsewhere, but that Ann was coming to spend the day with her. I felt too that Nancy would feel less jealous about not being with us at Christmas if she knew I was deserting Bunny.

Queenie and I enjoyed our day at the Buckinghams, and Queenie really behaved very well on the whole, tho' her society manners aren't good, she is restless and thinks all occasions have been designed to amuse her and barked a bit, teased on by Robin Buckingham. She got some turkey bits, and we drank Pimms No. 1 (horrid drink), sparkling Moselle which was too old to sparkle, Pouilly wine and port. Afterwards Robin and I took Queenie for a walk. She was very lively, and we threw her ball for her in Ravenscourt Park, and I slid down the children's iron slide which she thought highly entertaining. On the way back thro' the deserted Christmas streets, a rather wan gent with a Scottie hastily attached it to its lead when he saw Queenie bounding towards him – she was bounding after her ball – and said apologetically as we passed, 'He is very old now and nervous. Too old for shocks like that.'

I said, 'She wouldn't have hurt him.'

'Oh, is it a bitch?' he said, 'that's different,' and detached the Scottie again.

I patted the Scottie and wished the old dog a happy Christmas and prosperous New Year, and so we parted pleasantly.

Next day Queenie and I entrained for Haywards Heath, and reached it quarter of an hour before Nancy. A bitterly cold day. I'd never been there before, and looked about in the station vicinity for a little before Nancy's train came in, and asked a local for directions for a country walk, and ran Queenie about on some grass I found. It didn't look a very attractive place. I wanted to be home for dinner, which meant leaving about five at the latest. I saw Nancy's train come in, and Queenie found her first and went bounding to meet her with many a joyous bark. Nancy was very touched by the welcome. She looked pale and rather ill, and I walked her a bit first in the local public garden until opening time. I then realized that she was very upset about everything, Christmas, my flat and not being asked there and so on. I said I had asked her up, but she said it wasn't the same thing, and that she knew she was being kept out of the flat and it had become an obsession with her, that she had told me about all this before and had waited and waited for me to do something about it.

'If Ann could go there, why couldn't I?' she asked.

The answer was so obvious I forbore to make it.

'I suppose she stopped the night,' she said.

I admitted she had, but did not say she was to go on stopping.

'There you are,' she said. 'Why couldn't Bunny have asked me instead?'

I made noncommital remarks. She was crying a bit. However, I guided her to a pub, and we went in for a drink.

It was a very cold pub, and I give it to Nancy that she was doubtful about drinking and couldn't decide what. I said gin, but she hesitated a long time. It does produce hysteria in her, and I think she was afraid of that and didn't want to let go. However, stupidly I fear, I pressed some gin upon her. She looked at it dubiously when it arrived, then tasted it and said it seemed awfully fiery, was it a cheap brand? I said no, it was Gordon's. We finished it, but since the pub was so cold, I suggested we should look for a better one before embarking on the bread and cheese we had both brought. We walked out and found another pub at last. It wasn't much better – a fire, but a dying one. We ordered two more double gins, and I gave Queenie her raw meat which I had brought with me, and we ate our bread and cheese. Nancy was awfully sweet really. She had brought me in her haversack a pair of socks as a present, and some cheese. She drew attention too to her clothes – nothing warm enough for such cold wintry weather – only her old brown slacks, thin and much darned. I was horrified to think of her so inadequately clad – I knew she had saved up to buy a thing or two, but did not know what. I told here there was no difficulty there, I could easily fix her up in warmer clothes. I asked her why she had not put on her fur coat on such a cold day. But she said – I remembered at once that she had a feeling about it – that she could not wear a fur coat with slacks. I thought that silly, I must say, but women are women. I was wearing, on purpose, the last pullover she made me, which she had had great trouble over and had always refused to believe fitted. In fact it fitted very well. I showed it to her. She then said she was engaged on another for me. I asked her why on earth she didn't make something for herself instead, and she gave some explanation about the new pullover, which apparently had been meant first of all for her son, then reconstructed for me; but I was touched, as I so often am, by her making warm things for other people who don't really need them, when she would more profitably be employed making them for herself. She suggested a third gin, and that she should pay for it, so we had it, and at closing time – 2 p.m. – left.

Then the fireworks started. I knew that gin excited her, and shouldn't have allowed her to have it I suppose: in the cold air she went off almost at once into hysterics. Our brutal behaviour over Christmas, keeping her then and always out of the flat, if we could have had Ann, why couldn't Bunny have written her a nice little letter inviting her, but Bunny hated her, she was jealous herself, she had ruined Wendy – the happiest time of Nancy's life – by her hatred of it and anxiety to get back to my flat, and since then had treacherously set me against her. We were leagued together now against her, and our only wish was to get rid of her somehow, to put her somewhere or other out of the way. Bunny had poisoned my mind against her, and we were nothing but beasts, brutes, she hated us both – 'I hate you, I hate you, you're horrible, horrible, cruel, beastly, I shall kill myself and I shall haunt you, I shall haunt you.'

She was beside herself, alternately shouting in the street, or weeping hysterically and faltering up against walls and buildings. We had taken the Lindfield road – where her wholemeal bread is made – but I don't think she noticed anything of the route we walked along. It was an appalling walk, the worst I ever took, and it went on for nearly two hours. I had no notion what to do or say at all, and was, on the whole, angered and antagonized by it – had people any right to behave in such a way, and upset and worry others so much? I cannot remember half the things that were said. Nancy abused me and pleaded alternately. Bunny had had nine months in my flat – it wasn't fair – it was *her* turn – please let her come – she would not interfere in my life, she could not bear to go back to her lonely room in Worthing, she was frightened, she was lonely, she was ill – 'I'm ill! ill! – don't you see? – I'm ill!' I couldn't be such an inhuman beast as to condemn her to that.

And all the business about how much Bunny had told me, and whether she had talked about her, and what she had said.

'She said – didn't she? – that she didn't want me in the flat. She did, didn't she?'

I didn't say anything.

'It's no good your saying "No", I can just hear her saying it'. . . and so on. '*Why* does she dislike me so much? I've done nothing to her.'

I said, 'My dear, all that's between you two, nothing to do with me. But one reaps as one sows, you know.'

The hostess and other inhabitants of her house had tried to persuade her to participate in the Christmas festivities, but she had refused.

'Bunny promised that she'd never let me stay in a room by myself again. It was the last thing she said before she left. She knows I always go to pieces. You both know it. I've told you so. It's horrible of you both. It's horribly unfair. We may have had a few rows, but they were as much her fault as mine. She hated Wendy and was obstructive from the moment she arrived, only wanting to get back to London and your flat, and showing it. You don't know. And the only time she perked up was weekends when you were coming down. She was a different woman then. Personally I think I was jolly forbearing considering how difficult she made everything. And anyway, everyone has their rows. But she's been beastly to me ever since, writing the coldest most impersonal letters, and poisoning your mind. She's been horrible. I'll never forgive her. I would never have treated *her* like that, whatever she'd done.

'You were a sort of god to me always, a god, but now you've changed, you've changed, and it's that beastly Bunny's fault and your disgusting friends, they've all set you against me.

'What's the matter with me?' she cried aloud, throwing out her hands. '*Why* do you keep me out of your lives like this? I've done *nothing, nothing*. A few words with Bunny every now and then, but they didn't matter, and everyone has their rows, they don't matter, they don't make any difference to me anyway and my feelings for you both, so I don't see why they should make any difference to Bunny, but you've built this thing up, you've built it up and up, and now it's killing me, it's crushing me, it's driving me out of my mind. You're inhuman both of you, anyone would think I was a leper or something. You made me come here. And now you've got it. It isn't my fault. You made me come.'

I had no notion whatever what to do, and felt both miserable and hostile. All this horrible hysteria. And poor old Queenie barking and upset. What could I do? Bunny had asked me not to leave her alone with Nancy again – and I don't blame her; I didn't want particularly to turn Bunny out. I said we had no intention at all of keeping Nancy out, but that purely mechanically I couldn't have her in the flat.

'Why not?'

'What can I do with Bunny?'

'You could find a place to put her if you wanted – one of her relatives.'

I said I knew of no one, but that if Nancy was lonely and unhappy, why on earth shouldn't she come and stay at the hotel next door, as I'd suggested.

Nancy replied, 'I'll only come up in two circumstances, either I stay with you or in another place with Bunny.'

What does one do with people like that? I said it only showed how jealous she was, and therefore how unreasonable. She said that she wasn't any more jealous than Bunny – and then began again to try to set me against Bunny – 'She didn't love Mother at all, she hated her – I often remember seeing the hatred in her eyes as she glared at her. She pretends to have loved Mother and looked after her – but she hated her.'

'So did you,' I said.

'I didn't.'

I said 'Yes, you did. You even twisted her arm.'

'I didn't,' said Nancy, 'it wasn't anything. I wouldn't harm anyone or anything. It isn't in me.'

Women always lie like troopers to gain their own ends; Nancy was jealous of my mother and hated her, except when she became a very old woman, half blind and deaf, and was no longer a rival. And so the wrangle went on. Queenie too got hysterical and began barking. Sometimes I was stung to make a reply. Poor old Queenie begged us to play, but Nancy took no notice at all and, when I did, said, 'All you think about is that dog!'

To which I replied, 'She has as much right to attention as you.'

Nancy began again about Bunny and how jealous she was, and how she had gone out of her way to wreck Wendy by being uncooperative, and how it was not *her* fault but Bunny's that rows had occurred – indeed she, Nancy, had been remarkably forbearing, and hadn't done anything much anyway – everyone had their rows, and if she had picked Bunny's bed to pieces, she had remade it and apologized afterwards. And what about the knife you threatened her with? I asked.

'Knife? What knife? I never did such a thing. Did she say so? The beastly liar.'

She had never hurt anyone in her life. I don't know where we had got to by now, but it was a sort of scrublike wood that looked as tho' it had been shell-shocked or blasted by lightning – like one of those French woods, or what remained of them, near the trenches in the 1914–18 war. I thought we were headed in the right direction, back to Haywards Heath, for in spite of the misery and distraction of the walk I had kept my head about direction, wanting, indeed, nothing more than to be back in a train on the way to London. But in case we were lost, I asked a woodman, and he set us on the right track, walking behind us with his bicycle and speaking in a pleasant voice about the weather.

This exercised a calming influence, and Nancy began to talk in a quieter and more sensible way and to ask whether there was anywhere where we could get a cup of tea. The woodman said he thought no tea shops would be open, but that we ought to be able to get something in one of the hotels, and he named the bigger ones and described where they were. Personally I hoped to get away from Nancy without tea, for I had planned in my mind when starting out to take a return train at about 4.30 and it was getting on for four now. And what with the perishing cold and Nancy's hysteria I was less anxious than ever to prolong the visit. When we reached the High Street I said tentatively that I thought we'd better get away before darkness fell, especially since some fog had been threatening all day, but Nancy only said, 'What, without tea!' in a lifeless sort of voice. So we went straight to the station. But as ill luck would have it, there was twenty to twenty-five minutes to wait before a Brighton train was due, and since it was too cold to hang about on the station and the woodman had mentioned a hotel quite close by, we went to find it at Nancy's suggestion. I must say it was a nice warm comfortable place when we got into it – the first time we had been warm that day – and since Nancy seemed calmer then and I thought the gin had evaporated and that I oughtn't to terminate this awful afternoon until she had quite recovered, I resigned myself to the prospect of missing the next train. But I had omitted to ask the time of the following one, so after I had ordered tea and while Nancy went to the ladies' room to pee, I hared back to the station to find out and got back to the hotel lounge before Nancy had emerged from the toilet.

We had a quiet pleasant tea – tea for Queenie too and some cake – and Nancy talked a little, in a quiet way, about the difficulties of her life. But mostly we sat in silence. I was thoroughly stunned and tired by now, and had a headache, and only wanted to go home as soon as I could. But whenever I looked up, I saw Nancy staring at me appealingly with her great tear-stained eyes. At last I said, 'Come on, old girl. We must get off or we shall never get back,' and I paid the bill.

'Oh, not just yet,' said she, 'wait a little longer.' So we sat on in silence for a bit. Then at last I got her up and out. But no sooner were we back in the street and returning to the station, than she began again.

'Oh Joe, you're *not* sending me back to that room! Oh Joe, you *can't* do it, you can't do it. O please Joe, oh don't, oh I beg you. I can't stand it, I can't, I can't. I'm frightened! I'm frightened! I think all the time of suicide. I shall kill myself, I know. Oh Joe, *don't, don't!*'

This was dreadful. Those tears. The rising cry of hysteria. I put my arm round her. 'Dear old Nance. Dear old Nance. Not again.

Please not again. Don't start it again, old girl, or you'll make me ill too' – I was terrified that she would suddenly fall down or sit down in the road, or refuse to go, or insist on returning to my flat with me, where Ann still was camping out in Bunny's room. I said, ' I *do* see the difficulties of your life, old girl, and I will do something, I will.'

She said, 'No no, it's got to happen, now, now. I can't wait any longer. You're only fobbing me off as you always do. You'll just go back and forget all about me.'

I said, 'Listen, old girl, you do see, don't you, that except for offering you a room in the hotel next door, which I must say I *do* think you're unreasonable to refuse, I simply *can't, physically* can't, do anything *at once*. What *can* I do? You know my flat has only got two rooms and two beds, and tho' Ann camped out at night with Bunny on the sofa, it must have been jolly uncomfortable, and *you* wouldn't have liked it, and it would be absolutely awful for everyone if such an arrangement went on. And on the other hand I can't turn Bunny out into the street. I must have a breather to think it out and what will be best for everyone.'

'Oh no, I don't believe a word you say. You're just putting me off as usual with fair words which you don't intend to act on.'

I said, petting and kissing and supporting her, and wishing to God I was back safely in a London train, 'I do think of you, Nance, and your awful lonely life, and do think of it even tho' you imagine I don't, and if you were only able to think a bit wider you would see I've tried every sort of way to settle you happily – '

'Yes, just so as to be rid of me.'

'How silly to talk like that when I've told you so often that you could be of such immense help me if you only would, and that no one else could help me as you could.'

'It's not the same thing. It always comes back to me staying in a room by myself, and you know I hate that and that I always go to pieces. I've told you that over and over again. And Bunny too. She promised me when she left that she'd *never* let me stay in a room alone again.'

I said, 'All right, all right, I see what I must do, I must give up my flat at once, and take a house for all of us. Yes, that's what I must do.'

'But that will take time, Joe, and don't you see, I'm ill, ill. Oh Joe, do, do something quickly.'

'All right, old girl, dear old girl, I will, I really will.'

'But what?'

'Look, Nance, let's call it a day just for now. I'm so tired and have such a headache. Just leave it to me, trust me, I will do something quickly. Only don't ask me what at the moment, for I can't say.' But I said I would like to come down and stay with her on Wednesday night, and she agreed to book a room for me.

Eventually I got the wretched creature into her train. I kissed her goodbye, and she kissed Queenie goodbye, and the train carried her off through the foggy darkness back to Worthing. It was now 5.30. My own London train came in almost at once.

But I was dreadfully worried over the whole business. Besides the anger I felt against such behaviour, and the hatred I always feels towards her for this sort of emotional blackmail she so constantly subjects me to, there had been a sort of frantic note the whole time which frightened and worried me. Also I do feel so dreadfully sorry for her, so possessed by such jealousy, yet also so sweet with her gifts and her pullovers and her restlessly fidgeting fingers. It seemed to me that I really should have to give up my flat if she had reached such an extremity – but O God, what happiness could there be for any of us in another Wendy in London? Oh dear, oh dear, this endless problem. But her appeal had reached and disturbed me, and sitting there with my dog which I could fondle and kiss, returning to a flat where there was company to greet me, I thought with fresh misery about poor shabby old Nancy in her threadbare trousers – I must at once do something about that – with no animal or person to make a fuss of or fuss over her – her own fault if you will, but a poignant thing nevertheless – returning bleak and alone to an empty room in a boarding house in Worthing. I thought, I must get the old girl up somehow. I must take a risk on it. I can't just leave her to rot and go off her head. But what?

28 December 1948

But, of course, Nancy is right, one does fob her off. What else can one be expected to do but postpone decisions all of which seem equally dangerous and bad? The final solution is the one she won't listen to: that she should come to live in a room close by. Though that would be hell too – as she herself knows. 'I should react badly to Bunny being in your flat. If you didn't want either of us, I shouldn't mind.' But anyway she rejects it, saying now that she would be just as lonely living close to us in a separate room as she is in Worthing, which is manifest balls.

No, she just wants Bunny out of my flat. And with her dreadful appeals and threats and cries still ringing in my ears, I suppose I must do something for her, and I do go about it as I said I would, but although I think of the step I must risk, I delay making a definite proposal of it.

The step is this. I suddenly remembered that Nancy's birthday falls on 24 January. Obviously I must do something about that, and since we had let her down over Christmas, I felt I should make up for it over the second occasion. Bunny was very distressed over my news of my afternoon with Nancy in Haywards Heath, and my description of Nancy's frantic behaviour, and at once asked what I thought should be done. I reminded her of Nancy's approaching birthday, and the good old woman at once said, 'Perhaps you should ask her up, and I could go and stay with Ann.' Well, as I've said, if Nancy were a normal woman that would be a splendid plan, and one could even look further in an attempt to satisfy both, and have an endless game of Box and Cox, Nancy coming for a month or so and returning to Worthing to make room for Bunny coming for a month or so and returning to Ann – the only objection to it being that it would be rather uneconomical to keep Nancy's room on for such long periods, and of course she has no Ann or friend in her life, owing to her unaccommodating temperament, with whom she could put up. But, Nancy would never go. Never. Never. She is not that sort of person – the sort of person who gratefully and punctually and gaily terminates a visit and catches a train back to a less congenial surrounding.

However, it seemed to me a risk must now be taken. I accepted Bunny's offer.

Yet I could not at first bring myself to clinch the plan by telling Nancy of it. One always hopes – one has always hoped – that something else would happen to solve all one's troubles, that Nancy would make a friend, or find a man, or come to her senses, or suddenly see what a bloody nuisance she can be, and say, as she is sweetly able to say, 'It doesn't really matter, dear old Joe. I don't really want to turn Bunny out. It would be nice to stay with you, and tho' I know you are suspicious of me, I really would jolly well go.' How lovely, how simple life would be if that sort of thing happened. One would even persuade the poor girl to come up. Beg her to come. But as things are, one cannot help but temporize – as she clearly sees.

So the morning after Haywards Heath I did nothing more than send her a cheque for £50 with an affectionate note to say that the matter of her winter clothes could and must at any rate be immediately cleared up and that I was dreadfully grieved – as I was – that she had not let me know of the state of her wardrobe before, and said I was looking forward to visiting her on Wednesday night. I also phoned her on Monday night to clinch it. After that I fell into indecision about the plan, and, walking Queenie over Wimbledon and Putney commons, was always trying to think out how best to handle it, whether I should ask her up for one, two or three weeks, whether I should trust her to make things easy and gain my confidence by going punctually when the day of departure arrived, or whether I could think of some way by which I could make it harder for her to stay on. It could be very nice to have her up and give her a break and a good time for two or three weeks, if only one could count on her to play the game. Unfortunately there really was no reason why Bunny should not stay with Ann more or less indefinitely, but I don't want her to; the old woman has done me very well and fits in beautifully with my life. I want her to return, though I am willing enough to send her away again at intervals if Nancy is good. But I am sure Nancy will cling on, once she gets a footing. Compassionate tho' I feel towards her and worried over this constant talk of suicide, I do see that she is being a selfish pig – she does not care in the least what happens to Bunny, she can be shovelled into any hole, pushed out anywhere, no matter whether it is convenient or comfortable for the old woman or not; so long as she is got rid of and her place taken by Nancy, that is all Nancy cares about.

I meant only to write in this diary about Queenie, and the gay, lighthearted, joyful life we share together, the fun we have. But of course one can't avoid people. They connect, and that's all right, but they also interrupt and burst in on one's pleasure, and that's a bore. However, on with these relatives of mine I must go.

30 December 1948

How this business does go on. Awful letter from Nancy Wednesday morning, returning my cheque.

I haven't booked a room for you tomorrow because I don't want you to come. I couldn't say so over the phone because it is so public, and I don't want the people here to know I am in this state. They are suspicious already, and I knew you would argue and keep ringing up if I said no. I knew it would be no good going to Haywards Heath and having salt rubbed into my wounds but you made me. I couldn't stand any more of that – and of course I don't want this money you've sent this morning for clothes or anything else.

I told you on Sunday that this has all been too much for me. I shall never get over it and I can't stop thinking about it. It's been going on so long, you see – month after month I've tried to shove it away, to fill my life with other things when there was so little to fill it with, to keep on hoping and not believe the worst – it has been wearing me down for a long time. It was bad enough to be forced back into the life which both you and Bunny know I dreaded, but you didn't even stop at that. You have both gone out of your way to make me feel like an exile, no welcome in the only home left me to go to. I keep thinking of that ultimate cruelty which I got news of for the first time on Christmas morning – that you have asked Ann instead of me. You could never have me in the flat because there wasn't room, but you make room for Ann. Do you suppose I haven't thought of that alternative over and over again and longed for you to say, come up and sleep on the floor or a couch, or that you would borrow or hire another bed as so many people do at Christmas. You see, none of your reasons for not having me have been the sort of reasons that one couldn't get over if one had really wanted to.

It is all too much for my poor brain to cope with. I know you keep saying that you didn't think I minded about Christmas. Perhaps you didn't, although actually I mind very much and dread it more and more as the years go on and my life gets emptier than ever, but you did know that I was lonely and wretched and had been longing for you to have me to stay, so surely you must have realized that to leave me alone at Christmas and ask someone else instead was the most frightfully cruel thing to do. How can one believe in affection or kindly feelings in the face of such treatment?

I know there is nothing to be done now and I have nothing left to hope for – I might have spared myself the last humiliation of begging you to help me on Sunday.

Please don't ring up any more, or try to come here. I would much rather be left alone now.

Nancy

This dreadful misery and jealousy endlessly rapping at one's door. I can't bear it. I went out directly after breakfast and sent her a wire to say that I had an invitation for her to the flat and was writing, love Joe. But was that now a good - tactful - move? I worried as I walked morosely with Queenie over Wimbledon Common. Perhaps she would, now that she had forced out the prize, say it was too late. I was being rapidly put into the position, I felt, of having to beg her to come after all. Dreadful letter, dreadful tangle, what line could one take? How could she suppose that Bunny would invite her to the flat – an old woman of eighty whom she had persecuted with her jealousy and pulled from her bed at nine o'clock at night, pulled from her bed twice, throwing the clothes about, trampling on her things, and threatened with a knife until four o'clock in the morning? How much of that did she remember? She remembered getting her out of bed and treading on her things – but said she'd apologized afterwards and put everything back. She denied the knife. A lie? Or had she been *non compos mentis* at that point? Bunny had said she looked like a maniac. But even if she admitted as much as she did admit, could she really expect that to be passed over with an 'everyone has rows'? And the dreadful things she had said to Bunny: 'No wonder Mother died if you were looking after her', 'You've never done a day's work in your life', 'You shelter behind your age', 'We only have your word for it that you looked after Doc so well when he was dying.' Unforgettable, unforgivable things: could she really suppose they left no mark? And her persecution of the old woman, making her show the letters she received from and wrote to me; suspecting her of meeting and talking to the Wilsons [mutual friends] outside and calling her a 'liar' when she denied it. And the occasion when Mrs Wilson, seeing Bunny so upset and unwell when Nancy had taken to her bed because they could not find anywhere else to go after Wendy, had asked Bunny in for a glass of sherry: as soon as Mrs Wilson had gone Nancy remarked, 'You just go and have a glass of sherry with her, my girl, and see what you get when you come back!' Horrible behaviour, outrageous behaviour the whole time – yet to her mind now either forgotten or of no account. Poor old Bunny, when at last I managed to rescue her from Nancy's warder's clutches, was in a dreadful state of trembling nerves, and had nightmares for many weeks afterwards. Yet Nancy could suppose that she would be invited up to spend a Merry Christmas by her!

When I got back Morgan [Forster] had phoned, so I phoned him back and asked him to lunch and showed him the letter. He was horrified by it: 'unfocused hatred'. But said he did not think it gave indication of mental illness and that he did not think there was any urgency for me to run down to Worthing at once. He advised a short calming letter to say, lovingly, that I would not worry her with anything more at the moment, but wanted to see her and would like to come down soon if she would fix a day. He thought my wire a mistake, and recommended that I shouldn't refer again to the invitation to the flat when I wrote. I wrote that sort of letter, rather more than he advised, saying that I had promised her at Haywards Heath that I would do something, and had only asked her to trust me and have a little patience, and that now I had arranged it – I gave her a hint by saying it had after all turned out quite easy, for Ann's leg [recently broken] had just been freed from its splint, so that she was now more active, and I asked if I could come down on Thursday night instead. But I fidget in my mind about her. I keep thinking of her in her bedsitting room, day after day, week after week, with absolutely nothing whatever to do and no one to talk to, nothing to do but make her own meals, walk by herself, knit me pullovers and, in the evenings, what? She goes to bed I know at about 8.30. I shrink from thinking of her life, and when I force myself to, I feel quite ill.

So this afternoon, having got thro' my office work, and worried out of my mind, I decided to go down after all and risk it. In the train I wrote her a note of almost total capitulation. I said that she was my only sister and I her only brother and that, in spite of wrangles and rows and disagreements, she and I were knit together inseparably and that I needed her as she needed me and that I knew that in the end we should live together. Indeed, if only she did not persecute and blackmail me with her emotions, which I don't reciprocate and can't stand, to live with her is exactly what I should like, for she could be of immense service to me. Having given her that future prospect – something to look forward to, to hope for – a dubious prospect for us both, I fear, I added the present plan. That I had arranged for Bunny to go and stay with Ann in a couple of weeks' time or so, and that she (Nancy) was to come up for two or three weeks and stay over her birthday with me if she would. I said I would let her know the exact date when I knew it myself.

I wrote this note with the intention of leaving it at her house in case she should be out, or even to post it in Worthing if, when I got there, I decided not to upset her by making her see me after all. I was not quite sure what to do, what reception I should get, whether I was wise or not to force myself on her after her letter. I didn't want to bring her to hysterics in her own house. But I wrote my note, and decided to see how the land lay when I got there before determining on any particular course of action. I meant only to stay an hour in Worthing anyway.

As soon as I got there, I decided to go straight to her place by way of Miss Allison's – an old woman she visits – in case I came upon Nancy in the street. That seemed to me the most desirable solution – to come upon her in the street. It was about two when I arrived. I looked thro' the windows of the Salad Bowl, her restaurant, in case she should be there, then passed Miss Allison's house and walked down Shelley Road towards Winchester Road. No sign of her. I passed her house, but the luck of seeing her coming out or going in was not mine. Then I asked for the nearest public phone and, with an unspoken prayer, phoned her. She was in, and came to the phone.

I said, 'Nance, I've come down to see you. I'm in Worthing, just outside your house. Can I see you for a moment?'

She was surprised, and seemed pleased. 'Would you like to come here?' she asked.

I was delighted with this reception. She opened the door to me, and we embraced.

I said, 'I'm only down for an hour. Don't let us talk about the things that upset us.'

We went up to her room. I'd never seen it before; she'd only been in it some six weeks. It was a very nice room, warm, comfortable, cosy, friendly. She was awfully nice, as she can be. She asked me if I wanted anything to eat, and made me some tea.

I said to her, 'I've written you a little note in the train. I meant to leave it here if you were out. But I shall leave it here now, and you can read it when I've gone.'

Then she said, 'Joe, there's one question I must ask you. Do you think I'm a homicidal maniac or something?' I said, 'No dear, of course not,' and would have gone on to say what I did think, if she'd asked me, that she is a jealous woman with a tendency to violence, but she did not ask and did not even appear to listen. She then began, quite quietly, to talk about herself, that she was of a hysterical disposition, but that she was incapable of hurting anyone and so on. But that she was much thrown in on herself by the life she led, and things tended to assume a disproportionate size by brooding over them and having no one to speak to about them. She talked of her health and her stomach, how it never acted now unless she took an enema. She said she hadn't been to the WC since before Christmas.

She was awfully touching, sitting there rubbing her fingertips together, and every now and then smoothing her temple, another characteristic gesture she has, as though brushing away some worrying thought. She showed me a third pullover she had made for me, a red one, almost finished. She was awfully sweet. There was a gale blowing, and her bottle of milk had been blown off the window sill where she'd put it to cool. At last I said, 'Look, old girl, read my note after all, why not?'

'What, now?' she said.

I handed it to her, and turning her back towards me she put on her spectacles and read it. It was a short note, but seemed to take her a long time. Then I saw that she was crying a little.

'Oh Joe,' she said, and put her arms round me and kissed me. 'Are you pleased?' I asked.

'Oh yes,' she said. Then she began to talk, quite quietly but aggressively about Bunny and her heartless behaviour.

I said nothing at all, except occasionally, 'Don't let's talk about it, old girl. Some other time.' But she went on and on, quite gently and quietly, about Wendy having been one of the happiest times of her life because she had some occupation, and how Bunny needn't have been so beastly to her, and hadn't seemed to mind the rows they had had, but had made her all sorts of promises up to the last moment never to abandon her and so on. And how, again, everyone had these rows and, looked at as 'shouting matches', they did not come to anything or mean anything. If she only knew how I hated them and hated her for them!

There was nothing I could say – nothing safe – so I said nothing, until it was time for me to go. Then I said, 'Look old girl, I must rush now. I promised my editor I'd be back by five' (this was a lie, but Queenie had had scarcely any exercise at all and I wanted to get back to take her out), and Nancy was awfully nice and said how good it was of me to run down just for an hour and agreed to walk me to the station. She took my arm and we walked there. She went on and on about her worries, and I didn't stop her. Then she said, 'I was going to write to you today. I was going to ask you to come down tomorrow.'

I said, 'Well, tomorrow's a bit soon after today, isn't it?'

Fixing her great eyes on me she said, 'Oh Joe, do, to make up for Christmas.'

'I said, 'Oh my word. Of course, it's New Year's Eve, isn't it? Then I will come if you like, and we'll turn over a new leaf together. But I shouldn't be able to get down till a bit later, somewhere between six and seven, and shall have to leave first thing in the morning, for I've got a party on Saturday night which needs some organizing.'

She said vaguely, 'A party. What party?'

I explained that it was Morgan's seventieth birthday and William and I had put together a group of his friends, sixteen in all, to wish him many happy returns.

She said, 'Oh,' then after a pause, 'Then don't come, it doesn't really matter now.'

I said, 'Of course I'll come, old girl. I'd like to.'

In the station we sat and waited for the train. Then she said, 'No, don't come tomorrow. I'll be all right now. Come another day when you have more time.'

I said, 'One day next week?' She said yes. I said, 'Sure you won't mind seeing the New Year in by yourself?'

She said, 'Oh no. No, it's not that. I don't mind that. It's . . . '

'What is it?' I asked.

She looked straight before her at the railway lines, her thin fingers rubbing restlessly together. 'It's just that it's so dreary in the evenings.' Then, with a sweet smile, 'But never mind, I'm all right now.'

I waved goodbye at her from the train window until we were out of sight.

1 January 1949

Poor old girl. I thought afterwards that it would be a long time for her to wait for her evening talk until Wednesday or Thursday of next week – why not Sunday, tomorrow? So I phoned her yesterday to suggest it, and she was very pleased and agreed and booked me a room right away and had I had her letter – I said no – and I said I would wire her my time of arrival. And how were her bowels? Yes, they had moved. Her letter came in the afternoon, warmly affectionate. 'How sweet of you to come down and bring that wonderful letter. That was so like my Joe, my own real Joe . . . When you come again let us be hilarious. I feel it would do me good to be hilarious. And you are quite right; we will talk about nothing that worries us.'

Morgan's party in evening: Queenie is invited to Howards End by Miss Elisabeth Poston.

9 January 1949

On the evening of Sunday, 2 January, I went down to Worthing as promised, by the 4.35 train, to spend the evening and night with Nancy. I didn't feel at all like it. At Morgan's party the night before I had drunk a good many not very successful drinks – rather sweet sherry, rather sharp champagne and brandy, and I woke up on Sunday with a tired, unrested feeling after too short a night, heavy-headed and unwell. But in my sort of life there is not much rest. Queenie had to be walked, and well walked, for she had not had a great deal of exercise in the week, and would not get out again until Monday morning latish, for I was to stay the night with Nancy. So I walked the dog rather dully all over Wimbledon Common during the morning and, after lunch, would have liked to go to bed for an hour, but there was insufficient time.

I had had an amusing Picasso Christmas card from Georges, with a message for Nancy, which I thought would please her and remembered to take. I thought too that I would give her a picture of Queenie for her mantelpiece, which I had noticed, sadly, was quite bare of photos – no pictures of Paul her husband, Paul her son, me, Dad, Peter, Mother or Bunny. It was the only sad things that struck me about her room – no photos, as though there were no person, living or dead, of whom she wished to be reminded. I thought of Queenie's photo because Lilian Bowes-Lyon had sent it back to me.

Poor Lilian, I have shamefully neglected her, and have no real reason. I don't really think about people except the few of whom I am really fond, and additional reasons for not seeing Lilian are that she seems to have an emotional feeling towards me – and my family life has made me regard emotion as something to be avoided at all costs – and that she is not just ill, but one of the most appalling cases of illness that can ever have happened. To go and see a person who has had both legs cut off and is likely soon to lose an arm, and who has never been out of pain, night and day, for some six or seven years is not a pleasant errand, and one which a selfish man might seek to avoid. I keep my memoranda of things I want or ought or have to do on the backs of my Abdulla cigarette boxes, and Lilian's name has been transferred from one used box to the next full one for months on end. My conscience tells me I must go. In my busy, energetic and distracted life it is easy not to. I phone occasionally and promise. Nothing happens. Then one day some time ago – the day I called on Rose Macaulay – I did ring up and proposed myself and Queenie. But Lilian could not see me then, she was expecting her doctors. I said I would look in at Christmas. But though I thought of it, I didn't. Nor, worse still, did I send a Christmas card. For some reason I never can think of Christmas cards except in connection with the working classes. Anyway, to cut a long story short, on the morning of New Year's Eve I got a politely barbed letter from Lilian sending back to me, with an exquisite and painfully well-bred, almost Chinese, implied rebuke, Queenie's picture and some verses I had once sent her. I flew in to see her that afternoon and had tea with her and made, as well and affectionately as I could, my peace: but that is another story. The result was, that I had an extra picture of Queenie, and took it down to Worthing.

I reached Worthing at about 6.10, and Nancy was there to meet me. We greeted each other affectionately, and walked down into the town to get a drink. We thought we would go to the pub we used to drink at when I was staying with her before, but realized suddenly that it was only 6.30 of a Sunday evening and all pubs would still be closed. Where to go? What to do? A bench on the front? We walked there, but a better idea seemed to be to go into one of the seafront cafés and order a cup of coffee which we need not drink. This we did, and talked of this and that – the gale that had raged on the south coast on Friday and Saturday and blown a bus full of people over a bridge, and Morgan's party, which Nancy asked about. I told her how much we'd drunk.

'Oh dear,' she said, 'I bet you didn't much want to come down here today after that.'

I said, 'Well no, if the truth be told, I didn't.'

We then left the café for the pub, but it was still closed when we got there.

I said, 'How about buying half a bottle and taking it back to your place instead of drinking here? You get more that way.'

She said, 'Just as you like. I did suggest that on the phone (she had) but you put me off (I had).'

I don't know why I'd put her off – expense perhaps: but now, at the pub door, I recollected how uneconomical it is to drink spirits 'out' instead of buying a bottle, and how it is usually in my mind when I am wasting money in pubs. So we bought half a bottle of gin and a couple of small dry gingers and went to Nancy's room.

It was pleasant and warm there, and she had prepared everything very nicely – two nice salads laid out, with prunes, cheese, bread, fruit and a bottle of Algerian wine – at least, the wine was hidden away in her wardrobe, and when she went later to fetch it she pulled out a bottle of olive oil instead, which made her laugh. Before going up to her room she showed me mine, on the ground floor – hers was upstairs – and I left my coat and haversack in it. The gas fire was burning, and Nancy told me what a lot of trouble Mrs G. had gone to to air the room for me – the room in which her brother had died lately – and make me comfortable. I turned the fire down.

We poured out our gins and had a pleasant talk and I gave her Georges's p.c. and, since I pulled Queenie's picture from my pocket at the same time, I gave her that as well, and put them on her mantelpiece, which only carried a Sealyham calendar, a clock and a red jug. Sipping our gins I got her to speak of her health and dietary, and she told me a long history of the other occupants of the house – mostly old ladies. She was most amusing about them, and knew about their characters, lives and relationships, their eccentricities and jealousies and foibles. She explained that her room contained the airing cupboard of the establishment – a large cupboard in a corner – and that it was rather a nuisance. For the cupboard held garments and things belonging to the other tenants, and they had to have free access to it, to put things in or get them out, and were always popping in and out whether she wanted them or not, and using the cupboard to come in to gossip about each other or pry into her own affairs, so that she often locked her door. However she liked them all and was evidently amused by them – there were three or four elderly women, a younger woman and an elderly man – and the whole set-up and history quite diverted and amused me, and suggested to my mind – as I said to her – what a good stage device such a cupboard would make as a focus for getting miscellaneous characters together, and that she ought to write a play called *The Airing Cupboard*.

The younger woman – about her own age – who was staying there she had only lately met, and she had had a strange visit from her. The lady had come up, on New Year's Eve I think, rather tipsy and smelling of whisky, and had been very matey and had poured out her life history to Nancy. So far as I remember, she had lost her husband, but had a son who lived elsewhere with his granny, while she herself had this room here, and also a gentleman friend of whom she was fond, and some job in the town. Nevertheless while describing all this volubly and brightly, even gaily, in a hearty sort of way, she remarked that life was an awful bore really and she often thought of committing suicide. When Nancy went on to say that she herself, with nothing to live for, no friends, money or purpose, had spent a lot of time lately thinking of the same thing – that she would put her head in the gas oven – I interrupted to say with a laugh, 'You haven't got one.'

'Well this,' she said, pointing to her gas fire with its flexible pipe extension to a ring – it quite cheered her up to hear that someone else, and with apparently far less reason, had similar ideas.

After two strong gins I was happy and since it was now after eight and I had to get up very early in the morning, I said, 'Let's eat now.'

But Nancy said, 'Oh, not yet. I want another gin first.'

So I poured her another, and then sat to my salad. Nancy got out the bottle of Algerian, and we set to our meal. I praised her salad, and the stuffed prunes, which turned out to be the ones I'd sent her for Christmas. She said with a laugh that she'd only just opened the tin, she'd been so furious when it came. The wine was rather sour, I thought, but Nancy liked it, and of course I don't care myself what I drink, and had a couple of glasses, which made me tireder and stupider still. Now I wanted only to go to bed, but alas we began to get on to subjects – past grievances, future prospects – which I did not want to discuss. I had been wondering on the way down whether I'd say anything more yet about Nancy's prospective visit, but although it was a settled thing that Bunny should go and Nancy come for her birthday for a period, it was a subject that seemed to me so fraught with difficulties and anxieties that I thought it had better be left until I felt sure that Nancy had recovered from her Haywards Heath hysteria. I thought that if I alluded to it she might say, 'Why can't I come for longer than three weeks? Bunny's been with you for nine months. There's no reason why she shouldn't stay with Ann for ever,' and so on, and then a wrangle would begin and perhaps she would have hysterics in the house. But in fact she had been so calm and sweet and good so far and on my previous visit that it had occurred to me as a pleasant possibility that, feeling obviously so much happier now in the warmth of my love, she might even decide to make things easy for me by saying, 'Look, Joe, it's made all the difference to me just to be asked. I don't really want to turn old Bunny out, so won't come unless it really is convenient' – or 'I'll just come for one week, otherwise it will be too uneconomical you paying for this empty room and Bunny's expenses too.' How nice that would have been, but it did not emerge.

Instead, a querulous note in her voice began as we neared dangerous ground, so that I was much relieved when there was a knock at the door and Mrs Gray came in. I had never met her before, and liked her at sight – kind, practical, considerate – an extremely nice woman. I was introduced, and asked her to sit down and offered her wine or gin. She refused first, then accepted gin. She had taken a lot of trouble over my room, Nancy had told me, fussing about it, airing the sheets, and I thanked her for all that. She wanted to know what time I wanted to be awakened, and I diffidently said I would like to catch the seven o'clock train if possible, explaining about having to shave in London and take the dog out. Nancy said pleasantly, 'I told you, didn't I, that he'd probably do that, and come down without his razor,' and it was agreeable conversation, and Mrs Gray said she always herself got up at six, so there was no difficulty about knocking at my door at half past, and I said that would suit me fine, and I would just slip on my clothes and scram, and how to get out was explained to me, not the front door – difficult catches – the side door, just by my bedroom door was best, and then we talked a bit about Queenie whom Mrs Gray was nervous of having in the house because she herself has an old ginger cat she was even pottier about than I was of Queenie, and so she went.

It was now about 10.30, and I was almost drunk with weariness; but now Nancy began her stuff.

I said, 'Look, old girl, I'm awfully tired, and we said we wouldn't talk of anything worrying this time; say goodnight and let's go to bed.'

'But nothing's been settled,' she said, 'nothing, nothing. I knew it would be like this. You don't mean anything you say. Oh, why did you come?'

I concealed my irritation and said, putting my arm round her, 'Come, old girl, not now, it's too late. It's been such a nice evening, your lovely hospitality and salad. Don't let's spoil it now. Kiss me goodnight.' I kissed her head, for she sat slumped miserably in a chair and would not turn her face towards me. I did not know what else to say. The last thing I wanted at this late hour, fagged as I was and with an early rise and busy day ahead, was to begin any conversation of any sort, let alone one which would only end in trouble and take hours to get through; so I said firmly, 'Come along, old lady, see me to my bed and tuck me in,' and left the room.

I went downstairs, hung about for a little, then undressed, got into bed and turned out the light. I was almost asleep when she appeared, turning on the lights again. Oh dear, scenes in my flat returned to me, scenes at Wendy, tears and reconciliations in the small hours, why on earth couldn't she behave in a civilized manner? Grotesquely she carried a huge piece of cheese in her hand, which she placed on the mantelpiece.

'Here's some cheese for you,' she said. 'I knew it would be like this. You don't mean anything, do you, just placating me somehow.'

I said crossly, 'No Nancy, not now, do go away and go to bed,' and I turned my back on her. In a dim way I heard her mumble something or other. Then she put out the light and shut the door. I was asleep in an instant.

At 6.30 next morning I was startled out of a heavy sleep by a knock at my door. It was about fifteen to twenty minutes' walk to the station. In a rather stunned, somnambulistic way I turned on the bedside light and got into my clothes. Then I quietly opened the door into the passage, dimly lit by the light of an oil stove. Under my door, exposed when I opened it, was a note – a folded letter without an envelope. In a bleary way I picked it up, opened and read it. It was from Nancy, written in an erratic sprawling writing:

I thought you were going to help me, Joe – what did your letter mean? – just nothing. You know I am utterly miserable and frightened living by myself like this and you keep promising me that things will be different and pretending you are fond of me – then when I see you again you are quite different and I know you were only trying to lull me into a sense of false serenity – it will always be like this I know. I can't stand it any longer. This awful lonely life and a succession of bedsitting rooms. I have wanted to die for a long time. Now I am going to. I never wanted to hurt anyone – you least of all. I wanted so little – only to be near you and feel that I had something left to live for, to be able to do all the little things to help you that I did at Wendy which kept me busy and happy and not interfere with your life in any way – but you don't want me, and I can't go on alone. I thought you knew that, and have only pulled myself together these last few days, because your letter and visit gave me hope – But how many times have you raised my hopes lately and in the end it means nothing – You only want to go on as you are – leaving me here to be lonely

– ill – frightened – all the things I have been for years – and would go on being for the rest of my life –

I can't do it – even for you – my nerve and my spirit is broken.

I can't bear these letters of Nancy. I've had them, in varying degrees of jealous hysterics, over and over again for months. I can hardly read them when I have seen the first sentence and know from experience what will follow. Half-awake, tired, in the dim light, with a train to catch, I read it cursorily. 'Now I'm going to . . . ' Suicide again. Emotional blackmail. What a bore. Too much gin. 'Only to be near you . . . ' But I'd asked her up, over and over again, begged her to come and help, against my better judgement, and she'd only replied, 'I shouldn't like to come and stay in a room nearby. I should react badly to Bunny being in your flat. If you didn't want either of us I wouldn't mind so much.' Jealous cow. 'All the little things to help you that I did at Wendy . . . ' My God! Wendy! Passion-rent Wendy! Hell on earth. 'Now I'm going to . . . ' She was drunk, of course; she couldn't really mean that; I'd heard it so often before. . . . Nevertheless, I was perturbed and fumbled about in the passage for a light. At last I found one, and turned it on. Where was Mrs Gray's room? – she had just knocked at my door. I hadn't the foggiest idea. This passage on the ground floor was full of doors – Heaven knew where they all led to. No lights anywhere, no sound. Should I go up to Nancy's room? But where on earth was it? I couldn't remember where anything led, or where it was, or how to get upstairs. And would I not wake all the other ladies in the house, fumbling and fidgeting about. Oh hell, I thought, why bother? And I shall miss my train. I slipped out of the side door, and by hurrying caught it.

I read her letter again in the train and was worried by it, but not unduly worried. I did not really suppose that she could have carried out her threat, any more than she did when she returned from Haywards Heath, and added in my mind irritably that anyway if she killed herself last night she killed herself, and is now dead, and if she didn't she didn't and is now alive, and one can't upset a household of old ladies at 6.30 in the morning to find out which.

When I got back to Putney – at about 8.30 to 8.45 – having travelled there without even a cup of tea, for there was no restaurant service on the train, I found Bunny and Ann, at breakfast, and read Nancy's letter to them. 'So she may now be dead for all I know,' I said cheerfully. Ann was due to return to her own home this morning, she had been with us since Christmas and it was time she went.

Morgan rang up, and I told him about it and the letter. He was inclined to be worried over it, such rapid changes of mood, and thought she must really be ill mentally since she seemed now so totally incapable of controlling herself – 'Poor thing,' he said. But he too did not take the threat of suicide seriously. 'What will you do? You'll write to her, I suppose.' I said yes, and told him what I thought I would say. He said, 'I don't know; yes, you'd better say what you want to say, you will know best.' Having shaved and washed, breakfasted and walked Queenie on Putney Common, and said goodbye to Ann, I went up to my office, where my editor, who is a very sweet, sympathetic man and knows of my troubles, asked me about my sister. I told him what had happened in detail, and again added, with a shrug, 'For all I know she may now be dead.'

As this day developed, I felt more confident, supported by the lack of urgent worry shown by other people, but was worried in a niggling sort of way nevertheless, and decided that during the morning I would phone Nancy up and find out how she was. I had a good deal to do, however, and when midday came, I thought I'd better get lunch over first, and would perhaps phone Worthing when I got back. I had my usual rapid lunch at the Bon Accord in Great Portland Street at 12.30, and was back in my office before one. When I lifted up the receiver to put my Worthing call through, the exchange said, 'Oh, Mr Ackerley, we have a message for you.'

'What is it?' I asked.

'It's from the Stepney police – wait a moment.'

'Oh God,' I thought, 'she really has done it.' I was plunged at once into a state of nervous agitation. My heartbeats accelerated and my heart began to thump wildly against my ribs. 'Oh God, oh God,' I kept saying. And the telephone became maddening. PBX gave me the number of the Stepney police I was to ring. I phoned them, but they seemed unable to understand what it was all about and, after some delay, said they had no message for me and that there must be some mistake. I then began to put in a call for Worthing, Nancy's number, when PBX interrupted to say they were sorry, it wasn't the Stepney but the Putney police, and would I phone them. I did so at once: the police station said yes they had a message for me: would I go at once to Worthing Hospital where my sister Mrs Nancy West was lying dangerously ill from gas poisoning, and would I please call in at Worthing police station on the way. 'Oh God, oh God,' I thought, 'she's done it.'

I phoned poor old Bunny at once. I expected that the police had already phoned my flat and that she had received the first shock of the news, but in fact she knew nothing of it. I told her of the message I had got, and that I must go to Worthing at once. She was awfully agitated. I left my desk as it was, and hurried into a taxi for Victoria. At the station there was twenty minutes to wait before the next train for Brighton went, so I rang up Bunny again. I did not like to think of her left all alone in the flat with such news, and wondered whether Ann had already gone; if not I wanted her to stay on. Bunny was in tears when I phoned, but luckily Ann was still there and was going to stay on. I remembered, too, to give instructions for feeding poor old Queenie, who was obviously not going to get any more exercise that day. I told Bunny exactly what I wanted her to have at five o'clock.

I have what seems to me to be a rather contemptible faculty for self-preservation. It popped out more than ever in the 1941 days when I had shopped Freddie and tried later, without involving myself, to save him from the consequences of my actions. Now, travelling down to Worthing, it began to assert itself again. At first my mind was too confused and stunned for coherent thought, and I could only stare with horror at the day, the days, before me and think, Now it has begun, this dreadful day has begun, soon I shall be in Brighton and then in Worthing and then step by step this dreadful business will move me forward with it, through what, to what? I thought, I can't face it. I've got to face it. If she is dead I suppose I shall have to identify her. Oh my God. But I can't get out of anything now. I shall have to go through with everything, whatever it may be. The journey has begun and nothing can stop it or alter its course. I thought, poor Nancy, poor creature. I hope she's dead, and then thought, No, I can't hope that. The time for her to die was in 1938 when she had that hernia operation and I was summoned to her bedside. She has neither given nor taken anything from life since, only misery and worry, and it would have been better for her, and for everyone, if she had died then, in that accident of health; but not now when we are both, all, involved in her wretchedness and self-destructive action. Not that I should blame myself, I thought, if she is dead; she set me impossible problems and was always making me take sides – between mother and her, her husband and her, and now between Bunny and her. I was always on the other side, but I was fond of her all the same and though I could blame myself for impatience and irritability, I did my best on the whole in the dreadful dilemmas in which she placed me. Then I thought, Oh no, I hope she is not dead. I could have saved her. If I had been less impatient and irritable last night and had reassured her that the note I took down to her was true, she wouldn't have done this. But I turned my back upon her. Then I thought, but that doesn't justify such an action as she took. Oh God, how could she have done such a thing. She was drunk, of course; but then she'd said to me last evening, apropos of something, that she was afraid of drink, for although she thought constantly of suicide, she didn't think she could do it unless she was drunk. Of course I ought to have gone up when I got her letter this morning, I thought, and the letter began to worry me, it looked so callous, and I began to wonder what I would say about it and what explanation I could give for having gone off without doing anything when her letter had said that she was going to kill herself. I thought to myself, perhaps I'd better not say anything about the letter. It would be better to say nothing. One must protect oneself a little.

Now for it, I thought, when the train reached Worthing Central. Now what lies before me? This dreadful day begins. Now the first ordeal starts.

At the police station I had to wait while the duty man wrote down particulars of a white metal necklace which some woman had found and brought in. Then I gave my name and business, and was at once shown into a small office where a youngish constable met me. A sergeant was sitting at a desk writing up something in a ledger or charge book in red ink. They both began to interrogate me, the young constable in particular, while the sergeant wrote down my replies and every now and then put questions himself.

'You are Mrs West's brother? We understand that you were with her last night and left early this morning?'

I said, 'How is my sister, please?'

'We understand that she is showing signs of recovery, but we haven't heard from the hospital for some hours. We'll take you round there presently, if you would kindly answer a few questions first.'

I said I would tell them anything they wished, and sat down while they put me through about half an hour's interrogation – beginning with last night and going on to Nancy's life and recent movements since she entered Sussex, the places she had stayed at and for how long, her circumstances, the state of her mind, whether she had tried to harm herself before and every other sort of question. I didn't mind the young constable, but the sergeant seemed to me extremely hostile and unpleasant, severe and moralizing, watchful and suspicious. It crossed my mind that he suspected me of murdering her, or at least of having connived in her death, or deliberately brought her to it. I disliked him very much.

'What time did you leave the house this morning?'

'You didn't see your sister before you left?'

'Why didn't you go up and say goodbye to your sister first?'

'Had you any suspicion that she might have done such a thing?'

I was more than ever sure that the less said about Nancy's letter the better.

'What was her state of mind when you were with her last night?' and so on.

I told them the truth about everything, so far as I see it, her hysteria, jealousy, inability to fit in, except for her last visit to me in my bedroom and the letter. I said we had had a most happy and friendly evening, as Mrs Gray, who joined us at the end, would no doubt testify, but that I was afraid my sister had drunk too much.

As soon as I mentioned drink, I saw how important it was – drunkenness can get one out of lots of difficulties. The constable also seized upon this: true, empty bottles had been found in the room, an empty half bottle of gin and Algerian wine. How much gin had the bottle contained when I left my sister? About half. It was empty when found. There was also an empty phial that had contained Veganin tablets. And a letter, addressed to Joe, a long letter, which began with firm writing, and then straggled off into incoherency.

'She seems to have been jealous of your wife as well as your aunt,' said the constable.

'I have no wife; I'm not married.'

'Well, another woman is mentioned.'

I looked at him blankly. 'Who?'

'Someone called Queenie.'

'Queenie's a dog, my Alsatian dog.'

I never saw Nancy's letter. Piecing it all together, from the police's questions and information, one of the other guests in Winchester House had smelt gas at about 10 a.m. and this had been located coming from Nancy's room. The fact that her milk, too, was still outside had alarmed Mrs Gray, who had entered – how? The lock wasn't broken when I went there later – and found Nancy unconscious on the floor. She had at once sent for the police. The mixture of gas and alcohol, according to the young constable, had made things worse for her than they would otherwise have been.

The interview seemed a bit easier now – no doubt they had made up their minds that it was not a faked suicide covering murder, or that I had not deliberately driven Nancy to take her life. Further questions were left more and more to the young man, but the sergeant had not quite finished.

'Do you think it a proper thing to have left your sister down here with no one to look after her, knowing the state of her mind?'

I said, flustered, 'I don't know, one doesn't think, it's hard for a layman to tell the difference between a bad and a sick mind. She seemed well enough in herself. It's really only in the last week or two that it's struck me that a psychologist might be useful, but I hadn't got round to a steady view of that when this happened.'

The important question it all came to was, 'Are you willing to take personal responsibility and charge of your sister now, to prevent her doing this sort of thing again?'

I said, 'Yes, of course.'

While I was speaking the young constable went out of the room for something and the sergeant resumed his red-ink writing. He made no comment. His severe, grim, disapproving face was turned from scrutinizing me now, to scrutiny of his ledger. He had pronounced judgement on me and dismissed my case with a rebuke.

'Besides,' I said, trying to think back, 'my sister is a difficult person to cater for. No ordinary doctor would suit her; she only believes in nature cure people and I don't believe there is one in Worthing. I asked her, apropos of something else, only the other day.'

For a minute or two I doubted if he had even listened to me, then he said, 'I was not referring to doctors; I meant the employment if necessary of someone to look after her as a companion or even nurse.'

I said, 'I never thought of such a thing. I didn't even know such people were obtainable. Anyway, my sister's human relationships were' – I kept, for some reason, speaking of her in the past tense and then correcting myself – 'are so bad, that I don't suppose any companion would have stayed with her . . . ' Then I stopped. He was paying no attention to me at all. Bloody cheek! Why should I excuse myself to this monster? How like the law to pass easy judgements according to a code of conventional rules and morals without having had to endure the atmosphere, the worry, weariness, heat, strain and rancour of the particular case. Bloody cheek – sitting there, so self-righteous, ticking me off. He looked a pretty harsh and cruel man himself; what was *his* home life like, I wondered, and his relationships with his family and friends.

He took no further notice of me. The younger man returned with his hat and mac to take me to the hospital, which was about ten minutes' walk away. He asked for Mrs West at the entrance hall desk and was told C3 ward, so we at once proceeded thither down a long corridor. C3 ward was at the end of the corridor; an open doorway gave entrance to it. A number of screens hid the nearest bed, just inside the door. A nurse came. Mrs West was recovering all right, but was not yet conscious. Was she going to be all right? Oh yes, there was no danger now. Could I see her? Yes. The screens were drawn aside and there lay Nancy on her back, rather flushed and moist in the face, a metal half-moon surgical bowl on the pillow by her face to be sick into. Every now and then she turned and twisted spasmodically and uttered a sort of moaning noise. Her breasts were visible under her disordered night shift. I went over to her and kissed her. Her eyes were wide open and stared into mine. 'Dear old Nance,' I said. For a moment it seemed as though she recognized me, and her hand, which I had taken in mine, gave a little pressure. But she was not conscious, no.

I talked to the nurse and the sister; they did not expect her to recover consciousness for some hours, perhaps not until tomorrow. I asked if there was any fear of complications – pneumonia, for instance – they said no. She would be all right now. The young woman in a blue uniform whom I had first spoken to and took to be a nurse turned out to be a policewoman. She had to mount guard on Nancy – she and her relief – night and day to make sure she did not make another attempt on herself. Also she had to take a statement from her as soon as she came to. I asked if Nancy would be seeing a psychiatrist before she left hospital, and the nurses said they expected so. I said I thought it important that she should, and they said I should see the hospital psychiatrist about it at once if he had not already gone. It turned out that he had gone, and I was taken to the lady almoner instead. She said that the psychiatrist would certainly be going to see Nancy when she revived, but that would not be until tomorrow, when she was expected to recover consciousness. I did not see what else I could do in the hospital, and said I had better return to London and come back next morning. The policeman wanted me to return to the station with him to sign a statement; so I went along.

He said that Nancy would have to go before a court with me when she was able to leave hospital, but that it was a mere formality – she would have to swear not to do it again, and I would have to undertake care of her, that was all. He said they were anxious to get these things off their hands as quickly as possible so as to release the policewomen who were wasting time mounting guard on her. We made out a statement together, which I signed. I forget what the statement was exactly, but remember that, speaking as he wrote, he said that she had no means and that I made her 'a small allowance'. I said, 'Why small?' but he didn't seem to hear. We put the emphasis on drink. When he read the completed statement over to me and came again to the 'small allowance', I interrupted once more with 'But why small?'

He said, 'Oh, not small – all right, I'll cross it out.'

I said, 'Well, small if you think so. I give her £25 a month.'

He laughed. 'No, that's certainly not small,' he said, and corrected it to 'an allowance'.

I asked him then if I might make a phone call to London to the BBC. I ought really to have made two, to Bunny as well, but thought that was too much to expect. He said yes, if I paid for it.

I phoned my editor and told him vaguely what had happened – he guessed – and asked him to excuse me that day and the next. He readily agreed, and said if I wanted any personal help from him of any kind, I had only to ask. Sweet man; one couldn't have a nicer boss. I paid for my call. Should I tip anybody? I thought not. A lot of people were obviously being put to a lot of trouble, but it was all part of their day's work nevertheless. I left the station with thanks for their help and kindness and, returning to the station, took the first train home.

I phoned Bunny from Victoria with the news that Nancy was recovering. 'Oh, thank God for that,' said the old woman. When I got back both she and Ann were boozed up on gin, but had a nice warm drink for me. They had also the expected reaction from horror and tears: they became critical of Nancy – 'putting everyone to so much trouble' – now that she was out of danger. I had made three Worthing journeys that day.

Next morning I got up early. I phoned the hospital first, and was told that Nancy had recovered consciousness. I saw that poor old Queenie was not going to have much of a day, and thought I would giver her a two-hour walk anyway, before Worthing engulfed me again. But in the middle of Putney Common I was seized with a dreadful doubt which became almost a panic: I should have been there by the poor girl's bed when she recovered consciousness to welcome her back. How could I have failed to have thought of that? It showed how little I cared – how much even perhaps I hated her – that I had not considered that. I should have been there. I should never have left Worthing. What would her state of mind be when she came to? She had tried to take her life out of despair and loneliness and hopelessness and the belief that no one wanted her. How dreadful to wake up in a strange place, strange faces, to the realization that one has failed, that all one's insoluble problems, now worse than ever, still confront one, and the worse realization that, even after that, no love was waiting for her at her bedside. Would she not go out of her mind with the horror of it? She was almost out of her mind when she did it. Perhaps she would wake up now to real hatred of me and Bunny – 'I hate you! I hate you! I hate you both!' Her Haywards Heath cry rang in my ears – now it would perhaps seem clear that we only regarded her as a nuisance since we had not even troubled to welcome her back to life. To wake and find the police at one's bedside! Alas, too late, too late. But I must do what I could. I must fly down there at once.

So, although poor Queenie was hot on the track of a fieldmouse, I hurried her home after only about half an hour's walk, and rushed onto a trolley bus for Clapham Junction. I was in a dreadful state inside of nervous anxiety, and nothing went fast enough for me and the waits were torture. What a fool, I thought. How could you not have seen how important it was? But too late – too late – too late. The shock of realization of failure would have unhinged her mind, I thought, and I pictured her now as raving, weeping, and possibly fixated on me as the hated cause of all her troubles. I began to think of what could be done in such a case; it would be very important for me not to see her in such a condition; could I not retrieve the situation by getting the doctors to give her some opiate, and then arrange to be with her *this* time when she revived, so that she would come to in my arms? One could go on repeating this experiment, I thought, so as gradually to give the poor mind confidence, wear the horror down. But too late, too late, the mischief would by now have been done, the irreparable damage in her poor disordered brain already worked by waking back into the same nightmare of love-lessness which she had been unable to bear.

Additional to this dreadful anxiety in my mind was a growing worry about Nancy's farewell letter to me, which was still in my pocket. In a way I had lied about this letter; that's to say I had omitted any reference to it in my account of the tragedy, and I had stated that I had no inkling when I left Worthing yesterday morning that Nancy had meant to do what she did. But now it seemed possible that it might involve me in two explanations, one to Nancy herself – how could I have gone up to London without going up to see her after reading the letter? Obviously I hadn't cared whether she was alive or dead; and one to the police if she had mentioned it in the statement which would now have been taken from her. The more I thought about it; the more it added to my perturbation. Supposing she had told the police that she had pushed a letter under my door saying that she was going to kill herself? Or less remotely, she might be led into mentioning it by saying, 'Did my brother find me?' and when told no, 'But where was he? I pushed a note under his door telling him I was going to kill myself.' I did not see how I could be questioned by the police now about the letter, and admit it. Could I say, 'Yes. I got the letter, but I didn't really believe . . . ' 'Why didn't you mention it before? You stated that you had no inkling . . . ' I couldn't explain about that now, and admit to having lied. Could I say that I had put it in my pocket in my hurry and not read it till I was in the train? But then why had I not phoned up Worthing as soon as I reached London? No, having concealed the letter up to date, I must go on doing so; I couldn't admit having had it now. Should I tear it up – I took it out of my pocket – and throw it away? It would then be simply my word against hers if she had told the police about it, and since she had been drunk and demented it would be regarded as a hallucination. After all, what had it to do with the police anyway? It was a matter entirely between me and her, it was the climax of our relationship, the confronting thing for us both in any future there might be, that she had written me a letter saying that she was going to destroy herself – and I had taken no notice of it – and she had in fact tried to destroy herself. That was a matter between our two consciences alone: nothing to do with the police.

But then, what about her? If I were still in time, somehow or other, to save her reason, what could I say to *her*? Supposing she were now distraught with all she had been through and accused me with 'You didn't even trouble to come up and see! You didn't even bother to do that! That is all you care!' What could I say? Could

I pretend to her too that the letter had never been written at all? Or that I'd never had it? How about that? I might easily have missed it, I thought, looking back. There was a long curtain hanging on the door, and the letter lay between the door and the curtain, and was swept inwards a little by both as I quietly opened the door, and was noticed because it scraped on the linoleum, and might easily not have been noticed at all in the dim light. I could say I'd never had it. In which case it would still be there. In which case, if that were my all-round story, would the police go and look? Could I even go so far as to put it there, put it back? I should have to go to Nancy's lodgings to pack her things; could I perhaps, on some pretext, get back into the room in which I'd slept and lay the letter back where I'd found it, or ask to look if there was a letter there, and pretend to find it. Awfully touchy – the room would have been done out – but just possible. Conversations began to rehearse themselves in my head:

Nancy: 'But didn't you do anything after the letter I pushed under your door?'

I: 'I never saw the letter, dear, the police took it. But I thought they said it was on your table.'

Nancy: 'No, another letter, not that one. I wrote you another letter and put it under your door.'

I: 'Another letter? I never had a letter from you at all. Are you sure. . .? Then it must still be there. . . . '

Then with Mrs Gray, her landlady: 'Did your maid happen to find a letter in my room on the floor?'

'No I don't think so. I will ask' – or 'No, I did the room myself and saw nothing.'

'Could I go and look, do you think? My sister says she wrote one.'

She might say yes, or she might come with me. I must have the letter handy – in my sock perhaps – so that I could bend down by the curtain with my back turned and taking the letter unseen from my sock say, 'Here it is!' Tricky . . . tricky . . . but if it came off – if I were for any reason pushed to such subterfuge and it came off, it would be the best thing. Unless – another possibility – I said that my haversack had fallen to the ground off my chair and tipped its contents of papers and mss. onto the floor, and that, in sweeping them all back into it in the half-light of early morning, I might have swept in Nancy's unread letter too. . . . Not so convincing. I slipped Nancy's letter into my sock in case . . . .

As soon as I reached Worthing I went straight to the hospital. Yes, my sister was conscious. Did she want to see me? How was she? I was told to go to the ward. The policewoman was still there, standing as usual in the passage by the open door. The screens were round the bed.

'Does she want to see me?' I asked.

'Oh, I expect so,' she said, 'I'll find out.' She went behind the screens, and then opened them for me. She said, 'The police would like you to go along to the station again when you've seen your sister.'

I thought, God. Is it about the letter? I said, 'All right.'

Nancy was lying with her eyes closed and her head pillowed on her arm, looking dreadfully unhappy and worn. I ran to her, and knelt beside her, and put my arms round her, and, luckily I suppose, burst into tears. I sobbed and sobbed on her breast and arms. 'Dear Nancy, dear Nancy,' I said, 'is it really possible that I could have brought you to such a thing as that?' I said, 'I *did* want to be here to welcome you back. I did want my love to be here waiting for you.'

She was awfully sweet and gentle and tender and stroked my hair and told me not to cry, and when I realized that she was in a perfectly normal state of mind, I remember feeling self-conscious and thinking, I needn't have done this at all. But now I found it easy to go on, and thought it would be better for her perhaps if I went on crying for as long as possible. Poor old girl, she smelt very sour and stale with sweat – she knew it and said so.

She said 'Can you see my teeth anywhere? It's difficult not having them in.' I looked about and found them in a tumbler in some disinfectant.

'I suppose you're allowed to have them?' I said. I wondered whether the police had taken them away from for her any reason; but the policewoman said she could have them, so I gave them to her. She was awfully nice. I remembered asking Georges, one of her past lovers, what she was like in love, and he said, 'Gentle, sweet.' That's how she was. She was pleased with me crying, I think, and though I hate doing it, and resent being made to do it, and saw this even, in its way, as the last gasp of emotional blackmail, I was glad I had been able to cry so naturally and spontaneously, and let it go on since it was now easy, though I wondered what in the world the policewoman was thinking.

Nancy said, 'I know I shouldn't have done it.' She said, 'It was

the drink. I wouldn't have done it if it hadn't been for the drink.'
She said, 'I took Veganin tablets you know. It was those and the
drink. I didn't turn the gas on.' She said, 'I turned the gas on, and
then I turned if off.' She said, 'I don't remember much about it
now, or anything about coming here. Who found me?'

I said, 'Mrs Gray.'

She said, 'Didn't you get my letter?'

I said, 'No, the police got it.' She said, 'No, the one I pushed
under your door.'

I said, 'The police got it, I haven't seen it. But it was on your
table, not under my door.' I was looking at her when I said this,
but crossways; the line of my eyes crossed hers at rightangles, so
that we squinted at each other.

She said, 'No, not that letter. That was another letter. I was
trying to work it all out. But I pushed a letter under your door
directly after I left you. Didn't you get it?'

I said, 'No, I never got it. Are you sure?'

She said, 'Oh yes, I do remember that. I wasn't drunk then.'

I said, 'You may have imagined it.'

She said, 'Oh no.'

I said, 'Well I simply crept out, half asleep. Perhaps it's still
there. I'll ask Mrs Gray when I go round.'

I have a notion she knew I was lying, but I didn't care. There
was really no reason why I should have lied; it would have been
safe to say, 'Yes, I got it, but I didn't believe it', but I wanted to
spare her and myself every possible reproach. I said, 'Have they
asked you for a statement?'

She said, 'No.'

I said, 'The policewoman will, I think.'

She said, 'What shall I say?'

I said, 'You needn't say anything if you don't want. Say nothing
or what you like.' I thought a bit. I said, 'Best thing is either to say
nothing or to say you were drunk and don't remember. I shouldn't
bother them or yourself with details.'

'Yes, I suppose that would be best,' she said. 'Have you had to
see the police?'

I said, 'Yes, but it was no trouble.'

She said, 'Poor Joe. I've given a lot of trouble, I know.'

I said, 'We all do at times, dear. Don't worry. And it was largely
my fault. I could have saved it with a word, I think.'

She said, 'No, it wasn't your fault.' She said, 'Shall I have to go to court?'

I said, 'Nothing to bother about. Only a formality.'

She said, 'I feel very tired. I seem to do nothing but sleep.'

I said, 'I shouldn't say anything to the policewoman really, just that you were drunk and can't remember; it's the easiest way out.'

She nodded. 'Yes, I expect that will be best.'

Then I went out to the policewoman and betrayed her. Right or wrong? Good or bad? I can't disentangle. I said, 'She doesn't seem to remember much, she's all mixed up. She says she never turned on the gas.'

The policewoman smiled. 'She did that all right.'

I said, 'I don't think she knew what she was doing. She also says she put a letter under my door saying she was going to do it.'

The policewoman said, 'Delusions.' So that finished the letter, I hoped; I'd taken it to the end. Yet if Nancy asks me later whether I got her letter or not, I'm quite able to say, 'Of course I did; I just thought it better for us both if I didn't admit it then.' The police-woman reminded me that I was wanted at the station and said it wasn't anything much, only a formality, they wanted to be quite sure that I would take charge of my sister when she was discharged.

I went from the hospital to the police station, saw the new sergeant, rather nice, who said he only wished to make sure that I was taking responsibility for my sister's future behaviour and would call to take her away from the hospital as soon as she was ready for discharge – which would probably be on Thursday or Friday. He said that if she and I would sign a paper to that effect, that she would not attempt her life again and that I would take care of her, she need not go before a court. I agreed. Then I got from the policeman who had interrogated me yesterday the key of Nancy's room, for I had now to go and pack up her things. He had told me yesterday that the police had locked up the room on Monday and taken charge of the key; he also mentioned that he had noticed two £1 notes lying about in it.

With the key in my pocket I went to have lunch; then walked on to the Winchester Road. I wondered what sort of a reception I should get there, what the lodgers and landlady were thinking of the brother of a woman who had tried to kill herself after having had dinner with him – nice sort of a brute they must think me; and what the landlady must think of such goings-on in her respectable house; and how the other old ladies had managed, not being able to get to the airing cupboard for forty-eight hours. What a lot of trouble suicides give, I thought; and it does not make much difference, if any, whether they succeed or not.

But Mrs Gray could not have been nicer. Gracious, kind, sympathetic, practical, uninquisitive, she was the veritable friend in need. She said how dreadfully sorry she was over the business, and I apologized for all the trouble and worry and shock caused to her and her other guests. I told her a little of the circumstances of the tragedy, that Nancy was a hysteric upon whom strong drink had a bad effect, and that all the upset had occurred in the last ten minutes of the evening we had spent together. I said I had come to pack her things and clear her out of the room as quickly as possible. She asked if I would like her to help me – 'A woman is better than a man at packing a woman's things' – and I welcomed the offer with much gratitude. On the way up to Nancy's room, I said I was afraid that the other guests had been put to great inconvenience not being able to get to the airing cupboard, but she said she had had to borrow the key back from the police yesterday for that purpose.

Nancy's room was as it had been when she had been taken out of it. There were some pillows on the floor near her bed, and her fur coat lay on a chair nearby. She had lain on the floor near the bed, brought the tube of the gas fire across the room to her and covered her head with her fur coat. Mrs Gray said the coat had been saturated with gas fumes, and that it would be a long time before the smell of gas left it. I remembered that Nancy never has enough cases to shift her things from one residence to another, and the first thing was to find how many she had. There were only two suitcases, one medium sized, one small, and a roomy attaché case. Mrs Gray thought we might manage, so we started. Mrs Gray packed her clothes – separating with my help the things she normally wore, which I should have to take back to the hospital for Nancy to put on when she left; and I sorted out the miscellaneous belongings. There was an envelope containing some shillings for the gas on the mantelpiece, but no £1 notes lying about anywhere. I wrote those off as a dead loss: whoever had 'picked' them deserved pickings, I reckoned, for the worry and upset they had been put to.

We did not talk much as we packed, but Mrs Gray said how surprised she was that Nancy should have done such a thing, for though she knew her to be lonely and unhappy, she seemed to like the house, and had said to her, Mrs Gray, only a few days earlier when she was hanging some washing out in the garden, 'I do like being here. It is so nice and free. You let us do what we like.' It puzzled me rather, too. It was not a scene for suicide: warm, comfortable, cosy, and with such a nice friendly landlady, and with all the people coming in and out to the airing cupboard – how could one have felt 'frightened' and 'lonely' in such a place? And Nancy had been interested – as far as she is capable of external interests – in the other denizens, and in Mrs Gray herself. I recollected the amusing gossip, the 'play', she had recounted to me, so lively, that Sunday evening. And her kind visit to Mrs Gray's dying brother. And her care of the cat which constantly visited her. For some reason one expects a suicide to be careless and untidy, but here was the tidiest room of a person who took care not only of her things but of her health. All her clothes were nicely chosen though inexpensive, and neatly hung up or folded away. The cupboards were full of health foods – food-reform foods – quantities of vitamin products, nuts, fruit and vegetable extracts, charcoal biscuits and all the things Nancy liked. She had washed up the Sunday supper things before gassing herself, and put them tidily away. The latest Agatha Christie novel lay on the table – Nancy's favourite author – and a recent acquisition from the local library, for she had not had it when I had visited her on the Thursday. An alone person could not have had a friendlier room: the only oddness about it was the lack of personal history, the dead strained past and present – not a single photograph or memento of a fifty-year-old life. Alas, that was the key to the mystery. This was the room of my only sister, excepting for my aunt my only surviving relation; yet there was no photo of myself on the mantelpiece, nor of my aunt; no photo of her husband or her son; no photo of her mother or father; no photo of any lover or friend. Only Georges's Christmas card of the dreadful Picasso woman *Tête de Femme* and the photo of Queenie, which I had put on her mantelpiece on Sunday night. I put them both back in my pocket.

As I continued this melancholy task – what should I have felt like if she had been dead? – of packing up the belongings of this photoless, mementoless woman, I reflected sadly on her life and our relationship. She had started life with every possible advantage, with all the cards – beauty, money, health and a loving family – and this was what she had come to, attempted suicide in a Worthing bedsitting room. Why? She was a woman who had never been able to bear correction or criticism, and had always sought and found scapegoats for her misfortunes and failures; but

> . . . In tragic life, God wot
> No villain need be! Passions spin the plot.
> We are betrayed by what is false within.

[The extended reminiscence that follows is presented as though it were part of the diary. But, though Ackerley may well have gone back over all the events in his mind while packing Nancy's things, it is unlikely that the actual recording of them in writing can have been jotted down like the usual diary entry.]

Vanity, arrogance, jealousy, wilfulness and a stubborn conceit, a flashing temper – I was going to say that these were some of the things that had been her downfall, and no doubt they were, but deeper than these superficial maladjustments to life lay something else, the root cause, which has been diagnosed by friends as a fixation on myself. I don't know. She was a woman who, all her life, had obliged people to take sides. First – I am thinking of the twenties – the conflict was between her and our mother: cold angers, an overbearing arrogance. My earliest recollections of her are in our dining room of Blenheim House, Richmond, standing in front of the mirror above the mantelpiece, smoking, with her coffee cup or a liqueur before her, rowing my mother over her shoulder while she regarded all the time her own face in the glass. She spent much time examining herself in the mirror, and her thought was all for clothes. She treated her young men with the careless inconsiderate indifference of the spoilt beauty sure of her power. Fond of her tho' we were, we were fonder of my mother, and shook our heads over Nancy and her wilfulness and her displays of temper. My mother was frightened of her, and so was my father. My father was frightened of her for an extra reason, which became worse as time went on: her resentment of criticism and correction was such that she not only rejected them, but took all reproof out on other and weaker people – my mother – afterwards. After she had driven my mother from the room, as she sometimes did, and stalked out afterwards, my father used to sit silently at the table, with his brandy or port, never using, alas, the authority he had and could effectually have used I think, but sometimes saying sadly to himself such things as 'Nancy will never make any man happy,' or 'God help the man that Nancy marries.'

My father was a ladies' man, which I am not, and was therefore more sympathetic no doubt with female nature than I am. Considering what a large, powerful, dominating sort of man he was, it was curious how little he attempted to correct us, how lenient and indulgent he was. Instead of giving my sister a 'good hiding', as he must often have wished to do and which might have had a salutary effect upon her, he seldom pulled her up, but let her go her own way on the £500 a year he allowed her. He was fond of her, of course – and maybe realized early that she resented criticism so strongly that it was a waste of time.

Then she married, in 1926. In spite of his occasional remark, 'God help the man that Nancy marries,' Dad gave her a splendid wedding and she went off to live in Colon where her American husband worked. We were not surprised the marriage failed. We did not expect it to stick; her character was too subjective, a receiving not a giving character, and too stubborn, selfish and ruthless. And though she blamed all and sundry for its failure, her husband, his mother, sister and so on – we knew her character too well to sympathize in our hearts with her. She slapped his face once in public: it was the sort of thing she was liable to do. The poor fellow must have had a hell of a time. She had always done just as she liked, and she did what she liked with him, going into hysterics when he opposed her.

After some two years of married life and the birth of a child, he brought her, in a nervous state, and the child back to England, and left her here for a holiday. She stayed for two years, writing him angry, cruel or abusive letters when he urged her to return. We all disapproved deeply of her conduct and tried to get her to go back, but no one has ever been able to influence her, and few have even attempted it, one is too afraid of her temper and her tongue. She has a curiously vulgar streak in her, not obvious in either our father or mother, which enables her to say to people the cruellest and most cutting things.

No doubt her husband had too few memories of conjugal happiness, or they were outweighed by the dreadful scenes and rows which we did not need the exercise of any imagination to know must have occurred: at any rate, he at last instituted proceedings for divorce. Then she came to her senses – but, as always, as the victim; through all the losses and misfortunes of her life – attributable, all of them, to the 'falseness within' – one has scarcely even heard her blame herself; she has always been the injured party, the victim of the jealousy or treachery of others. An effort to retrieve the situation failed; and we were so sure, from our experience of her, in our hearts, fond as we also were of her, that what she had lost she had justly lost, and that no reconciliation of any durability was possible, that, though some of us took her side, and acted as her emissaries, we could not hold up our heads when confronted with the case of the other side – it corresponded too well with what we knew to be the truth. Our friend General Charlton, who accepted the task of meeting the husband in New York and trying to persuade him to reconsider his decision, sympathized with him too much when they met to press it; Nancy had hysterics at this news, I remember, and Leo was the sick traitor in her eyes for a long time afterwards; and I myself proved a broken reed in my two meetings with Paul's sister Jane, when she confronted me with her genuine anxiety for her brother's happiness and her exhortations to me not to trifle with the situation, but to speak my honest and truthful opinion. Indeed, I did not believe, and I do not believe, that Nancy cared for her husband at all – simply because she has no real feeling for other people. She behaved as if she disliked him, and she actually said she disliked him, she even said she disliked him sexually: later she explained all that on the grounds of her nervous illness, and what did *we* know of a woman's post-pregnancy nerves? But in fact she chose between her family and her husband, and chose the former; and it was only when she lost him that she thought she wanted him.

But he'd had enough. She took the child back to him, but nothing came of it. He allowed her to divorce him, and she got alimony and the custody of the child. Later, she brought the child home for good.

My poor old mother, who was living quite happily by herself in Richmond, said she must take them in. I begged her not to, and reminded her of how ill they had always got on; but she was sentimental about poor Nancy's plight and was determined to lodge her. Nancy and the child stayed with her for two years, and how dreadful those years were. They left an indelible mark upon my mind; for, although I had my own flat and life in London, I was a weekly or twice-weekly visitor at my mother's house and endlessly involved in the troubles that disturbed it. Indeed they all now fell upon me, for my father was dead, and as the only surviving male in the family the burden of desperation and appeal was narrowed and focused upon myself; it was upon me only that the wretched task endlessly fell of attempting to protect my mother and keep the peace.

Life at 159A Sheen Road, my mother's small house, which used to be so pleasant, with cheerful visits from myself and my friends, like Leo [Charlton] and William [Plomer] and Harry Daley, had now become positive hell. There was pretty well always a row in progress, and an endless business of 'She said this . . . ' and 'I never said anything of the sort . . . ' and '*I* heard what you said on the telephone . . . ', 'I suppose you've been running to so-and-so for sympathy' and 'You're always talking about me behind my back and poisoning people against me.' Like all jealous and temperful women, my sister had developed a strong persecution mania, and my poor old mother's life was no longer her own. Suspected all the time of telling tales about my sister and putting others against her, she was not even safe in her silences; if she looked ill, as she frequently did, that was playing for sympathy, or if she said when asked how she was, 'Oh well, never mind,' or something like that, that again was implied criticism of Nancy. I longed to help and rescue my mother from this torture, but the situation was extremely delicate. I could not even openly take my mother's side, for then the poor old woman got an even worse time afterwards for telling tales to me; and indeed she was so frightened of her daughter that she scarcely ever did say anything, but when I saw her ill, or she looked worn, or deadened from the overweight atmosphere, or I noticed other signs that there had been trouble and, my sister out of the room, I asked my mother what had happened, she would usually say in a nervous frightened way, 'Never mind, dear, don't say anything, don't say anything, that's the best way. It doesn't matter.' When things got so bad that my mother sometimes took to her room and bed with a headache, and I attempted remonstrance with Nancy, she would say, 'Of course you would take her side. You never think anything's her fault, but you don't know what she's like when you're not here. She behaves quite differently to me from what she does to you, because she's always been jealous of me and hates me, she always has.' Years later when my mother was dead, she was to say, 'I never had a mother.'

Another reason why it was a difficult situation was that my sister had no money, for her alimony never came, or did not come for some time afterwards, when I – it was always I from now on – got lawyers onto it for her. One could only therefore get rid of her from this small house by giving her an allowance, and this eventually my mother and I did between us. I sometimes asked the old lady in her distress to come and live with me, but she wouldn't. She was not the sort of person to do that sort of thing. 'Oh, couldn't they go somewhere else?' the poor old lady begged me at last. 'I'd willingly pay anything to be rid of them. And she's not happy here, so why does she stay?' But it was two years before I managed to separate them. I should have done it earlier, for my old mother never recovered from the misery and strain. Indeed things had got to such a hateful pass that my sister even went so far as to twist my mother's wrist. My mother never recovered her gaiety or took the interest in her home that she had had before. She became eccentric and slovenly and took to drink. Her faculties began to deteriorate. Later, when she was going deaf and blind and was losing her locomotive powers, she used to say to my aunt, 'Don't let her (Nancy), come near me, she's cruel, cruel.' At this time, the old woman being so old that she was no longer a rival I suppose, my sister was 'looking after' her. In the last year of her life, when she had hardly any faculties at all, she would sometimes say after my sister had visited her, 'Who was that woman?'

I often hated my sister during those Sheen Road days, and wished her dead. I hated the emotional demands she made upon me and the endless frictions and rows that inevitably arose wherever she – and only she – happened to be. Yet so careful did I have to be and so kind must I have appeared – and indeed so sorry was I often for her – that she now postdates my antagonism towards her some ten years later. However that is understandable, for the more characters that fell out of our domestic drama, the more we two were left to confront each other alone. Yet she had early indications.

I remember once sitting with her in a pub in Richmond in the war. I had come down as I did once a week to visit – *she* thought to see *her*, but in fact to see my dear old mother, and I was having a drink afterwards with Nancy. She said, referring to mother, 'She was a bad wife and a bad mother.' The remark shocked me profoundly. It shocked me for a number of reasons: first, it was a lie; secondly, it was a filthy thing to say about an old woman who was now so far gone that she could no longer speak up for herself; thirdly, it was a filthy thing to say to me who, as my sister well knew, loved and was loved by my mother; and fourthly, it was the grossest piece of criticism as coming from *her*. *Even* if it had been true, she herself was the last person in the world to utter such a judgement. A wonderful wife *she* had been, and a pretty dubious mother too. She had already wrecked her own life very thoroughly – and her son's, by depriving him of his father – and though I never liked the rather troublesome little boy, I felt dreadfully sorry for him, for I was quite unable to believe that the jealous possessive temperament that characterized my sister was going to be any more good for him in the long run than it had been for anyone else with whom she had been emotionally involved. The fact that she loved him – if she did – was what worried one so much. The remark, indeed, like an electric shock, struck sparks off me, and if she had been in any sense a discovering person she might well have wondered what was going on behind my mask of cordiality and kindness, if such manic and unwelcome reactions could be produced. I simply let fly, and told her that it was a disgraceful lie, that our father had never ceased to love mother even tho' he had been unfaithful to her, and that she had never ceased to love and care for him. The most united couple with scarcely a wrong word between them in all their forty to fifty years of married life. An abominable slander. Up to the day of his death he had ventured to make love to her in all those little ways of thought and remembrance that people who are fond of each other cherish, mementoes on birthdays and anniversaries, presents, presents all the time, and at the end of his life, 'Look after your little mummy,' he had said to me. A bad wife and mother indeed! She had borne him three children, and had worked for them all her life. 'She was a bloody sight better woman than you!' I said in a furious temper at the stupid arguments my sister persisted in putting up as proof of her accusation, and eventually reduced her to tears.

From 1935 when her husband died, until about 1940 when the house was rendered uninhabitable by a land mine, Bunny had lived with Mother at 159A. Nancy was by then in a Key Flat at Lichfield Court, Richmond, and the nextdoor flat to hers was now taken to contain mother and Bunny. The three of them lived there throughout the rest of the war, until the rates got so large that they all left. Mother and Bunny went to live in Carshalton, Nancy went to stay in Hampshire with a woman friend.

Before she did that she came to stay with me, and it was far from a happy experience for either of us. Her mixture of feebleness and fault-finding was very disagreeable to me. With no resources of any sort of her own, no hobbies, friends, interests, she was the kind of guest who is a continual responsibility because she had no means of entertaining herself. I know very well that I am not an easy person to live with, but then I have lived alone and looked after myself quite successfully since I was a boy, and don't want to be lived with, though I don't mind being stayed with for a specified and not too extended time. Nancy is not an interesting person; since she has never bothered to read anything but detective stories, and is so little interested in the world that she does not even know what is going on in it, politics, art, the theatre, music, anything, the subjects for conversation were naturally limited, our talks endlessly about the stale and boring problems of her life, her alimony, her son's future, or about health – her one great topic – food reform and getting one's bowels to work. She is a woman with no initiative, and, one might say, no capabilities except for knitting and for food-reform cookery, at which she is undoubtedly good. It wasn't much to occupy a day, in fact it was so little that she noticed all the time that I was paying insufficient attention to her.

Some time later a woman doctor who was attending her in Brighton – a German woman – said to me on the only occasion I ever met her, and then only for half an hour, 'You know what the trouble with your sister is, don't you?'

I said, 'I know a number. Which have you in mind?'

She said, 'She doesn't fit in.'

It was a brilliant diagnosis; it was absolutely right. Nancy expects other people to fit in with her; if she ever attempts to fit in with them she can't keep it up.

In the autumn of that year her son returned. She had sent him off to his father at the latter's suggestion when war broke out, regretted it ever afterwards, and not seen him since. He had spoken of coming over at last and eventually he came. He came at the same moment as Nancy herself came along to make a second stay with me: she now had a cottage in the country – not much of a one, but a home anyway and a friend next door – and I thought perhaps I hadn't behaved awfully well to the poor girl last time she stayed and invited her again, meaning to make up. Her son, just arrived, was in my flat when she appeared. It was rather touching: she dropped her bags outside on the mat, crying, 'Paul!' and ran forward to embrace him. But oh dear! If the previous visit had been a failure, this one was a disaster.

It was, of course, a trying business for her, granted that, a testing time for any woman: if ever a moment had come for her to exercise control and sacrifice herself and *fit in* – not merely because there was nothing else to do, but from diplomatic motives, as the only hope of gaining her ends – here it was; but she couldn't take it. The boy was almost unrecognizable – nineteen as against twelve when he'd left us, over six foot tall. He was dull, unemotional, stubborn, good-mannered, conventional. But he meant well. It was a case for the most careful delicate handling, the most selfless, considerate

'The beautiful Nancy Ackerley' — with her brother in Richmond, *c.* 1920

Ackerley and E. M. Forster on holiday in Dover in the late 1930s

ckerley with Jack (Sebastian) Sprott and his sister Velda

kerley with an Athenian kitten

Ackerley with two Japanese students

Ackerley with his dog Queenie (Tulip in *My Dog Tulip*)

Ackerley and his sister Nancy

(portraits by Don Bachardy)

Above left: Siegfried Sassoon in 1915

Above right: Siegfried Sassoon as an old man

Right: James Kirkup

treatment. Grievance No. 1: his father and stepmother were also over here, and he was rooming with them. Nancy thought he should be rooming with her – but where? No room in my flat, and I now had Queenie, so couldn't very well leave myself. And although he expressed himself as willing to go down to her cottage, she didn't want that. I think she was afraid of having this strange youth all to herself in a rather uncomfortable cottage. Uncomfortable? She made him far more uncomfortable here. Grievance No. 2: Instead of having come over to live with her for ever, he was only over on a holiday and wanted to return. Grievance No. 3: even in his short stay he meant to take time off and away from her to go to Europe – France and Switzerland – to try to make a little money out of the exchange rate. He'd heard money could be made that way.

Poor Nancy; one sees that she was being put to a severe test, but how badly she came out of it. I begged her to control herself. I explained that her only course, if she really wanted the dull young man, was to acquiesce in all his boyish plans and projects, not attempt to hinder him in any way, give him a good time to equal the good time he was getting from his father and stepmother – dinners, theatres, drinks, fun, etc. – and make no complaints at all. She said, 'I know you're right, but I can't.' She couldn't. She rebuked him for having left off loving her. She was always in tears – the emotional blackmail that I always get. She only took him out once and then lost her temper with him – couldn't fit in with his ideas of eating and drinking; it wasn't food reform – and, worst of all, ran down his father to him. Oh, I begged her not to, but she would. How dreadful, how boring it was. Then, having failed with all other weapons, she fell ill – it is her way – of a mysterious complaint, a temperature, lumps that wouldn't go. What a time the poor oaf had. He came regularly, punctually, and every time was met with reproaches, hysterics, sickness, and the sense of guilt. I sympathized with him profoundly. Why shouldn't he live the life he desired? These possessive, jealous, clinging women: he was being put thro' the hoops I was all too used to myself. However, less sentimental and weak-natured than myself, he was not deflected from his course. Though his reunion with his mother must have been absolute hell – and must have pointed a very striking contrast with his gay life with his stepmother – though he was considerate, affectionate and unfailing in his engagements to Nancy to the end, he caught his train and boat back to the USA, leaving her on her sick bed. Oh my word, and all in my flat.

If the boy got a poor time, it was nothing to what I got when he'd gone – attempts at suicide and all the rest of it. From every point of view – even practical – it was a deplorable exhibition of utter un-self-control. I am told I behaved heartlessly. Very likely. I didn't believe in any of it. I didn't believe in the boy as anything worth bothering about; I didn't believe in my sister's love for him (she had agreed he was deadly; but when I reminded her how deadly we'd agreed he was, she said, 'You don't understand a mother's heart!' Alas, I understood such parasitic organs all too well) and I didn't believe in her illness. I didn't and I still don't. It was one of those undiagnosable temperature illnesses – taken seriously by medicos, true, oh yes, genuine enough – which hysterics are always able to induce in themselves when they can't get their own way. If the boy had suddenly returned, cast himself at Nancy's feet and said, 'I repent. I will live with you for ever,' her temperature would have vanished in twenty-four hours.

As it was, she was carried from my flat in an ambulance to Putney Hospital. She was there, rather expensively, for nearly two months – complaining as usual, and trying to food-reform the hospital ('A difficult patient,' said her doctor) and was then carried off to a convalescent home in Brighton. Here she made more fuss than ever. 'Your sister doesn't fit in.' Thence she went to a vegetarian hotel, and then as a lodger to a house in Hove, where she began to receive treatment from Dr Latto, a naturopath, and then to Miss Clark, a fellow-thinker, on the Littlehampton Road.

My little mother had died while Nancy was in Putney Hospital, and my Aunt Bunny, her sister, who had been caring for her in her decline, came to stay with me. Penniless, there was nowhere else for her to go. She came to stay, and stayed on. (During all this time, of course, I was constantly seeing my sister; critical of her tho' I was, I always kept in touch and friendly, and fidgeted down to see her in her Hampshire cottage, her vegetarian hotel, her Hove lodging and her place with Miss Clark.)

Now that I owned Queenie, it was convenient for me to have someone in the flat with whom I could leave her, and Bunny and I seemed to get along well together. Moreover, she had some friends, and among them Ann, who had a flat in Thornton Heath to which my aunt was able to go when I wanted my own friends to come and stay. So the spring and summer peacefully passed, while Nancy lay recuperating in her various hotels or houses on the south coast. At last, having quarrelled with Miss Clark, she rented a bungalow called Wendy in Beehive Lane, Ferring, for the winter months, and this was a useful piece of news for me, for I had been invited to Italy for my holiday and I was now able to accept. So Bunny, Queenie and I drove down to Ferring a few days before I was due to fly to Florence; we went down just for that period of my holiday, a month – but we stayed for more than six. Wendy! Nancy afterwards described it as one of the happiest times of her life. How extraordinary! – and yet not how extraordinary. She enjoyed it, by contrast, because she was occupied, had something to do, preparing meals and taking out the dog; she was mistress of the house. The fact that we did not want to be looked after, especially by her, did not matter. The important thing was that we afforded her occupation. Having lost her husband and failed to retrieve her son, she now had us willy-nilly to supply the depressions in her life. She looked after us – and she gave us positive hell.

But this happened gradually, though the term of our bondage was established from the beginning. For we found her in an overwrought and near-hysterical condition, afraid of her bungalow now that she had taken it. She dreaded staying in it alone. She had thought of finding a lodger or companion to share it, but did not know how to set about it. (Afterwards she was to say that she had never wanted us to stay on and that we had in fact spoiled her game, which was to start out in her career as a landlady. By staying on we had prevented her from getting lodgers.) But she set about me – almost on our first walk. It wasn't fair. I had everything, my flat, my work, friends, aunt, dog. She nothing. She was odd man out and it was very unfair, and she couldn't stand it, her lonely purposeless life with no friends or future, it was making her ill, she only wished she were dead. Both Bunny and I were very sorry for her, and agreed we could not leave her like that, we would have to stay on and help her out, see her through. But I made one condition, and that was that I should have to take Queenie back to London in February for her next heat and mating, for I had made all plans for her there and had a prospective sire. And since I could not properly look after the dog alone, I should have to take Bunny too to help me. This was agreed to. So instead of staying at Wendy, for the period merely of my holiday, we remained on – indeed we stayed till the lease came to an end, that is to say Bunny and Nancy stayed there, and Queenie, while I spent the weekdays between my office and my flat in London, and went down to Wendy for weekends.

It was proper hell, but more hell for poor Bunny than for anyone else. She was not by nature suited either to Nancy's companionship or to Nancy's kind of life: they are woman of entirely different character. Bunny is a confirmed townee, a Londoner even still at eighty, she has a childish response to the life and glitter of a town, the lights at night for instance, and always, when I have taken her out in Putney across the bridge to dine at Bertorelli's, she has exclaimed with pleasure to see the ordinary street lighting – the red, yellow or green traffic lights, and the street lamps, and the moving lights of the buses and other vehicles, shining and moving and making patterns all round her, and reflected in the water of the Thames. Oh, look at the lights. How pretty they are! How beautiful!' She is always quite moved by them.

Then, too, she is a sociable woman. And boozy. She had friends in London with whom she had always kept in touch, and she adores being taken out, anywhere, to anything, a drink in a pub, a cinema, to lunch or dinner, a play. She loves all that, and dresses up to the nines, in clothes often, especially hats, more suited to a young girl, Dresden shepherdess hats, high heels and so on. She wears gloves, even long kid gloves, just for shopping, she would not like to go out without them – and in fact and in short loves life and a good time, and takes an immense interest in it. Again this laudable wish to enjoy herself, this appetite for pleasure and life is reflected in her taste for food and drink – she loves exotic foods and strong flavours, spices and herbs, tasty sauces, and in her cooking spices everything, stews, fish, soups, etc., with a lavish hand.

It was scarcely to be wondered at that the poor old girl hated Ferring. There was nowhere for her to go, the pubs were too far for her to walk to, the buses scarce and inconvenient. To go to a cinema or into Worthing was an expedition. The roads were gravelled and uneven, very trying for her high-heeled shoes. The nights were pitch dark. She was cut off from her relatives and friends. And, to crown matters, she was subjected by Nancy to a health diet, vegetarianism, and no drinks except at weekends when I came down. She therefore spent most, if not all, her time in the bungalow, grating nuts and raw vegetables against a grater, while Nancy went off shopping or took Queenie for long walks on the downs.

But there is another trait to Bunny's character, and that is that she fits in. She may well have shown and said that she disliked the country and wished herself back in town, but she toed Nancy's line and did what was expected of her as good-naturedly and uncomplainingly as anyone could expect of her. She is a very ardent

100

feminist, one of the few women I've met who actually likes other women, admires feminine prettiness and beauty without jealousy, has all the old-fashioned ideas about chivalry and gallantry to women, the weaker sex, stands up with immense loyalty for all her, often awful, women friends, refusing to allow a word to be said against them. She is also a woman who reacts instantly to friendliness and kindness in others; a positive gush of sentimentality and sweetness is at once called forth from her in response to any little affection or kindness or graceful action from others. On the other hand she has a belligerent streak in her nature, she does not take rudeness or insult lying down, though her responses even here – and this is important – are always dignified and correct. Like my mother, in fact, she is a lady, dignified and correct.

All this is most important, for if one was confused over the rights and wrongs in Nancy's disputes with her husband, and if one even also allowed some provocative element of jealousy on my mother's part as some small excuse for Nancy's behaviour to her, Bunny was as fine a test case as one could imagine. If Nancy had treated Bunny properly, Wendy would have been harmonious; the fact that it was a positive nightmare was, without any shadow of doubt, due to Nancy's jealousy and bad nature. This is not to say, of course, that Bunny is a perfect character. Who is? There are a number of things that are irritating and boring in her – her boastfulness first and foremost. But however exasperating it may be to hear her continually referring back to her early triumphs as a vocalist, etc., any one with any sensibility would understand and ignore all that, for it is something to pity, the nostalgia of a person who knows she has been a failure.

Nancy behaved abominably to her. She was jealous of her, for having done what she herself had failed to do, live harmoniously with me, and she was determined that she should not return there. It was the same thing over again as 159A Sheen Road, only worse. She bullied and persecuted the old woman, and frightened her out of her wits – the snake and the rabbit. No wonder my poor old aunt looked forward more than anything else to my weekend visits – someone more human to talk to than this dreadful sergeant-major schoolmistress of a woman, humourlessly grinding at her raw vegetable salads, reading my aunt's correspondence, and keeping her up to the mark from morning to night. Also my visits meant gin and wine. But the poor old girl wasn't even allowed to look forward to me. This was interpreted as provocation and jealousy on her side.

'You don't know what she's like when you go. Idles about and refuses to do anything – leaving all the work of the house to me. But as soon as Friday comes, oh, that's a very different matter. She perks up then all right, and even offers to help,' and so on.

The rows were endless and awful. I got them, too, major rows, at least every other weekend, rows that went on for twenty-four or forty-eight hours, rows about anything or nothing, all based on jealousy. At the beginning, I remember, when I was walking with Nancy I began to praise Bunny. I had learned a good deal about her from having had her live with me, and was much interested in her character and, especially, in her learning, her memory and her wisdom. She had a solid foundation of good literature, which I hadn't suspected, Shakespeare, the classics. She'd read them all and remembered them and could quote from them; many of the things she said to me about life and people were astonishingly wise. I said all this to Nancy, out of interest, while we walked; and Nancy staged a major twenty-four-hour row that evening because of it, accusing me of having deliberately tried to make her jealous. What pettiness! What stupidity!

There were jealous rows too over cooking. Condemned to a food-reform diet during most of the week, Bunny would look forward to cooking for me our meat rations, or fish at weekends, and presumably it made Nancy jealous to see this link between us. If we had herrings, for instance, she would open the windows because she found the smell so offensive; and Christmas Day produced a disgraceful exhibition of childish rage; we had acquired a goose, and Nancy spoiled our pleasure in it by sulking over her beans or whatever she ate, and saying that neither of us cared in the least what *she* ate, we had monopolized the kitchen, and so on over *our* food, and she, of course, could eat anything, *that* didn't matter. God, how awful she was.

Every weekend I used to go down in a state of anxiety – what was I in for? At least every other weekend I got it in the neck – over something or nothing, the wrong answers, the food, the dog's food (Nancy was trying to make poor Queenie a vegetarian too) or anything else.

And then the dreary tiresome rows. The usual pattern – fault-finding remarks from Nancy because she had too much work to do, or we didn't poke the stove properly, or something; some gay or pert rejoinder, or a raspberry from Bunny, or a laugh, anything, then a storm of rage from Nancy, who would go out, banging all the doors, sulk in her room or go out into the night with a cold, white, set face, looking like a sort of suburban Medea, for immense walks, whether it was raining or icy cold or not. We would try to placate her. No good.

'I hope I *do* catch my death of cold. Neither of *you* would care, anyway.'

Off she'd go, a handkerchief round her hair, seething with hatred. Time would go on. Poor Bunny would begin to fidget and worry.

'Don't you think we ought to go after her? What *can* she be doing all this time? It's really dreadfully worrying.'

Visions of Nancy's corpse floating in the sea. I was so enraged by these exhibitions myself I didn't care, then anyway, whether she drowned herself or not. What right had anyone to make so much trouble? Queenie of course would be very upset, always affected by hysteria – and contributed herself to these hysterical storms, I daresay, for although she would go out with Nancy for walks during the week when I was away, she would never leave my side when I was there. ('Queenie is a different dog when you aren't here. Subdued and well behaved. It's only *you* who have such a bad effect upon her.') Then more banged doors and Nancy would be back, shut into her room.

Bunny and I would huddle miserably in the kitchen.

'Don't you think you ought to go in to her, Joe?'

'Oh, fuck her' – but I would go in at last, one had to break the wretchedness somehow. 'Nance dear, come and have a drink and be matey.'

'Go to hell.'

I would retire to the kitchen. Then, nothing else to do, I would return to my room to try and read, Queenie dutifully following. But how could one read in such an atmosphere? At length we would go back to the kitchen and begin to prepare our evening meal. Nancy would burst forth. Enter the kitchen like a tragedy queen – God how silly she looked – seize whatever health food she wanted, Slippery Elm or something, perhaps prepare it there without a glance or a word, and haughtily return, banging the door again. If one ventured some mild reconciliatory remark, one was shouted at. Then, in the middle of our own dinner she would burst in again – now on the verge of hysterics.

'You hate me, both of you. There you sit whispering about me, and you're driving me mad, mad. You're beastly, beastly, both of you. I can't stand it! I shall kill myself. I shall kill myself!'

Then, of course, one had to do one's stuff – the usual stuff – the stuff all this was an emotional blackmail to get – one had to put one's arms round her, and kiss and caress her, and say loving things, and so calm her down. This was the required emotional reconciliation. This I've had to endure all my life. Disgusting. I hate it. It seems to me degrading, filthy, and yet she calls upon me for it all the time.

Once, after a row, Nancy shouted out that I hated her, that we both hated her, and that she meant to end her life, and in the kitchen, tore off every stitch of clothes she had on and ran out into the back garden to catch pneumonia and die. Stark naked. In Beehive Lane, Ferring, at nearly midnight. I loathed her for it, of course, but what could I do? I had to get her back out of the garden. So I set up a wail of 'Oh Nancy, dear Nancy! Oh, come back. Oh my God!' putting tears – far from being felt – into my voice, pretending to wail and weep – and eventually she returned. I turned on a hot bath for her, and brewed her some hot drink – after, of course, the usual petting and kissing – and so, worn out, managed to get to bed. A fine weekend in the country. Next morning I felt like death – but she appeared to be none the worse for her suicide. The only reference – quite casual – to it was 'Oh Joe, I think I must have left my cardigan in the garden last night. Do go and get it for me.' I felt like saying, 'Go and get it yourself, you silly cow,' but dared not.

But I was concerned and puzzled too. In a similar hysterical storm one evening, when I had gone in to soothe her, she said, 'Go on talking, that's it. Talk about anything. Go on talking. You used to get me out of these attacks, but now you don't, you only make me worse. Go on, talk to me about something, anything.' So I went on talking about something or other to her, and eventually she calmed down, and accepted a drink. I was drinking my own drink on the doorstep of Wendy, looking out into the night, and she came and joined me there. I put my arm round her.

She said, 'Joe, do you think I'm weak in the head?'

One so seldom hears her criticize herself that I was taken by surprise and said, 'No, Nance, I don't.' But I was touched by the question – and concerned. Perhaps, through never having attempted to control herself, and through having nourished herself for twenty-five years on hatred and resentment, she now was simply unable to exercise self-control, in short perhaps she was now mentally sick, not just a capricious, jealous, bad lot.

And all this time we were hunting about, Nancy and I, for some other residence, in the Worthing district, or on the downs, or even nearer London to carry on into when Wendy came to an end. It was dreadful – the grimmest time I ever spent. Everything was grim and humourless – as tho' one's life depended upon it – the house-hunting, the cooking, exercise; there was a feeling of strain and agitation running thro' it all, nerves; it was the most neurotic six months I ever spent. My charm, kindness, efforts to be loving and gay, efforts to help, were all of no avail. The thin crust of civilized life cracked and cracked here and there, like the roof of my Putney flat, and one was always patching things up.

When Queenie's heat drew near, I made an effort to take her away. It was a noble effort on my part, for I proposed to leave Bunny behind; and to look after Queenie in my flat single-handed and on heat was a formidable task. Nancy resisted it, of course, with might and main – she saw in it the beginning of the end of that family life which she 'enjoyed' so much and made so awful for everyone else. I told her what she would have to contend with if Queenie remained there, that the bungalow would be ruined and that it wasn't fair on the owners – but women, and Nancy in particular, have no powers of reason when they want their own way. In the middle of it I took Queenie off at last. A successor to Wendy had still not been found. Nancy's hysteria and panic increased as the end of the tenancy drew near. She behaved more and more like a lunatic. One night at 9 p.m. thro' some disagreement or other she hauled Bunny out of bed, threw her personal belongings about and trampled on them, and, turning the bed upside down so that she could not get back into it, took her off into the kitchen.

'I shan't sleep tonight,' she said, 'and neither shall you.'

She bolted the kitchen door, and taking some knives out of the drawer, threatened the old woman with them – 'I shall cut your throat first and then my arm.' After some time she relented, remade Bunny's bed and tidied up her room, but when Bunny got back into it she hauled her out again. 'Oh no you don't. I shan't sleep and nor shall you,' and kept her up till four in the morning.

I went down once or twice with some difficulty, leaving Queenie alone, and tried at Nancy's request to get an extension to the Wendy lease until Nancy had found another place, but without success. Nancy then, in the last few days, did her usual stuff of feeling ill, just to make life more difficult, with her kidney – and the last time I saw her then was lying in bed, weeping and reviling us alternately, with poor old Bunny running to and fro like a frightened hen getting her hot drinks. I never saw a more lamentable sight, and would have like to have taken a stick to her, temperature or no. It was decided than that I should finally book some rooms in Wimbledon which I had already found for them, not very nice, but they would do to begin with. Mrs Wilson came in to see 'poor' Nancy and ask if she could do anything to help, and Bunny was reviled afterwards for having allowed her in. Mrs Wilson sent an invitation to the old woman, for whom they were extremely concerned and sorry, to ask her in for a sherry if she could be spared.

'You go, my girl,' said Nancy, turning her Medusa face upon her from the bed, 'and see what you get when you come back.' That was the kind of way she spoke to Bunny throughout.

But Nancy, still determined to have her own way and not fit in with us, did not wish to come to London, and this resolve so restored her health that she was able next day to get up and continue her local search. Meanwhile I booked and paid for a week of the Wimbledon rooms – only to be phoned that evening by Mrs Wilson on Nancy's behalf to say that she had found something else. It is thought that I was awfully angry about this, but of course I wasn't, though I dislike having my time wasted and also my money. But my real anxieties were two: I wanted to rescue poor old Bunny from Nancy's clutches, and I also wanted help with Queenie. So I pretended to be angrier than I felt, and said that since I had paid for the Wimbledon rooms, one of them must come and occupy them; but Bunny too misunderstood all this rather foolishly, and thought I wanted to stick her in a strange lodging all by herself, whereas my real wish was to get her to London where she wished to be, and away from Nancy's jealous police supervision.

They found a woman to take them in, and then Nancy discovered a flat she liked and moved into it and Bunny came to me. The poor old girl was quite shattered when she arrived, and had nightmares for some weeks after. Nancy had developed, out of her guilty conscience, her usual persecution mania towards her, accused her of seeing people, like Mrs Wilson, whom she had not seen – 'You're a liar' – and had kept a close supervision over her correspondence with me.

'I thought I would write to Joe.'

'There's no need for you to do so; *I'm* writing to him.'

I myself was still enraged by the last sight I had had of Nancy, lying in bed sipping slops and alternately crying into her pillow and accusing me of everything under the sun – not doing this, and not doing that, thinking more about the dog than her, not trying hard enough to find rooms for them, pretending I had work at the BBC when she didn't suppose I had any at all . . . and so on and so on, ought, ought, ought; as tho' I were some sort of servant or poor bloody henpecked husband instead of a person on whom she had *no claim whatever* for anything, and should have been humbly grateful for the smallest kindness I cared to show her. I ought to have put Queenie into a kennel, I ought to give up my flat, I ought, I ought – bloody cheek – it took me many months to get over it, indeed I never shall, and wrote Bunny at about this time a letter, which I knew Nancy would read, in which I said that, whatever solution of their problems they cared to make, I would have no more passion-rent Wendys, so Nancy need not trouble herself to look for another. Bunny said that that left Nancy rather quiet, as well it might.

So Bunny came up to me, and Nancy stayed at the seaside, which she preferred to town. She had to move soon to another room, in Portland Road, and there she stayed until the move to Winchester House. I saw her from time to time, and did what I could to organize her into my life – partly because I needed her help and partly because I was sorry for her. But there were two solutions I could not any longer entertain. One was that she should live with Bunny again – indeed Bunny had begged me when she arrived to put her in a poor house rather than in Nancy's power again; she said she didn't at all mind seeing her, but was frightened of her now and did not want ever to be left alone with her again. Even if she hadn't asked me this, I wouldn't have allowed it. The other thing to avoid was that Nancy should come and stay with me. I knew she would never go if she did, and I did not want to be persecuted by her possessiveness again, any more than Bunny did. Nancy eventually interpreted all this as beastliness and hatred and a sort of combination against her, but of course it wasn't. She herself in one of her rare enlightened moments at Ferring said to me, 'I never could live with my relatives,' and this seemed to me an absolutely correct and intelligent diagnosis. But she did not remember having said it afterwards, and even denied it. She is dreadfully stupid really; never having used her brains, how can she expect to have any? She said later that we had 'built up' things against her, but it was she who did the building-up. After Wendy, I wrote her a number of

107

letters in which I tried to make her see reason as I saw it myself, but it was of no avail.

In order to attempt to smash this dreary jealousy and emotional possessiveness business I told her that I did not love her, I only liked her, and did not wished to be loved by her, for I simply couldn't reciprocate it. I also told her that she could be of immense help to me but that we should get on much more peaceably together if we lived separately and close together instead of under the same roof. I also told her that she had a hell of a temper and that it was about time she tried to control it. But what's the good of talking to people like that? If one says anything at all that isn't a gush of sentimental affection, one is being cruel. Yet I did all I could to make use of her. I asked her to come and live nearby. No. 'I should react badly to Bunny staying in your flat. If you didn't want either of us I shouldn't mind.' A normal woman would have said to herself, 'Poor old Joe with that dog and all his work, and poor old Bunny with a neuritic hand: I'll go along and help them both.' Then I asked her to get some place where she could take Queenie for her pregnancy. She looked in vain, and was eaten up with jealousy because Bunny was in on the business here instead of her. Even when Queenie had pupped, I hoped Nancy would find a place where she could take the puppies, and sell them, and begin a life as a dog breeder. But nothing happened. Then I told her to buy a bungalow if she could get a cheap one, and help me by taking the stored furniture – and Queenie from time to time. I tried again to bring her to London. Then I hoped she would at any rate take another room – for she had to clear out of Portland Road – where I could park Queenie on her; but she went to Winchester House. And this was the end of that.

[The reminiscence ends at this point.]

What a woman, I thought, clearing up her things – and what is the cause?

'Know thyself', that is the only road to happiness. Understand oneself, know oneself, accept oneself for the weak thing one is – how otherwise can one help oneself, control and conceal one's bad impulses, attempt to improve? Clearly if one is always blameless, a victim, there is nothing to improve, and one never gets any better – indeed one goes from bad to worse, for one is always blaming other people and therefore disliking or hating them and therefore living in a constant state of resentment, bitterness and even revenge. Nancy has nurtured herself for twenty years or more on resentment and hatred – her husband, his in-laws, mother, her son, Bunny, and now me. She is poisoned with her own poisons of hatred and bitterness and anger. No photos on the mantelpiece – bitterness and anger. She was *not* unhappy in this room. I thought, she hated it because she hated her son and Bunny and me, out of jealousy and resentment and rage that she could not possess us. She tried to kill herself in anger, in hatred, as a gesture of rage against me. Against me, because she loves me and wants to possess me, and cannot bear that anyone else should be preferred to her. How dreadful, I thought. And what do I do now? What indeed?

When we had packed up both suitcases and the small dressing case, there was still an immense amount of stuff over – food, shoes, utensils. Mrs Gray thought Nancy had brought it in a blanket, but I could not take it away in one. What a bore. We had dispatched the business so far pretty rapidly – and things could not be rapid enough for me, for my chief object as always was to get things done without delay and get back into a train to poor old Queenie, shut up in my flat. I saw at once that I should have to buy a trunk or outsize expanding case, and Mrs Gray told me where the nearest suitable shop was. I hurried out at once, but the shop did not have what I wanted. I had less than £5 in my pocket, and the nearest thing in size and cheapness to my purposes would have cost almost all that. But on my way to the shop I'd noticed one of those surplus WO stores that have sprung up everywhere and which I have found so useful in clothing myself since the war. So I had a brainwave, and repaired thither to see if they had an army kitbag. They hadn't; the nearest thing was a naval kitbag, about half the army size. So I bought two of those, and another naval receptacle, a sort of valise, very commodious, rather like a large cricket bag. All these together only cost about 25s., a cheaper proposition than the four guinea cases in the other shop. As I hurried back with them, I ground my teeth over Nancy again, and the troubles she put one too. Someone was always clearing up after her, helpless, useless woman. It used to be dresses and clothes always lying about when she was a girl, dropped on the floor or thrown carelessly onto chairs, for domestics or my mother to pick up and put away. Now and for years it was her general belongings.

In about another hour, this time unaided, I had crammed all the rest of her belongings, except empty tins, cheap books and periodicals and perishable foods which I left behind, into the naval bags. I was unable to remove them to London that day, but Mrs Gray kindly said she would keep them until I could return and clear them out of the house. It was all done in less than three hours, and at Mrs Gray's request I called in at the stationer's where Nancy got her papers and paid the bill there on the way back sweating to the hospital, taking one small suitcase with her necessary clothes, etc., with me, and some make-up, her comb and one or two other oddments she had asked me to bring.

I told her I had packed up her place and she seemed quite surprised.

'Why did you do that?' she asked.

I said, 'Well, you couldn't go back there, could you?'

She said, 'Wouldn't Mrs Gray have taken me back? Was she angry with me?' Extraordinary remark!

I said, 'No, of course not. She sent her love. But *I* wouldn't like you to go back.'

I spent about half an hour with her. Dr Brodie, the psychiatrist, had been to seen her, she said, and wanted her to go to his nerve hospital at Graylingwell, near Chichester, for a time as soon as she left Worthing Hospital, which would probably be on Thursday. She had said she would, but was now worried about it because she did not know if she would get her food-reform diet there. Also, since it was 'orthodox medicine', it was all contrary to her beliefs in health.

I told her how immensely helpful it would be to me if she did go to Brodie's place until I could get ready to receive her, and she only asked me to have a word with Brodie before leaving to make sure she could get vegetarian diet. She was very sweet, and so was I. When people have tried to kill themselves, and failed, there are innumerable subtleties of treatment and behaviour to be thought of. Love to begin with. One has to put that out, as much as one can, more perhaps than one feels or wants, to anchor them back into life; yet at the same time one has to reassure them somehow that everything is quite ordinary and natural, that they aren't being a nuisance, or putting one out, or forcing upon one arrangements that wouldn't otherwise have been made.

Fortunately the way was fairly clear for me then, for the invitation to the flat had already been made before Nancy tried to destroy herself – though it was true that even then she had forced the pace and I was far from happy in my mind about it. But anyway, it was easy to say to the poor woman that the whole wretched business

110

was simply a nightmare which should never have been dreamed; and that I blamed myself (which she wouldn't allow) that it ever had been; that she wasn't a nuisance at all, or no more of a nuisance than any sick person was, and that everything was just the same as it had been before she drank too much gin, the invitation to my flat had been perfectly genuine, and she could still come and spend her birthday there, as had always been intended, as soon as she had had a rest at Graylingwell. What was going on in the poor creature's mind I don't know; was she glad to be back? or sorry she had failed? did she know why she'd done it? did she believe anything I'd said?

At any rate, she acquiesced guiltily in everything, and so I left her to see Brodie. This took up another half hour of my time. He was a young man, with a keen face and a dogged, challenging look. I tried to tell him about Nancy's dietary peculiarities and that she was afraid Graylingwell might not cater for them; but he brushed all that aside.

'Your sister made a determined attempt upon her life,' he said, 'and it would be very wrong for her to go back into life without rest and treatment. Besides, she's already agreed to go to Graylingwell.'

He seemed to think I wished to prevent it, so I made haste to say it was exactly what I myself wanted. At that he returned to his papers, observing that they would find her the sort of food she liked in Graylingwell. It was all fixed up in his mind. I hurried off and caught a train back to London at about 5.30; the police had told me not to bother to come down again tomorrow (Wednesday) – 'You don't want to go running down here every day; we'll phone you up and tell you what time to come on Thursday if you'll tell us when and where.' I had done a lot of travelling since yesterday, and was only too happy to think that I had a day off ahead.

I felt very unwell in the train going down to Worthing, as I had on the Tuesday too – reaction perhaps – and kept thinking to myself, You mustn't break down. You must pull yourself together. Think of Queenie, and what would happen to her and to your work and everything if you cracked up ... I'm sure I'm in for a nervous breakdown, I thought, I feel so queer and dizzy – but you mustn't break down, you really mustn't.

Early yesterday therefore, round about 10.15, I was at Worthing hospital and broke the news to Nancy that I couldn't accompany her to Graylingwell. She did not seem to mind. I then flew over to Winchester House to collect her two suitcases and tell Mrs Gray that I would call for the rest later.

111

Mrs Gray said, 'By the way, I remembered after you'd gone: Mrs West has a bicycle here too.'

That was a blow. What on earth was I to do with a bike? I remembered then that Nancy had once spoken of selling it, and I decided to try to sell it in Worthing as soon as I had seen her off. Mrs Gray also began to air a grievance of her own. The publicity – for it was sure to get into the local paper, she said – of Nancy's suicide would be bad for her from a business point of view, she said; people would fight shy of coming to a house where guests did that sort of thing, and she felt she had little prospect of letting the room now for some weeks. I did not know what substance there was in that, but she had been very kind to me, and it seemed to me that I was morally her debtor anyway for all the worry and trouble and upset Nancy had inflicted upon her house, so I not only agreed at once with her proposition to impound the week's rent in advance which Nancy had deposited with her, but I gave her an additional two weeks' rent on top of that besides paying the current week. The sum involved was not large, under £5.

I then took Nancy's suitcases and hurried back to the hospital. The police sergeant was awaiting me there with a document for Nancy and me to sign; a declaration by her that she would never make an attempt upon her life again; a declaration by me that I would be responsible for her and see that she did not make another attempt upon her life. We both had to sign four copies of this, and kept one each. Then it emerged that the police were expecting me to go with her to Graylingwell. It also emerged that the hospital was not after all prepared to send a nurse. I said I simply could not go; but while the lady almoner was trying to arrange for someone to be spared (they were short-staffed), the sergeant stepped in with great severity and said that I *must* go with her, that I had taken responsibility for her out of their hands, and that if I did not go the police would be obliged to regard themselves as still being responsible and have to take her to court after all. Faced with this ultimatum, I was obliged to give in, with as good a grace as possible. Luckily the whole business went off with greater efficiency and speed than I expected.

Nancy by now had been got up and was dressed, the car – it was a private car – was waiting at the main entrance, the sergeant (who was really a decent, conscientious sort of man) shook hands with her and said, 'Goodbye, Miss, and don't worry. It will all pass away like a bad dream,' and we got ourselves and luggage into the car and drove off. Once again I wondered how much I should be charged for all this, or whether I ought to tip someone or other; but no one seemed to expect anything, neither the hospital nor the police, not even a voluntary contribution box was put before me; indeed, as soon as Nancy was out of the bed, someone else was put into it, and we were taken no further notice of at all, but trailed away, myself feeling rather ashamed, as tho' one had been silently expelled from school, down the long corridor to the waiting car. It was all very extraordinary and remarkably civilized; one could try to kill oneself without cost or reprisal; medical skill, hospital care and psychiatry were all at one's disposal, without reproach, free of charge. But surely I should have to pay for the car? A lively, bustling but untalkative man of about thirty-eight drove it, nondescript, in a civvy suit and a mac. What on earth he could be I had no idea. He drove us off with great rapidity and ability through a fine but heavy drizzle of rain. There was little on the road, and we reached Graylingwell within the hour. I said I was hoping he would drive me back, and he said, yes, of course, those were his instructions. Graylingwell also received us with efficiency. We sat in a bleak waiting room, like the general waiting room of a railway station, for some fifteen minutes, then a young doctor came in and summoned me out and, taking me into another room which looked like some tribunal chamber (a crescent of curved table and chairs and president's seat on a rostrum), got me to sign the paper which permitted them to break Nancy's bones. We were then taken over to another building, where an efficient sister said to us, 'Well, now say your goodbyes.' She was obviously thinking only of me, and the trouble I was taking, and asked where I could get my lunch. I said in Worthing. Nancy behaved very well, she made the whole task very easy for me by her courage and restraint.

I then returned in the car with even greater speed to Worthing, and tried on the way to elicit from the driver what my liabilities were, without asking point blank. He said he drove for the hospital when they were short of transport, as a part-time occupation; he had a café in Worthing which did all right, tho' better in summer than winter. He did not have much to say, but asked me where I would like to be dropped. I said Worthing Station. He put me down there at about 1.30. I thanked him very much and asked him if I could stand him a drink, and offered a 10s. note. But he refused it politely but firmly.

11 January 1949

Visiting days at Graylingwell are Sunday and Wednesday, and I
had told Nancy I would go down today, but I have felt so exhausted
and unwell lately – reaction to the shock and worry and emotional
strain – that though I do have, I know, an immense resource of
nervous energy, I felt that if I was not to fall ill myself I ought to
rest this weekend. So I wrote her on Friday to excuse myself, and
phoned Brodie yesterday to ask if he thought it would be OK if I
didn't go. He was extremely reassuring about it, and said Nancy
was perfectly all right and would not be at all disappointed if I
didn't come, that she was quite calm and settling down well.

How nice to have had a quiet Queenie weekend. It has been so
peaceful, tho' in my walks I have worried a great deal too about the
future and my responsibility towards Nancy, and, I feel, my inability
to undertake it. I am not the right person – indeed, I am the very
wrong one.

A beech tree creaked sharply and ominously today in the wind on
Wimbledon Common as Queenie and I passed beside it. It stood
over the tracks that lead down towards my shrine. It had funghi
growing out of its stem, I noticed. Yesterday, when we passed again,
it had fallen, broken clean in two, but not across the track. The
beech tree is a brittle affair, I believe, and a number of them have
been snapped by the winds. Many of them, too, I've noticed since,
have these hard porous funghi, like petrified sponges, papillae, growing on their stems. Dangerous. But better to have one's skull cracked
open by a falling tree in the midst of happiness and beauty, like the
man in Morgan's story, than to end up in a gas oven.

30 January 1949

I have not added to these notes for some weeks. A rather worrying
life, weekly visits to Graylingwell, two Wednesdays, and Queenie
not very well.

I kept having panics over Nancy but they have passed now.
Panics about myself have taken their place. But to begin with, how
does one re-approach a person who has voluntarily entered the
Valley of the Shadow – and on one's own account? She says very
little, all through she has said very little, but remained quiet and

docile and sweet. What has been in her mind? She tried to leave life because she thought she was not wanted. (Queenie has just quietly collected from the floor and walked off with my spare fountain pen, held gently in her mouth, her tail swaying from side to side. I have rescued it. Now she is capering up and down the passage with a bit of Bonio.) What does she think now? Does she not see how really this new fabric of care and concern for her is an artificial thing, even a false thing, cast upon us by her act? Does she lie awake at night thinking, They don't really care. This is just pretence. I forced this out of them. Everything is just the same really as it was. I am no good. I am not wanted. And my failure to take my own useless and unwanted life has obliged them to take steps, make arrangements, they wouldn't ordinarily have taken or made. Bunny doesn't want to go. Joe doesn't want her to go. They got on well together. Now he's got to have me, whether he wants me or not, and he *doesn't* want me, he's told me so, plainly, many times. I've forced a situation upon them. I've upset them. They're doing their best. They're awfully sweet and kind. But it's all a fake. And now something exterior to ourselves has taken charge of it, through me. Now I'm even homeless. I've nowhere to go, except to Joe, who doesn't want me. I can't get out of it, and nor can he. I've got the thing I wanted, and it's something dreadful, something horrible, I can't carry. I don't want to live. I'm a nuisance. I should have died. I should have died.

I had constant panics, imagining her lying awake thinking like this – tho' whether she did, I don't know. She says so little. And since it's all true, it shouldn't have happened, it isn't the right pattern, I don't want it, it is a strain upon me to have to think out the right lines for pretence, the best things to say. First of all, I said, I shall be ready to take you in two or three weeks' time. Then I thought, That won't do, it only accounts for me, what about Bunny? In order to reassure Nancy and give her confidence now in a new life she must have the invitation she wanted at Christmas, to us both. So then I wrote again to say that although it would on the whole be more convenient if she came in two or three weeks, when Bunny had had time to pack, etc., she could of course if wretched in Graylingwell come any time, immediately. And that in any case she might like to come a couple of days or so before Bunny left, so as to have a little time with her too – I could go and stay in one of the hotel rooms next door. I hoped that her considerateness and good sense would reject such a proposition – and indeed she did not take it up. But even that wasn't enough, I saw. Women, of course, are tougher than men, hard as steel, implacable: Aunt Bunny had taken no notice of Nancy at all since her attempted suicide a fortnight or more ago. She can't forget or forgive. I saw, at length, that that wouldn't do; if Nancy was to be supposed to have resurrected from the grave a would-be different and better person, she must be welcomed home from both sides – not, anyway, be left by one with the same problem she tried to escape from into the grave. Yet, I did not like to oblige Aunt Bunny, who always seems to me correct and wise, to take a step against her inclinations. But I asked her if she considered writing to Nancy. She said, 'I meant to ask *you* about that. Do you think I should? I will if you like. But she should write to me.' I did not press it, but she did produce a letter for me to take, which ('If it won't do, you must tell me what to say. It's the best I can do') wouldn't have done at all. Chilly, remote, 'I only hope you will make Joe happy' . . . and told her to tear it up. But a week later I saw that something must be done, one simply had to offer Nancy a clear field, a new chance, and told Bunny so, and why. I wrote out the letter for her, taking the blame myself for its lateness – 'I did write to you before, but Joe said he would not carry any letter from me until he had seen and spoken to you' – something of that sort. I didn't oblige the old lady to say anything that I felt she couldn't truthfully say – just sorrow for what had happened and hope for a happier future. (I had said to Nancy in Chichester, the first Wednesday I went, that Bunny had sent her love, which she hadn't, and had burst into tears and been dreadfully upset over Nancy's reaction. Nancy said, 'Bunny was?' as tho' she didn't expect, or perhaps, believe it. When I left she said, 'Give Bunny my love.' So clearly something had to be done there. I couldn't go down again without a letter.) So I wrote Bunny's letter for her. Bunny approved of it quite sincerely and I took it.

Nancy didn't read it at once, we were in a hurry to leave the hospital for Chichester, but I am sure it was a burden off her mind to get it. It had to be written surely? She had to be given her new chance? Or was Bunny right to sit back and do nothing? To leave the first step to her? Am I feeble? I don't know. I simply don't know. I am not good at seeing into people's minds. Such things as Nancy said were nice, as showing that she was thinking now about us, instead of about herself. 'What is going to happen when Bunny comes back to your flat?' – that I took as meaning to show me that she did not wish or mean to oust her altogether. I said I would be glad of her help on that problem when she came, that I had already put my name down at house agents with the idea of buying a house for us all.

'Do you mean you will give up your flat?'

'Yes, if necessary.'

'But you don't want to, do you?'

'No, I don't. I like it. But I will if it's necessary.'

But I didn't want to put any worries upon her; for, of course, it was scarcely possible for her to think far without seeing that it was she who was turning my life upside down. I was even afraid that at any moment she might say, 'Joe, I don't want to come to you really. I don't want to turn Bunny out. I'd like you to find me a place nearby.' Although it would have been the thing I once hoped for from her, now I could hardly have borne it; I was so dreadfully upset about her after her action, and felt I *must* make her think she was definitely and even urgently wanted.

The hospital was called euphemistically a 'nerve hospital', but it was really a 'mental home', a 'loony bin', full of neurotics and cranks and hysterics and, in other buildings, the insane. It was dreadful really to think of her there, my sister, who had once had the world at her feet, and I felt that she must at all costs be prevented from thinking that she too might be a lunatic, that I must get her out of it as soon as I could, urge her to come without delay as a favour to me to help me with Queenie, give her something to live for. So I kept saying to her things like 'The sooner you come to me the better, I shall be pleased', 'Don't stay a moment longer than you must, for you can be of great use to me', and so on; at the same time thinking in my mind, Is she going to be difficult? Will she now fit in? Shall I be able to keep it up when she is once with me? Will it be absolutely awful again as it was before? A little of the old Eve was already showing, even at Graylingwell – not much, but a little; the little one might expect; complaints about the food – white bread instead of brown, no vegetables, no freedom. However, it was all much milder than it had been in the Putney and Brighton hospitals of two years ago. I sent her brown loaves and herbs and various things from London, and bought her olive oil and cheese and Ryvita and Marmite in Chichester. But altogether she was gentle and mild; if she were always like that how nice it could be.

Graylingwell was more like a prison than a hospital. She was allowed no money, and her exercise was confined to the garden in front of her own particular house: she wasn't allowed to walk in the grounds as she liked. Later she was given a white card and was allowed to walk anywhere in the grounds. The discipline was strict, times of rising and eating and so on; there were social evenings and a weekly dance and 'handicrafts' every morning and afternoon. Poor old Nancy. Anyway, she'd managed to get a room to herself. She was not being subjected to the electric treatment after all – they decided there was no necessity for it in her case – and apparently received no treatment at all except typhoid and insulin injections – the latter made her very hungry. Now she has gone to a convalescent home [the Acre] in Worthing for a fortnight. Perhaps at the end of this week she comes to me. Bunny goes to Ann. How will it work? Oh, how will it work? Will she fit in with my ways or not? Bunny sees scarcely anything of me; I am shut up in my room with Queenie all the time that I am not working or walking or eating. Will Nancy object to that? I fear she will. And I fear she will want to walk with Queenie and me wherever we go, and will spoil Wimbledon Common by talking about alimony and bowels. If she *does* fit in she could be of great use to me – more useful to Bunny. I wish I could believe that she will.

Frost and fog. Wonderful lighting effects on Wimbledon Common. An incandescent world sometimes, with the sun burning unseen against the thick white mist and, in patches where it was thinner, sending shafts through to turn the dull, brown, dead bracken a shining copper. Sometimes the woods seemed full of pale bluish smoke. Very still. And twice the fog was so thick I could not see twenty feet in the depth of the woods – though we had left a fairly clear world above; but I found my way without the least difficulty, reading my path back from various landmarks – a bench, a bush, a piece of broken pottery, even a button – things I have seen over and over again in my rambles.

Lying awake in bed afterwards, Queenie beside me, I thought, if Queenie died tomorrow, what should I do? I tried to think of my life without her, returning day after day to the flat without her welcome, sitting in my room without her company . . . I thought, it would be the end, the end. There'd be nothing to live for at all. I couldn't even write about her, for my book is to be a gay book, about happiness, fun; there'd be no book if she died. I should want to die, too. But could I, like Nancy? No, I supposed not. Nor could I go abroad, to live abroad, an entirely different life and scene, not with these two women to keep. I should take to drink, I expect; and spend the money and my health that way.

9 February 1949

Bunny went off to Ann's in Thornton Heath on Sunday. Good and remarkable old woman, she made no fuss or trouble about it at all. When I had one of my panics about Nancy some two to three weeks ago and asked Bunny how quickly she could move, she said she really ought to have a couple of weeks to get ready. On Friday evening when I wandered into her room it did not look to me as though she had got very far, the place was still choked and littered with her multitude of things. And indeed, it turned out when I questioned her, that she hadn't even begun. All she had done in a fortnight was to arrange for her old age pension to be transferred to the Thornton Heath PO. She had not begun to pack and had only one and a half days left, and the sight of her room would have daunted even me.

I was quite perturbed, and said she would never be able to do it.

'Oh, I'll bustle about tomorrow,' she said.

'I'd better hire an ambulance instead of a car,' I replied. After all she is over eighty years old. Moreover there was a film in Putney we had been trying to see all the week, and I decided to go to it on Saturday afternoon as my last chance. I asked Bunny if she'd like to come – felt I ought to but expected she'd refuse: not a bit of it, she would like to go very much. It was a long film and lasted from 1.15 to nearly four. We had lunch together first at the local Greek restaurant. I went out to dine with Morgan that evening, and when I returned the old woman had not only packed all her belongings, without help, into about four suitcases and one of the naval holdalls I'd bought for Nancy's kit, but was busy darning the remainder of my socks. I thought it a wonderful performance – and contrasted her again with poor old Nancy, who, to begin with, would never have gone to make way for a rival, and confronted with such a task would have fallen ill. Dear Bunny, so good and considerate. She darned all my socks before leaving, washed everything up, and was neatly dressed and cheerful and ready to go on Sunday afternoon when the car came. I had bought her what provisions I could muster, and a bottle of gin, and accompanied her to Ann's.

Not an attractive place, though Ann had done her best with it.

And a camp bed ready for Bunny in the sitting room, where a coal fire was burning. Too many stairs, mostly steep, up and down. The remainder of the rooms cold. No, *not* a place for a woman of eighty. Nancy would have disliked it very much – the discomfort and cold. But Bunny fits in to any frame – it is her genius – and was all the time thanking and complimenting Ann, herself a cripple, on the welcoming touches which Bunny at once noticed. Let us praise her as she deserves, a selfless, sweet old lady, courageous and uninhibited, generous to a degree. She had given up her comfortable home here, and my company and care which meant a great deal to her, without a word of complaint or bitterness, and parted from me without even an embarrassing tear. Just warmly and tenderly. She had reacted with understanding and sympathy to the whole situation, always thinking of others – Nancy, me, Ann – before herself. A unique old woman.

And Nancy didn't come.

At 4 p.m., as arranged, I met her train at Victoria, with a hired car to drive us back to Putney. I cannot truthfully say that I met the train with enthusiasm; indeed, I viewed the future with the gravest doubts. I had written to a friend at the end of the previous week, saying, 'Nancy comes on Monday: pray for me,' and that was the state of mind in which I set forth.

Alas, how often do we kill people in our hearts; she wasn't on the train. To have one's wishes granted: is not that the most dreadful thing of all, as poor Nancy herself, I had for a long time feared, must see? I was at once seized with dreadful worries. Would she have thrown herself from the train on the journey up? But there was no spare luggage about, and no agitation among the other few passengers. I began to inquire about future trains in case she had missed this one, but soon saw that my only sensible course was to phone the convalescent home [the Acre] in Worthing for news. I did this at once from the station, and was told by whoever answered the phone that Nancy had had a relapse the previous Friday and had gone back to Graylingwell. And no one had told me! 'What was the matter with her?' I asked – though I knew the answer in my conscience alas – but the voice rather brusquely said that I would have to phone Graylingwell for further information.

14 February 1949

A dreadful, dreadful week of worry and self-torment. I have not been able to sleep at night without aspirins, and only patchily then. It has gradually emerged, from phone conversations with Brodie, that Nancy's present condition is little better than that of a lunatic, that she can hardly walk or hold her water, has gone quite out of her mind. She is having this electrical convulsion treatment. Dr Brodie would not let me see her; he told me that he would send me word when I might go if I would keep in touch with him.

Alas, in my guilty mind, I see what happened as surely as though I had deliberately willed it to come to pass. She has been accusing me lately of never being the same, as always being different whenever she sees me; and of course it is true. I am deeply attached to her, my sister, in my way, and in emergencies, when I am deeply touched by her, or frightened for her, as when I took my letter down to Worthing after Haywards Heath, or burst into tears in Worthing Hospital, or saw her, so gentle and sweet in Chichester, I can love her and am ready to do or promise anything. But then I leave her, and remember the past, and become worried and anxious, and see, for instance, old Bunny, quietly and uncomplainingly packing up her gear to go and live elsewhere, and my consideration and affection or feeling turn elsewhere, or simply withdraws, and Nancy sees it going, and feels it gone.

19 February 1949

All through the past night I could not get it out of my head that I had failed her, and saw now, as it seemed to me, that this was the end, it was a thing I could never put right. She will never come now, I thought, never, never; I had my chance to help her and I botched it, I lost contact, I withdrew the prop; now she will never come, Graylingwell will be her last home, poor old girl. How could it be possible for me to raise once more this shaky edifice of confidence and so bring her to the point of once more believing that I wanted her, welcomed her to my flat; of actually making the journey? What could I say to her now that I had not said already and which had failed for the second time because I did not really believe in her or the things I said, and she now knew it? 'I don't believe a word you say now,' she said to me in Worthing. How was it possible to try again? This collapse, as I saw it, was a self-protective mechanism against all this, the 'me' she didn't want to face any more, the 'me' who did not love or want her, who disapproved of her and only wanted to shove her away somewhere handy and be rid of her and her problems, the 'me' who had now to pretend all the time that this was not so, but couldn't for long keep it up, the 'me' who was always therefore 'different' whenever she saw me, the 'me' in short in whom she could not now believe and feared – 'me' the focal point of her conflicting, anxious and tormenting thoughts. How could I help her now – I who had in a way again struck her down?

An immense pity for the poor creature took me, thinking back over her dreadful ambling life. She had begun with every advantage – and now had nothing. When Queenie, sitting on my bed, looked suddenly so sweet that I was impelled to go over and kiss her, I would think, poor little Nance, she had no one to kiss, not even a dog. I kept writing little notes to her, to put in a photo, of Queenie and me that I decided to frame (but not in glass) and talk – would it not help her to find a photo of us, she who had no photos of any sort, on her bedside table when she 'came back'. 'Poor sweet little lady, who has had no fun, a love, a happiness for too long; come soon to your poor old Joe and his Queenie, or you will break his heart.' Once again through these wretched days and nights, unable to sleep, tramping with my self-torturing thoughts over Wimbledon Common, without joy, without noticing any longer the branches of the woods or the happiness of my dog, my wretched mind, as it had done so often before, turned right round once more: the problem now, as in the Worthing Hospital, was how to get the poor woman to me – to get her now to Putney, to have her in my place, to care for her and help her with kindness and love, to make reparation somehow for the unkindness of the past and give her back her self-confidence in the last thing, me, she had lost – this was now my one desire and preoccupation. But how was it to be done? What would happen to her wretched mind if and when they dragged it back from its remote retreat – to be confronted with the same old weary tormenting problems again? Would she not shrink back again at once? Would she not find even the sight of me unendurable – me and my double face?

21 February 1949

I went to see her yesterday. I dreaded the visit. What should I find? Would she have hysterics at the sight of me? Would my visit bring about another collapse. Before going, on the Friday, I'd had a new crisis of nerves – something James Kirkup had told me, that the electrical treatment was a dreadful thing and a mistake. I ought never, I felt, have allowed it – these medical experiments. Perhaps she would have recovered and recovered better if I'd had her straight to my flat, and a nurse to look after her, and Queenie's love and mine to draw her back, and even her Dr Latto to attend her. In any case, she should not be allowed to recover memory in Graylingwell, if she were to recover it all all. Of that I felt absolutely sure. It would be a fatal, dreadful mistake. She *must* come to in my flat, and nowhere else, if ever she was to be fit again. I phoned Brodie, and upset him I think. Could I take my sister away on Sunday when I came? He said it would be most unwise, that in any case she would not come. I did not perfectly comprehend her state, he said. I wanted to ask him to stop the treatment – convulsing this wretched, senseless body, this body that wanted no sense – but had not the courage for that. 'There's nothing to worry about, Mr Ackerley,' he kept saying. 'There's really nothing to worry about.'

Down long stone corridors, led by a nurse, who unlocked and relocked doors behind us, and thence into a large bare ward, full of beds, all empty except one, at the end, in which Nancy lay. The nurse said she was a bit better today – not so 'dopey'. Brodie had said she was up and went about, staggering I expect; perhaps he had put her to bed in case I tried to rouse her. She was propped up against some pillows, and had on her spectacles. She peered at me over them as I came in. I waved and flickered my fingers at her in a jolly breezy gesture as I approached; she flickered her fingers back.

'Well, you wicked woman,' I said, 'in bed again.'

'Wicked woman,' she repeated, and gave a little laugh.

The nurse then left us, telling me to tap on a door outside when I left, since Nancy was not to be left alone. I sat down beside her. She was wearing a pink woolly shawl. Her hair had been done for her, and was very frizzy – the electricity I suppose – and rather bunched up on her head, insecurely held by a row of tin Woolworth combs. She looked rather fat and well. I told her so.

'How fat you've got,' I said.

'Have I?'

I kissed her, and took her hand. I kissed that and her arm, which also looked fat and strong, as did her hand and fingers too. She had some papers on her lap – *Woman* and *Picture Post* – and was reading one of them upside down. She seemed to forget me as soon as I was beside her; but as the nurse left, she said, in a thick, trembling voice, and with a smile, 'What a lot of locking of doors.'

'How are you?' I asked.

'All right.'

'Nice food?'

'Not very.'

We had that kind of conversation, and every now and then I kissed her, or smiled at her, or made some little laughing remark. Whereat she smiled or gave a little laugh back. But she volunteered nothing herself, except suddenly to say laughing, when someone I had not noticed begun to sing in a distant ward, 'I can do better than that.'

'Why don't you?' I said. 'Do.'

But she went dead again. I asked her if she would like some chocolate, and she nodded. But she seemed unable to take the bit I broke off one of the bars I'd brought for her, so I put it in her mouth. She sucked it, unable to munch or chew it seemed. Her hands fidgeted a good deal – the old fluttering gesture that used to worry and touch me – fidgeting at her breast or with the papers or touching her temple as though she had a headache or something pressed there intolerably to come out. I kept feeding her with bits of chocolate all the time I was there. It seemed awfully long. If I said anything she usually responded, but mostly she just sat silent, playing with her papers. She would take one and raise it slowly in the air in an aimless wandering way, higher and higher, above her eyes, her head, and then rest its edge against her forehead, and so remain for a long time until she slowly lowered it again.

I said, 'I thought of bringing Queenie down to see you, but didn't think it would do.'

'No,' she smiled, 'I don't think it would have done.'

Bunny wasn't mentioned by either of us.

There was a small abrasion on her forehead, where the belt went I expect that fastened her to the electrical machine; I kissed it. Every now and then she fixed upon me a wide-eyed, contemplative look.

'What are you thinking?' I asked, rather fearfully.

'I – don't – know,' she murmured. But later she said, 'You've cut yourself.'

I'd forgotten it, a small cut on my chin.

'Is it bleeding?' I asked.

She made no reply.

For long periods we sat in silence. I wondered whether to say anything to her about the past, but could not bring myself to. How awful if tears came into her eyes.

And so we sat in silence, every now and then I would kiss her or take her hand, and she would play with mine for a moment, before going back to her game with the papers, lifting them slowly, wanderingly up in the air and she would begin to fall sideways in her bed towards me, as though her head were too heavy to carry. This was my sister, the beautiful Nancy Ackerley, who had come into the world with every advantage of looks and money and position, this was what she had come to at the age of fifty.

23 February 1949

When I woke in darkness at between 5.30 and six this morning, I said to myself, 'It is your fault that Nancy is like this. You have been persistently cruel to her for the last year; you have hated her, and have produced evidence of it at every move she has made; you have driven her out of her mind.' In the darkness I lay looking at this and knew that it was true. I have really hammered at her a good deal in these last twelve months, holding my mirror to her face and endeavouring to get her to recognize and acknowledge the image – and to change it. Cruel, yes cruel, the result speaks the word, points its finger at me. I have tried to get her, for once in a way, to look at herself critically and acknowledge her faults, instead of endlessly accusing others; and then I have been asking her to change, to exert a few controls, to make some friends, to find some occupation. And in my heart, true, I have hated her for her assaults upon my own personality. I have driven her out of her mind.

'You were a God to me, a God.' 'I would do anything for you.' 'Say it isn't true!' '*Don't* send me back to that room! You can't be so cruel!' Alas, the cries for help echo in my ears. And now I cannot reach her. And even if I could, what should I say?

But there are so many viewpoints. She was my sister only, my only sister, but my sister only, and her assault upon me was more the assault of a lover, a wife. Was I to give up everything for her, my independence, my life, my own character? As a lover, indeed I see I failed her. But as a brother, did I do so badly? I never wanted anyone to live with me. I have a right to my independence, have I not? I wanted to live alone, with my dog, visited by my friends, her indeed too if one could have trusted her not to abuse one's hospitality, to have my flat to myself for Freddie's visits or those of any other similar friend I might make, to have my other friends to stay when they came to town, Jack [Sprott], Georges [Duthuit], Leo [Charlton]. And in between whiles to have the solitude I am used to and enjoy, to read my books and write if I feel inclined.

My sister, not my lover or my wife.

Dear Nancy, I know you did love me, and I know you did try, so far as you were able time and time again. I am so grieved and so wretched over your state – aye, and so ashamed. If I could help you now, I would.

Would I? Whenever you are in real trouble, whenever I feel I have gone too far and am becoming cruel – because you don't seem to understand, whenever you touch me or I think of you in the way that you would wish, I fly down to you and kiss and comfort you or weep over you. But as soon as you are well, I get wary again – 'the shutter comes down over my face' as you once said – I begin to temporize, to withdraw, to fob you off. Even if you recovered from this, poor darling, would I not once again kill you with my doubts?

Morgan dismisses you easily, 'awful woman', and says I do not dwell on the things I might dwell on, the troubles you have caused; but life is not as easy as that. I am so sorry for you, old girl, and for the punishments that have fallen upon you. I would help you if I could, but I am no good to you I fear. We are frightened of each other now; it will never come right I know.

Yes, yes, conscience has me; the poor thing was ill, this was no way to treat her, and though I was kind and solicitous too, and indeed worried to death, this no longer worked. She was sharp enough to see: 'You only want to put your conscience right, when you feel you've gone too far or said too much. That's why you're so nice when one's ill, that's your nicest time. But when I'm well, "The Home Counties for Nancy".'

Much truth in it, yes. It was indeed the truth. In all these outpourings, how much real love do I have for Nancy? How difficult to know. I have said, from time to time, that she should have died

126

on that occasion when she almost did die, in St Mary's Hospital, when I was sent for. Then, because no one was involved in her illness, it was an Act of God, we should none of us have suffered from remorse, and she herself would have been spared those subsequent painful and useless years in which she has made so little contribution and been only unhappy, and we should have been spared all the trouble and worry she has caused. We should have been dreadfully sorry, and then, as one does, forgotten about her, poor thing, continuing our own lives with an easy conscience, we had done our best. But now, we are involved, we blame and accuse ourselves – or rather I do – and this 'love' I now put frantically out from the depths of my rent and tormented heart – does it come from there, or from the dark recesses of a guilty mind? Do I not only beseech her to come back from the remote place to which she has retreated so that I shall not go forward with this remorse, this conscience, that I helped to drive her there?

Yet, I don't know; why should I have done anything? I am only her brother, her only brother, but only that. I might have been a married man with children, living possibly in India or Africa. What then? She would have had to do without me. But I am a bachelor, the unattached male, fair game for relatives who find themselves without money, shelter, friends or occupation. Like William [Plomer] with his father, John Morris and his mother, Francis Bennett and his sister. Considering this, and that I am homosexual and have made my own life and have my own pursuits, did I do so badly? Testimonials: Leo [Charlton] writes: 'Do not blame yourself. Never was there so solicitous a brother.' Mrs Wilson: 'Pam says she only wishes *she* had a brother like you.' Bunny: 'I hope she has learned at last that she has the best and kindest of brothers.' Jack [Sprott]: 'Don't blame yourself, you have always done everything you could.'

One always hoped of course that something would happen to her, as things happen to all of us, that she would meet someone she liked, find by chance some new interest. How was it that she never did? What did she want of me? Morgan said, 'Even if you'd committed incest with her, do you suppose that would have made her happy?' He meant that nothing short of that – and not even that – would have.

I used to say it to myself before, when she had her senses, and now I say it to myself with no less horror. What *does* she do? What does

127

she do, poor girl? How does she pass her day? Sitting, or shuffling from one part of a room to another . . . I can't bear to think of it, any more than I could bear to think of her days in Worthing, returning night after night to an empty room, making her solitary dish, and crying herself to sleep. One *can't* allow – one *shouldn't* have allowed – such a thing to go on, and I *ought* to have intervened. After all, I know, I have felt, the horrors of loneliness myself, the dreadful feeling of turning, evening after evening, the key in the lock of an empty flat. She told me she cried herself to sleep, she told me she used to sit thinking of suicide, she told me she went to pieces if left alone, she told me because she had no one else to tell – it was the truth, but one doesn't harken to the truth, one writes it off irritably as something else, tiresomeness, blackmail; but one should believe what one is told, face value, just as I now know that Queenie, for instance, is entirely reliable, she always speaks the truth – if she pricks up her ears and barks, there *is* a reason; if she ferrets excitedly round a clump, there *is* something there, she is not showing off.

But I *didn't* hear the truth with Nancy – not seriously. Previously, when she said, 'I can't live alone, I always go to pieces,' one just thought, Well, you'd better find someone to live with, old girl, or, What a bore all this is. But in fact it was the literal truth the poor woman was speaking, and if one had understood, *heard*, that, one would have said – had to say – indeed *wished* to say, 'Oh, but I can't allow that. You must have whatever you want at once. Come and live with me' – for that is what I am saying *now* in my heart, when the truth of the poor woman's words are all too plainly proved. The truth then, and now – I didn't listen, I didn't believe or want to believe, not to the extent of a loving reply, of opening my arms; I gave only makeshift replies, tired replies, tinkering with this and that, hoping that the mere sound of the tinkering would be enough to divert and console her.

No, this isn't quite true either, it makes me out too unfeeling, and I did feel for the poor thing, and tried to get her up here when she could not have been so lonely; but alas, the sorrow and unease one felt for her on one's visits didn't last long upon one's return to town, to the toil and worry of life here; then one forgot, or only remembered, from time to time, and certainly one didn't hear the canker eating further and further into the fabric of her life. But anyway, it comes back to the same thing that I did not hear the truth of her appeals, nor the urgency, until Haywards Heath, and then everything happened, oh dear, with such dreadful rapidity. Haywards

Heath was the day after Christmas: this frightful and total collapse has occurred within only a few weeks of that.

And this *was* suffering, that is the point. The suicide – that could be explained away – drink; but nothing except great suffering, dreadful tension, could explain this, this crack-up of the mind – and *that* was what did not break through to me until too late.

The more hysterical she got, alas, the less desirable she became; and the more undesirable she saw herself becoming, the more hysterical she got. That was the dreadful seesaw. It wasn't her character (the thing Morgan seems to see and write off) one thought of and judged; I have no opinion of my own character, and don't judge other people's, and expect she is just as nice and nasty as I am and as most people are; but it was the hysteria one minded, either the row in progress or the row in prospect, and that was what frightened me and guided my conduct, how to fit her in to my life and give her *some* occupation, without involving me and Bunny in these dreadful rows.

'Do you think I'm weak in the head?' Poor darling. It was the ominous creak before the tree fell, snapped by the winds of hysteria. A dead tree, perhaps, like that silver birch on the common, the wood had rotted and perished.

Would-be suicides set themselves apart from us; one speaks to them afterwards as over a gulf. Their suicide has shown that one was inadequate; how could one make further conversation with someone who has already dismissed one with a final goodbye?

She said, 'Let us be hilarious. I feel it would be good for me to be hilarious' – and then tried to take her life. I thought afterwards that she hadn't smiled or laughed much for a long time; she was always serious and anxious and tense. She used to have a rather trenchant sense of humour, but that had all gone.

But I should have seen sooner, acted quicker. I remember her on the day I took down my letter of welcome, how gentle and sweet she was. And how nervous. On Worthing station. Could I come down and spend New Year's Eve with her? Yes, of course, but I'd have to come late and leave early. Well then never mind, another evening. I'll come if you like, old dear. No, don't come, another evening would be better. (She was thinking of me and giving trouble.) We sat on the station, her eyes moving restlessly, her fingers fidgeting. And what did she say? It was the dreariness, that's why she needed company, the evening dreariness. But (she pulled herself together) I'll be all right; don't worry.

Alas, how unkind, how cruel we are to each other. I *was* cruel to her, no doubt of that, trying to get her going over this and that – jobs, bungalows. But then it was for her good as well as mine, so I thought; I wanted her to make a new life, but not with me. But she couldn't, not her character, and only flopped. And my cheerful, practical, rather unsympathetic manner, how she must have hated it. Poor girl. Poor me too. And now she's mad, and the doctors, who know nothing about her, try to clear it up.

Yet it was all quite simple really – only not for her. No, not for her, poor thing. For she couldn't be ordinary, cheerful, practical, helpful, pallish, the things I wanted. She couldn't take a train up for a day to visit us, for instance; it wasn't her character, no initiative; one always had to go visiting her. When I asked her up for Christmas, to the hotel next door, why didn't she just say, 'Righto, good idea,' and come and have a merry time with us? We would have been nervous of course – would she make rows? – but that was for her to brush aside, ignore, overcome, show how nice and easy she could be. One couldn't really say anything to her, that was the trouble; she resented anything.

I went again to Graylingwell last Sunday. Graylingwell, oh Graylingwell.

This time she was not in bed, and I was directed to a huge room, the theatre, set out with small tables and chairs like a whist drive. All the tables were already occupied, so I sat at the side of the hall where quantities of wooden chairs were stacked. A strapping Jewessy nurse, heavily made up, occupied a table in a commanding position looking down the hall, like the president's place at a meeting. Nancy was sent for. It was some time before she arrived. Then she came, shuffling slowly in, supported on either side by nurses. She could only take little steps, and would have fallen, I think, if her supports were withdrawn. Her hair was all fuzzed up on her head; her head sunk in her shoulders. She peered round with a vague, big-eyed, apologetic, sweetish look. She was like my mother, her appearance, her state, as the old woman had been in her last year. This was my sister, destroyed by me. I hastened forward to receive her, and guided her to my chairs. She sat slowly, with difficulty. I arranged chairs beside her to support her in the armpits on either side, in case she fell sideways. There she sat, woodenly, her legs and feet close together. She was wearing coarse brown woollen stockings and a cotton dress with blue flowers on it; her own grey tweed coat, bunched round her by its belt, Paul's shoes. She allowed herself to be kissed on mouth and forehead and hands and arms, but paid little attention to me. Most of the time her head was turned away as she vaguely watched the other patients and their visitors.

I had brought her various things, dates, prunes – the same sort of prunes I gave her at Christmas and which had made her so angry but which she had liked later – a breakfast food, a chocolate cake, some tins of prune essence. I gave her a prune to eat and she made some remark I did not quite catch about it not tasting very nice, and spent much time during our one and a half hours trying to get rid of bits of the skin which she could not masticate and which clung to her lips and teeth and fingers. She ate with slowness and difficulty. I had also brought down a photo of myself with Queenie, which I had had framed for her, with a mica front. She seemed vaguely interested in it, peering at it, and picking it up again to look at in a sort of wonderment. But she made no comment on it, and did not ask after the dog or Bunny, nor send any messages.

What did we speak of? I hardly remember. I said, 'I've decided not to mate Queenie again after all.'

'*Quite right*,' she rejoined with emphasis and distinctness.

'Are you happy here?' I asked.

After a pause she said, 'Yes, quite happy.'

'Don't be too happy,' I said, 'or you will stay.'

'What do you mean by that?' she asked. But paid no attention to my reply.

'When are you coming to my flat?' I asked.

'Well, I expect that depends on the deep insulin.'

'Are you having electric treatment too?'

She didn't reply. Towards the end she suddenly said, 'I was wondering.'

'Wondering what?' I asked, when she paused.

She said nothing. I tried again. Nothing. She plucked at her fingers a lot, and those fingers, how they upset me. I had to convey the food stuff I had brought to her ward to save the nurses trouble, so it was arranged that I should walk her back, with the help of one nurse, when departure time came, and leave the food there. We were late in starting, and she walked very slowly; I thought then mostly of missing my train, and rather hurried her poor, shuffling steps. Alas, even in the midst of such tragedies one has to catch one's train. Queenie had to be taken out.

She gets little mention now, that blithe spirit. If it were not for her, how could I survive? She is in excellent health, and radiantly beautiful in her new spring suit. Almost all the old coat is now out; her tail, last thing to moult, still sheds some feathers. I found that combing and brushing her weren't the best way of relieving her of her loose hairs. The best way is with one's bare hands – leather gloves might even be better, but mine are new and I don't want to dirty them – stroking them pressingly down her body and sides, the way of the hair – that draws the loose hairs out better than anything – they accumulate round her tail – and gives her much pleasure. Nice long walks with her, nice for *her* anyway, plenty of rabbits, but I am too preoccupied to enjoy them myself or take much note of anything. She is due to come on heat in about three weeks.

Lunches with Kenneth Walker and Dr Ed Glover. How kind they both are, the latter in particular, for I have never met him before, though he reviews for me. He asked me to lunch and took the whole story from me, and said he would write to Brodie. He doesn't mind the insulin, but doesn't think well of the ECT. I showed him Nancy's photo. 'It's a *nice* face,' he said.

Interview with Brodie in London. Tiny man, shabbily dressed; obviously very energetic and, one would say, sincere. More like a junior games master at a small private school than a doctor. Small red hands, little pointed fingers. Wiry Scotch hair, difficult to keep tidy. No hat. Carrying a copy of *Madame Bovary*. He said Nancy had had seven or eight shocks and would get a dozen more. Admitted she made hardly any progress – indeed had regressed further – but was quite confident he would have her back with me within six weeks. I can't believe this. And in the same condition in which she was before her 'relapse'. I can't believe it – and don't like it at all. I don't think he has any imagination: he thinks of cases entirely from the physiological point of view. It is from the moment that Nancy begins, if at all, to recover her mind, that I begin to be terrified. I cannot believe she will just calmly enter my flat after all this, in a few weeks' time. She will collapse again at the prospect, or as soon as she gets there. I asked if some analytical help could not be given to her there at once as soon as her mind returned. He said the digging should begin after she came to me, because it was a mistake to have *two* analysts on a patient. I see there is sense in that. But if she waits till she reaches me, it will be too late, too late. I wish I could get her to Guy's – Glover speaks well of it – it would suit me in many ways: it is nearer to me, it would get rid of this difficulty of two analysts, and I could *ease* her into my flat from there by motoring her over for visits first.

28 February 1949

Graylingwell again yesterday. Graylingwell, oh Graylingwell. She was brought in to the 'whist drive' room again, supported by a nurse. She wore her fur coat, a dilapidated thing it looked, buttoned up to her throat (to secure, as it turned out, the ends of the tartan scarf that had been hastily thrown over her dishevelled hair); she wore woollen gloves, the same cheap cotton dress and stockings and her American shoes, much stained. At first I thought her better, her recognition and welcome more emphatic, but afterwards I doubted whether there was really any progress. She had a black eye, but did not seem to know it or how it had happened; she had had a fall, I expect. She shuffled slowly in as before and we sat at a table. She was chewing something, which eventually she took from her mouth, a piece of meat; part of her lunch, no doubt, and no doubt she had been chewing it vaguely for some time. Yet when I asked her what she had had for lunch, she did not know. A pitiful sight, her large blue sorrowful eyes, sunken now in her head, devoid of sight or intelligence, wandering heavily over the room; her head sunk in her shoulders. She slid farther and farther down on her wooden chair during my visit and piddled on the floor without knowing it. She played with my hand a good deal, beginning sentences and never finishing them. The beautiful Nancy Ackerley, the beautiful Mrs West. She was raised from her chair with difficulty when I left, and began her infinitely slow, swaying, tottering return journey down the stone passages supported by nurses upon whom she heavily leaned.

A small dark greyhound passed up on Wimbledon Common today. The declining sun was behind it, and it was just as if it carried some small bright lantern with a reddish golden flame at its belly. This curious effect was produced by the sunlight pressing the thin membrane of skin that attached its pale grey penis horizontally to its stomach.

4 March 1949

One of those recurrent nights, when I wake too early and lie awake in the crepuscular cold light, and say to myself, 'You didn't come for her, and she went out of her mind. She loved you and the last year of her "life" was spent in lonely bedsitting rooms making pullovers for you, but you didn't have enough sympathy for her, and she went out of her mind. You must have hated her really; although you did a good deal for her, it was more because you felt you had to than for any other reason; you always spoke against her, propagandizing against her in a way, and putting even the newly met against her: yes, you hated her really, and though she tried to believe otherwise she knew it ("Say it isn't true! Say it isn't true!") and went out of her mind.' Huddled in front of my fire with a teapot as dawn breaks, I go over the last scenes, the last letters in my mind, a substitute for the coldnesses, the unkindnesses, the luke-warmnesses, the words and phrases I wish now I had used. In course of time, I daresay, I should have come to think I really did use them – if this diary did not confront me with the truth.

6 March 1949

Snow today. I brushed Queenie's teeth, which she is doubtful of, liking, I think, the taste of the paste, but not enjoying the scrubbing, brushed her, and took her out early – 8.15. She loves the snow, but it does not 'love' her; her beautiful grey legs look rusty and dingy, dirty even, against the whiteness: a yellow dog, and my Abdulla cig-box looked yellow too when I took it out for a smoke. Just the right amount of snow, about two or three inches, enough to carpet the ground and lay a thin layer on branches and twigs, little blobs on the leaves, without overloading everything. Very beautiful as we got farther, a Chinese world, painted in tea. Tea-colour, the dead world under a thin coverlet of snow; tea-colour the branches; and tea-colour my dog also, and the leaves of the holly pale jade.

I dread seeing the poor thing this afternoon, now that she may be recovering her senses, more than I did when she was bereft of them. What can I say to her? Nothing? Only pretence. And she knows that. For I don't want her. I have an immense pity and compassion for her, and a guilt feeling too – my not wanting her, and my refinements of cruelty helped with everyone else's to bring this on – but I don't want her, and have nothing really to offer her, only a certain amount of housekeeping work.

As I trudged along on the creaking snow I thought of myself and my own character. I am a bad character too, cruel, hateful. I treat Bunny, for instance, very badly; I hate Bunny half the time, she irritates me, as she irritated Nancy; perhaps the only difference between Nancy and me is that I do just manage not to let it loose, she gets from me gruffness, abruptness, monosyllables, silence – but not reproach or abuse. She maddens me, but I don't say so, as Nancy did: 'You madden me!' I shut myself up in my room instead and spread an air of irritability instead of exploding. She is frightened of me, no doubt – Mother was too, perhaps Nancy – but I expect she refuses to interpret my behaviour as hatred, and explains it to herself as 'Poor Joe is so worried.' She is a good old woman, I see that, but I have no affection for her and am often cruel to her, pretending not to notice, taking her for granted, refusing to praise the things she does, the food she cooks and so on. I try not to be horrid to her, and am always attempting to pull myself together over it, but I am irritable most of the time. I scorn her so much that she has renounced all initiative, and does nothing at all without consulting me. That annoys me more.

'Shall I put the kettles on?' she said this morning at 7.15, for instance. What a question? Maddening. The early morning cup of tea, it is the only longed-for thing. Usually I am up before her and manage to get my pot of tea and shut myself up in my room with it before they wake; but they woke first today, that irritated me too – as it used to irritate me when Nancy stayed; I hate people fidgeting about and 'looking after me' first thing in the morning, women should stay in bed till ten or so. Anyway, why not put the kettles on, without asking? Idiotic question. I could not just say yes though, and didn't say, 'Of course, you silly cow.' What a stupid question. I took a middle line and said, 'I should think so indeed. Full pelt.' Even then she only put the gas burners on half cock, and when, going into the kitchen and seeing this, I flared them up to full with an irritable movement of my hand and demanded, 'Why not full on for heaven's sake?'

She said, 'I didn't know if you'd be quite ready yet.'

She has this thing about kettles not boiling until one is ready for them – the water changes character or some balls. Anyway, surely only hatred could have prevented me from just saying yes? I do hate her, I know. Why? I never look at her if I can help. Why? Is it that I feel so guilty over Nancy, and wish she was with me now instead of Bunny – not because I want Nancy, for I don't, but just so as to ease my conscience? Or is it just because I don't want anyone? for I don't – just a housekeeper, deaf and dumb. I am just a bad character, that is all, cruel and heartless. I don't care for people,

135

only a few; I am bored and irritated by people generally. No good. No good. V. used to say: 'Are you cruel?' Little Forrest Reid said, 'Do you really care about people, Joe?' I don't. And if I don't, I can't help it.

As I trudged along, I thought, Good heavens, poor old Nancy may have been right all her life, right and nice, how can one tell? I am no judge at all. Perhaps nothing has really been her fault, perhaps she really was victimized by Paul, Mother, Bunny and the rest, and her only fault is that she hasn't taken things lying down. And now she has seen that I am a shit and hate her, as everyone else has hated her, and that Bunny is jealous of her and hates her, and that we have both and all always poisoned the minds of others about her, so that everyone everywhere is critical of her, and she could bear it no more. Certainly Paul has turned out a disappointment to her, and Bunny always said Mummy was jealous, and as for Bunny herself, well I hate her too – so perhaps we never have been fair to Nancy; and have at last killed her. She can, I know, be awfully sweet. With all this hatred in me – Jack [Sprott] found it out over Irene – I have no right to criticize her.

Still, I thought, even if I am as nasty as I think I am, and even if Nancy is nicer, or even if the main difference between us is that I only *think* my hateful thoughts while she expresses hers, there is an extra important difference between us, and that is that I am independent, and she isn't. Awful though I may be, I do less harm. I don't need company, as she does, I am content to be alone; I have my interests and consolations – reading or scribbling in this book or playing with my dog – I do not therefore bring my bad qualities to hurt and disturb other people. I am by nature now a recluse. I like it. I prefer it. But Nancy needs company and companionship and entertainment – she has an empty life, and needs it filled in. That is why, if she came to me, I should be worse off than I am now, for she would never put up with the way I treat Bunny. Bunny is jolly good, I do see that – almost as good as it is possible for anyone under my roof to be – and now that she has Ann with her it is even easier for me to ignore her. I manage now to have my afternoon tea, as well as my morning tea, shut up alone in my room. Oh, the bliss of being alone, of not having to talk or listen. The only time really that I now exchange or wish to exchange a word with my aunt or Ann is in the evening when we sit down to supper. Otherwise I live alone, wish to live alone, and am irritable if any kind of attempt is made to disturb me or look after me at those quiet moments when I prefer and am perfectly capable of looking after myself. This is the life I have to offer poor Nancy – the life she disliked before. I cannot, though now somehow I must, look her in the face and tell her I want her.

Alas, Wimbledon Common has shrunk. I no longer get lost in it, nor ever can again; we reach the farthest boundary in no time, and have to turn back, and all the tracks, which once seemed so numerous, and various, and bewildering and mysterious, are now few, familiar and stale; there is nothing to do but trudge back the way we came. The way back always seemed different from the way we came, but now I see that it was only a trick of the imagination; it was always the same.

9 March 1949

I distrust myself so deeply, that is what I mean. How does one know what one is like? I hide from other people. I hide, too, from myself. The savage, the monkey within me, it cleverly conceals itself. That is civilization, of course. But not cleverly enough. Crises occur, and the façade breaks – as Jack [Sprott] saw with me over Irene: 'Why this hatred, Joe?' – the grinning ape looks through. 'Joe is so kind,' people say. Some people. 'People are frightened of you,' William [Plomer] has said. What am I really like? How do I behave, on balance? What do I do in secret, concealing it from myself, so that even I shall not look into the dreadful depths?

I woke in the middle of the night and thought, She cried herself often to sleep. She told me so. Oh dear, oh dear, that was dreadful. I should have never allowed that. I should have done something at once. I did feel for her too. When I visited her in that wretched sort of room in Portland Road, and saw her washing up in a tin basin on the wash-hand stand, I used to think to myself with a dreadful pity, compassion, Oh no, this mustn't go on. It's too dreadful. This is death. But I let it go on, out of fear. And of course she herself could do nothing. She had no initiative, no 'go'. I ought really to have given that its true value. It was simply her character not to be able to do things, not to be able to pay a day visit to London, or move, or go to lawyers by herself. It was part of the weakness of her character not to be able to do these things. And I – judging others by oneself, as we always do – thought it just tiresomeness, and that she should be driven, forced to do these things, obliged to do them by not being helped. But she killed herself instead.

The truth – that is what is so worrying and impenetrable in these matters, and fills my notebooks with such miserable arguments. Whatever Nancy may be, she is not a liar, a calculating schemer, a person one can expose. It is much more difficult than that. Bored and tired by her perverse – apparently perverse – behaviour, her capacity for looking always for scapegoats for her own mistakes, I said to Morgan once lately, I remember, that I didn't know whether to tell her the truth or not – that *she* was the troublemaker, and that the disorders of our life were due to her uncontrolled bad temper and jealousy – and Morgan said, 'I should certainly tell her the truth, why not?' Jack [Sprott] on the contrary shook his head, and said it was no good. Jack was right. I did try to tell her the truth. How, I thought, was it possible for her ever to improve if she did not see her own faults, and admit them? So I tried to tell her the truth, and in the end she went out of her mind. Why? Because she saw the truth too – but her truth was different from mine. She was not making, consciously, any case for herself; she simply saw herself as ill-used, cruelly used, betrayed, abandoned. Her husband deserted her. He betrayed her to her son. Her son deserted her. Mother and Bunny, in spite of all her efforts to tell me the truth about them and their jealous characters, poisoned my mind against her. In her own eyes, and in her vehement accusations and self-defences, she is the victim of the world; that was her truth – nothing invented, or put on, that is what she *saw* – and every now and then one got a glimpse, a dreadful disturbing glimpse, of this vehement truth, as she saw it, that she constantly stated, that she vehemently tried to get me to see – so that one had yet again to revise one's own judgements. That is what is so dreadful – she believed everything she said, it was her truth – and one had to ask over and over again, and has never really stopped asking – was it the truth? Lacking confidence, as I have always done, in my own judgements, have I been wrong?

13 March 1949

It is quite possible, I was thinking as I walked, that something quite small, if indeed anything at all, brought Nancy to this collapse. Obviously her mental health has been bad for years, and getting increasingly so, and I think she has realized it at times, though not all the time, and been unable to help herself. I was remembering some of her remarks, all with regard to her 'bad moods' and hysterics, such as: 'I've asked you not to take any notice of me when I'm like this.' 'Talk to me, talk to me about something, anything, to take my mind off.' 'You used to be able to talk me out of these attacks, but now you goad me and make them worse.' 'Do you think I'm weak in my head?' 'I don't want Mrs Gray and the others to know the state of my mind.' 'I'm a hysterical person, I know it.'

I shouldn't be surprised if she didn't feel something physical happening in her head, like a snake uncoiling, something she didn't want to happen, was afraid of, but increasingly couldn't prevent. She tried to walk it off – long, lonely walks – but without success. I've often seen her touching and rubbing her forehead, as though she felt some tension inside. It must have put a great strain upon her, I see now, trying to restrain, control the thing, trying to prevent the mad snake uncoiling. And her suicide was a sort of abdication, a giving up of the struggle. So the least thing, or just nothing, may have set her off. The snake was in charge – perhaps it always will be now.

If this is the case, no one can blame her. One can't even say that the execution of more self-control as a child and girl would have prevented this sad culmination – for she might not have been able to help herself then – and on Dr Glover's theories she could not, for whatever set her wrong set her wrong then.

It is a curious business certainly. Here are three doctors, three strangers to me and to Nancy, Drs Brodie, Glover and Walker, and I run to them for help in a matter which covers, includes and exposes the whole of our family life. In a few letters, half an hour's or an hour's conversation, I have to convey to them somehow our characters and history and personal relationships – everything that constitutes our half century of life and beyond. They make up a sort of tribunal to which I have to take my own and the family guilt, the family failure, and they are expected, on what I care or choose to tell them, not only to withdraw my sister from her self-imposed psychosis, but rearrange our shabby and unsuccessful personal relations, in such a way that we shall not destroy ourselves or each other again. What I am saying to these doctors, in effect, is 'Comfort me in my guilt. I have mismanaged my domestic affairs so badly that my sister has preferred death to my care, in which she no longer believes. Can you somehow pull her out of it, so that I shall not feel responsible, for the rest of my days? Can you, without knowing any of us, or anything really about any of us, create an atmosphere in which we can all live?' No wonder Dr Brodie seems to me not to understand or give due importance to the dreadful subtleties which seem to me involved. Yet I expect him somehow to launder this half-century-old dirty washing.

14 March 1949

Graylingwell again yesterday. And I was astounded by the improvement which Nancy showed since I last saw her. She walked in, not altogether steadily, but by herself and sat with me, and conversed in a comparatively sensible way. Though still vague in many respects, she was now in possession of much of her mind. She asked for some money, complained about the food, and seemed to expect to be able to come and join me quite soon. Some of her luggage, she said, was missing, and she was concerned about that. She asked after my health, and seemed to take an interest in my replies. Her head was still too heavy for her neck and hung forward rather, but she was altogether, excepting for a cold, a well woman compared with what she had been before. She had even written me a letter, which I had not then got, but have since received – uncertain in writing, and rather rambling in thought, but wonderfully encouraging. She said she was having insulin now every day except weekends. I asked her if she had had electrical treatment too; she said no, not to her knowledge.

Oh dear. *What* was it that sent her down and out at the Acre? What thought, what anxiety, what revulsion – if any? And when her mind is able soon to embrace once more *all* the problems of her life, will she come up against that thought, that anxiety again, and fade out once more? At the moment there seems no reason why she should not be with me in a week or two – as Dr Brodie prophesied.

21 March 1949

I visited Nancy again yesterday. Every Sunday I see her shows a marked improvement in her physical and mental health. Yesterday she had been moved into a 'higher' ward – C1 to B1 – as one goes up in forms; she was much more her old self, dressed in her own

140

clothes, and held her head erect. Conversed perfectly normally – until one spoke of the past, and then she couldn't remember. I asked her what had upset her at the Acre to cause such a collapse. She did not know what the Acre was. I asked if she recalled visiting Worthing Hospital to retrieve some garments she'd left, and then going to the wool shop to get some more wool to finish up the red pullover she was knitting for me. She could not recall either of these expeditions, or even that she had knitted for me a red pullover.

'Was I allowed out then, in the Acre?' she asked. 'My memory is awfully bad,' she said.

I ascribed, as a possible cause for her breakdown, change of life, and told her how Mrs Gray had written to me and said that 'women of our age' (hers and Nancy's) went through difficult times.

Nancy said, 'Was she the matron of the Acre?'

I said, 'No. She was your landlady at Winchester House.'

'Winchester House?' said Nancy vaguely.

'The last place you stayed in in Worthing,' I said.

'I don't remember,' she said. 'What did I do there?'

I didn't pursue that. She has blacked it all out, poor creature. Better leave it so, surely, if one can. I said I could take her in my flat the moment the doctors released her.

It was a depressing atmosphere. We sat in the garden, and loonies of all sorts – all women – passed by, perambulating the paths – talking to themselves or behaving oddly, stroking their hands, like Lady Macbeth. One woman stood for a long time like a statue in the middle of the small lawn. It can't be very pleasant to 'come to' in a place like that, surrounded by lunatics. Is it right for a woman like Nancy? What does one think, recovering memory among mad people? 'I am mad, too.' We joked about it. She was awfully sweet, touching. She said she slept badly; the loonies talked so much, in their sleep too, and wouldn't be silenced. She said that she was only worried about coming up because she didn't know what help she could be to me just yet. Also she couldn't still retain her water properly. Poor old girl, she was very sweet.

25 March 1949

Beautiful days, cloudless, windless, cool in the night, warm by day. Faintly misty. The sky pale blue. On Wimbledon Common every morning immense orchestration of birds. How they pipe and trill.

A rabbit this morning fled out of a clump of bracken almost under my feet. Queenie was hunting elsewhere and did not see it. I began to give a shout to attract her; but the day was so beautiful, why stain it with blood. We had the place quite to ourselves from eight until ten; just ourselves and the birds, and the rabbit. Queenie had a meal of dead bracken. I never saw her do that before, she tore off and munched quite a lot. Perhaps a rabbit had pissed on it.

There was a certain amount of new broken glass about, which I tidied away. Spring and summer – they mean broken bottles, and perhaps cut feet. Still, one can't stop it, one can only pick up the glass when one comes upon it.

28 March 1949

I took Bunny to Graylingwell yesterday to see Nancy. Nancy had been sending her very affectionate messages, and I thought it might be beneficial to her to see the old woman whom she had not seen for a year but round whom she had built up such a structure of hatred and jealousy. It went off very well. Nancy much improved and allowed out into Chichester until six – to which we took her, although it meant abandoning our nice through train back. We gave her tea there and she saw us off by the 4.50. Poor old girl, standing smiling and waving at us through the carriage window, and wishing she could come too. And, of course, the blessed train wouldn't start – one of those trains that simply won't move but remain as though glued to their rails long after doors have been slammed and the guard has waved his arm.

Nancy's memory for what happened at the Acre and back was still extremely, and perhaps luckily, vague or blank. But if you can be called normal in such a condition, she was otherwise normal.

This morning, hearing voices by Queensmere as we passed and catching sight of a nude figure, I mounted the slope with Queenie to see the early bathers. It was a very cold morning after a frosty night, though fine and still; the whole air had a sort of cold greyness, though not a greyness ominous of rain; there were three young men at the water's edge, one, separate from the others and older than they, stark naked. The two younger chaps were talking together, and one of them was very attractive I thought; dark and lively. He was drying himself – a beautiful spare body, muscular, but not overmuscular, hard and glowing with warmth and health, a pink tinge – from the cold water and the scrubbing he had given it. A working chap I should think. I hoped he would take off his bathing slip so that I could see his cock and bottom, and this he soon obligingly did, standing there with no inhibitions stark naked drying his belly and arse, with one leg up on a bench, talking to his companion. A nice bottom, and a nice cock too, dark and curved, tautened and rubbery from the icy water. A neat little bush. Over-head a tall willow had begun to bud alone among the other still wintry trees, the palest of pale green its tiny drooping sprouts. The boy noticed me looking at him and smiled. I smiled back. Once upon a time . . . But the young male body is very beautiful; I must go again at the same time before nine. After that bathing is forbidden.

2 April 1949

James Kirkup came and sat with me on Tuesday evening. I like him. I think he is very intelligent and sensitive, and will be some-body someday. Queenie makes a fuss of him, and he of her; he admires her and has no fear. He mentioned that he thought he should go and see a psychologist, because he suffered from anxieties. Who doesn't? I had lent him Edwin's autobiography, and though I had forgotten the passage, if I ever got that far, Edwin had himself psychoanalysed with helpful results for anxiety.

We did not speak much of it while he was with me, but when I walked him back he returned to it again when we reached his gate. He said he suffered from persecution mania and thought people were following him, in a hostile manner. They did it in his lunch hour in the city, he said, where he works, and they had done it this evening on his way to me – some young men in the High Street milk bar had detached themselves from their conversation and fol-lowed him on his way to me. He had at last taken to his heels and run. I hardly knew what to say. He looks rather like an exhibitionist, the way he dresses – cord trousers, sandals, white socks – he likes white socks; I remembered I used to too – a waterproof khaki tunic jacket, zipped up to the throat, and a muffler round his neck and caught inside it. Odd dress, and with this his homosexual gait, a quite good-looking face, and golden hair, with an immense wave, very carefully arranged on his wide head. No wonder people follow him – one might almost say he invites it – but even if he doesn't, he is an obvious young 'queer' that any corner boy would be liable to try and take the mike out of. But I didn't quite know how to discuss all this, and only made vague reassuring remarks. He is young, after all, and I am not very well acquainted with him, though we do now call each other by our Christian names, and he has asked permission to inscribe his next book of poems to me.

Dinner to Morgan, ———— and Cecil Day-Lewis (Monday). Wrong order. It was originally a dinner to Cecil, but then Morgan appeared on the scene and we had difficulties in fitting in any other meeting, so I invited him, and then ———— asked himself. ———— is the sort of person who asks himself, and then asks for more wine in a roundabout though pointed way – 'Why, Morgan is the only one with any wine left!' – after one has already been generous. Bad mannered. Cecil is a charmer. I asked him, when I invited him, if he happened to have a poem for my paper, and he wrote back to say he had no short poems at all. But when he arrived, worn out with work and worry, he said, 'I have something for you, Joe,' and gave me a poem he had specially written. What could be nicer than that – especially in an eminent man? He reminded me of Morgan: 'By the way, Joe, would you like a new short story of mine for the *Listener*?' What a remark! I said, 'You are offering me a nugget of gold.' He gave it to me, just out of love.

Dinner with Rose Macaulay. Dear creature. Lunch with Elizabeth Bowen. How nice *she* is too. She too complained fretfully about ————, whom she likes: he comes to dinner and simply won't go, has to be turned out by her husband at two o'clock in the morning. He really is quite rude and irresponsible.

Living as a bachelor in my flat I have got into bad lonely habits such as farting loudly in order to hear the noise – for company. Even with Bunny and Ann here I do it still, without thinking. Do they laugh? They are awfully unobtrusive and good, but must be somewhat taken aback sometimes to hear resounding explosions from my room.

15 April 1949

Bunny and Ann go off to Thornton Heath tomorrow, and I go to Chichester to bring Nancy up. She is to live with me from now on.

24 April 1949

I have not added to this for a week. It has been a week of some responsibilities, but the weather has been very beautiful and life has passed easily and quietly, though at some sacrifice of leisure. Nancy has been very good and pleasant and useful, though 'deadish' – she was always a little so, lethargic – and as though blunted in her receptive and affective faculties, happy I think, but not gay, certainly not enthusiastic or eager or responsive, quiet, dull, acquiescent, vague, slow, dragging. No doubt this was to be expected. I have given her much attention, affection and help. There have been no frictions at all, except a curious passage over Velda Sprott, who was spending a few days in London and whom, weeks ago, I engaged to dine with me one evening, she and a friend of hers. Her arrival in London synchronized with Nancy's almost, and I remembered that Nancy, at Wendy and after, had picked on 'those awful Sprotts' in particular as treacherously responsible for what she regarded as my change of heart towards her. I did not know if this delusion persisted, so having fixed to take Velda and her friend to dinner on Wednesday, I sounded Nancy about it. I told her of my engagement, and said I didn't quite know what to do about it, that if the food situation were simple I would have liked to invite them here instead of to a London restaurant. 'Oh, don't ask them here,' said Nancy at once. She might have meant because it would be too much trouble to feed them, but I think she meant because she didn't wish to meet them. I asked her if she'd care to come and dine with them with me, but she refused. However, she asked quite agreeably if I'd enjoyed myself and what sort of a dinner we'd had. Later, looking through her things, which have been here since she last stayed, and finding an old address book, she said it contained all sorts of addresses she'd forgotten 'including Jack Sprott's. I can't think what that's doing there,' she said.

Her memory is a little better over the last year than it was, but not much. She recalled suddenly the name of the man, Hextable, with whom she had been friendly in Worthing, and which she had been unable to remember before, but still cannot remember Miss Allison, the old woman who lived in the same house and whom she saw almost daily. I don't like this business of remembering, yet can one have a black period in one's mind like that and be whole and healthy?

Queenie being on heat has complicated matters, for of course

Nancy can't take her out during the day, and she doesn't seem to have any independence at all, no pleasure in walking alone. At present I sense some discontent and resentment over my routine, for I am pursuing once more the course I thought best when Queenie was on heat before – that's to say I take her up to Putney Heath first thing in the morning, before breakfast, drinking just a cup of tea, and starting off at about six. Nancy has shown an inclination to accompany me on these early walks, and though I have not refused her, I have been discouragingly vague about my plans. 'What time are you going out tomorrow?' or, when I return, 'Queenie weenie, you've been out without your Auntie Nancy.'

I *don't* want to take Nancy or anyone else on my usual morning walks with Queenie. I want to go alone, and mooch about with my own dog and thoughts, without the company of anyone. I want to think of Queenie, study her, and jot down notes about her, and – if ever I have the leisure – take out my sketching block and try to draw her; and I certainly want no company in this. But Nancy, poor thing, is lonely and entirely without interest and occupation; her focus is entirely on me, how worrying that is; how shall I manage, I wonder, to get my own way, to get solitude, the solitude I want, which is a great deal. This sounds as though discordancies had already occurred, but they haven't; only the intimations of discordancies – as when I can't walk out of the flat without explanation or excuse – 'Where are you going?' – I hate that – and surely I *may* hate it, I do have a right to my own life and my own idea of freedom. What I really want, of course, is a simple housekeeper; no housekeeper would venture to say, 'Where are you going?' or 'May I come with you?' But I must do my kind best with the situation as it is, helping Nancy as much as I can without losing my own freedom.

I do think she is rather jealous of Queenie. She criticizes her – and me – though not as much as she used. 'You pay too much attention to her.' That sort of remark. 'It's not necessary for a dog to have all those blankets to lie on you have in your room, and unhealthy for you. You should have some straw for her.' Why bother about such things? I explained that the blankets, on chair and ground and my bed, were *her* blankets, and their object was to keep bed and chair and carpet clean, especially now when she is dripping blood. The explanation was unanswerable really – straw, I added, makes such a filthy mess itself – and no answer was forthcoming – but why interfere? I must say I *do not* care for women. They simply can't let one alone. However, I must keep everything smooth and quiet, at any rate until we have visited Dr Post on Wednesday. I must have his opinion before I start to assert independence – if I ever now may.

Yet Nancy looks remarkably well and, except for a sort of lethargic drag, and loss of memory, seems normal. I have seen her once or twice in her combinations, vest and trunk drawers, and was struck with the healthy-looking robustness of her figure. Like a young woman's, sturdy and strong. I said so, and she replied, 'I only wish yours was the same' – meaning I was too thin and an object for concern. Yet when Freddie and Irene came in for a drink on Sunday night at eight and overstayed their welcome, I was quite struck by Nancy's appearance of fatigue, her pallor, the white lines under her eyes, the rapidity of the transition from liveness to deathliness.

29 April 1949

A cold day. Rain last night and the common very wet. But I got up at 5.30, when I woke, and though I had rather a headache, walked Queenie for two and a half hours nevertheless. Nancy had breakfast ready when I returned. I gave Queenie some warm milk with a raw egg in it. One of a dozen fresh eggs Diana had given me.

'Did you give her one of the fresh eggs?' asked Nancy.

'Yes, I did.'

'You louse!'

Never mind. I washed and shaved and breakfasted and went to work, getting horsemeat on the way. Felt rather unwell at midday, so came back home after lunch for a nap. Nancy's bedroom door was closed. She was napping too presumably. I took an aspirin and went to bed, with Queenie, who seems always now to spend the whole day limping after every morning run – though whether it is just cramp or rheumatism I don't know. I rub her leg and it gets better temporarily. First thing in the morning it is always all right, so that I suppose it is nothing and take her out and then it is bad again.

I got up just before four not having slept much, and risked taking Queenie out for ten minutes to get some fags. A dog eventually bothered us, so I brought her back. Nancy was up and was preparing the tea. I hailed her genially and asked her if she'd like to come to the Royal Academy with me after tea to help me choose pictures for the *Listener*. This is third and last private view day, and a convenient moment.

'The Royal Academy,' she echoed rather blankly.

I said, 'Yes, it's the annual show of paintings, and I have to choose some for the *Listener*. You might come and help me.'

'Where is it? It's in London, isn't it?'

'Yes, Piccadilly.'

'Oh no. I shouldn't like that.' At tea she said, 'Do you have to go today?'

I said, 'Well, yes, I have an invitation card for three days and this is the last of the three.' I showed it to her.

She looked at it without interest. Then she said, 'I haven't been to the lavatory again today. I expect it's because I don't get enough exercise.'

I said, 'I don't suppose it's that really.'

She said, 'Since I can't go out with you in the morning I hardly ever get a walk.'

I said, 'Don't you like walking by yourself?'

'No, I don't really. I prefer company. Anyway by the time I get the shopping and housework done there never seems time.'

I said, 'Need you shop every day? Can't you lay in enough twice a week?'

She seemed to think not. One couldn't keep vegetables indefinitely. 'Anyway I hate the Putney walks. I don't mind telling you I'm fed up with the place already.'

I was rather shocked by this remark and her discontented face. What a thing to say after all the trouble she has given and exacted from me.

But I only said, 'Why not come to the Academy? It would be a change for you and quite amusing. And it is exercise walking round looking at the pictures. And if that isn't enough, we could walk back down Piccadilly afterwards.'

'I hate walking in London.'

How very disagreeable! How Bunny would have jumped at it! Dear me. Morgan once said, 'You will never please Nancy whatever you do.' I suppose not. I remember she said yesterday what a bore the towing path was, and what a pity Wimbledon Common was so far away, and what a pity we didn't live in Wimbledon. Is she going to ask me to move? Yet here she is with nothing to do but make me an evening meal, keep the place nice and bright for me, and keep Queenie company. There are masses of books for her to read and cinemas to go to. London with all its amusements half an hour away. Yet she goes about with a dull discontented peevish look, thinking how awful and boring everything is. 'I don't mind telling you I'm fed up with the place already.' I can't get over that remark.

She then went on to say that she'd tried on some jackets in a shop along the road and wanted my opinion about them and they'd said they wouldn't keep them after this afternoon.

I said, 'But I'll go with you after tea, my dear, I'd be very glad to.'

She didn't say anything, but later, when she'd washed up and when I said, 'Well let's go and see these clothes,' she said, 'Don't bother to come, it doesn't matter if you've got to go to the Academy.'

I said, 'But I can catch a bus outside the shop. It's quite easy. Besides I'm thrilled to see what costumes an odd little shop like that can produce to please you.'

On the way I thought I'd better scrap the Academy after all; I can easily go on Monday with the rest of the world. She tried on two suits, and I gave my opinion and bought her one, £7 10s. 0d. Then I told her I wouldn't bother to go to the Academy after all and could easily go on Monday. She made no demur about it. So I trailed round Putney with her, doing some shopping. A dispiriting afternoon, in fact, and bad augury for the future. She really has no interest in life at all, I fear – except perhaps, in a dull sort of way, to be as much as possible round my neck. Yet I've done everything I possibly can since she came to make her happy and cheerful.

30 April 1949

I said I would make an omelette for lunch today, and when it came to the point suggested I should make it of the foreign ration eggs, of which we had five, instead of Diana's fresh ones.

'The foreign ones!' cried Nancy. 'Let's have the fresh ones.'

I said, 'Just as you like. But it's a good way of using up the foreign ones.'

She said, 'Why don't you want to use the fresh ones?'

I said, 'Well they'd be nicer than the foreign ones hard-boiled in salads. And also I thought you liked an egg beaten up in milk for your lunch.'

She said, 'Oh yes. I suppose you want to keep them for Queenie.'

I said, 'No that wasn't in my mind at all.'

She said, 'You gave her two of them yesterday anyway' – fixing me with her eyes. I said, 'No, only one.'

She said, 'Well, how is it there are only eight left, for we have only had two? You did give her two, didn't you?'

I said, 'No, only one,' and took the eggs down to count. There were nine. She didn't apologize for this. Simply said nothing. But I didn't care for it much. Fancy counting the eggs anyway, to see how many I was giving Queenie. *My* eggs anyway, and her position here might be expected to make her more diffident and careful. Strange woman.

I went to a wedding in the afternoon and when I got back I found that Nancy had taken Queenie out, and looking down the embankment from my balcony I saw them both, so I hurried after them to join them.

Some time later Nancy said, 'There was a letter for you from Paul Junior, this afternoon, and I opened it. I couldn't wait. You didn't mind, did you?'

I said, 'No.'

But of course she shouldn't have, even though Paul is her son. My letter, not hers. Bunny would never have opened a letter not addressed to her in such cases. Nancy should have waited. Patience. Anyway, it was the thing I foresaw happening – a letter coming while I was out – so it was a good thing I told the truth about what I had written to the boy.

1 May 1949

'Have you got the darning-wool box?' asked Nancy at 12.15 today, coming into my room where I was sitting in my chair doing some work.

I said, 'Yes, there it is.'

'I don't see why I shouldn't sit in here, as you've got the fire on,' she said.

I said, 'Do, of course.'

But it wasn't the way to put things. You know. And that is why I don't believe I ever shall *really* get on with her. 'Should I disturb you if I come and sit in here?' – that is what I would have said.

Tea at Freddie's this evening. Nancy was asked too, but didn't want to go. So I went alone. I had not visited them for some time. Molly was there, and Irene, and the three children, Richard, Pamela and Nicky, and the other son's child Mona (fourteen), a silent sly-looking little girl. Freddie looked awfully nice with his hair all tumbled, taking his ease in his armchair by a large coal fire, his younger son Nicky, who dotes on him, never leaving him alone. Richard clung to Molly, who brought him up and whom he still loves best, his 'Nanny'. Tea was bread and butter, lettuce, tomatoes, and two kinds of cake. Everyone was so nice, the family group touched me very much, pretty sturdy children being told they mustn't have so many sweets given them, the family cat, a little female, said to be pregnant again, sleeping in front of the fire. A nice homeless cat.

'What's its name, Freddie?'

'It 'asn't got one. We don't call it nothing.'

Freddie had bought a new suit from the tally man – a 'spiv's suit' he called it – hopsack, eighteen guineas. We asked him to show it us, which he was pleased to do, and put on the jacket – very nicely cut, very smart. Irene brusquely dispensed tea . . .

Sitting with them there, this pleasant happy family group, I remembered the past and the passions that had rent us all. My love for Freddie, my 'shopping' him, the dreadful remorse and anxieties that flowed from this bad action, and the troubles and expense too, my enticing of him to desert, how I kept him, his marriage with Irene and the increase in my expenses, the birth of the children, Irene's nasty jealousies, the dreadful rows by which the house was rent, in which Freddie and Irene assaulted each other, Molly's love for me, Bob's jealousy, Freddie's career as a burglar, and his apprehension, trial and imprisonment, my row over Queenie with his mother. All these turbulent waters had flowed under the bridge, and the flood had passed and subsided. Looking round at the happy family group, peace and calm now restored and established, in which I was an old friend liked and welcomed, I saw in the hackneyed phrase, that we had reached harbour and without loss, with gain indeed, for we all knew the best and worst of each other, and had accepted both. I was touched and moved by it all, the friendliness I felt and got, the nice people, and wished to do something really nice for them all. I kissed Molly, as usual, on entering and leaving; and saying goodbye to them all recollected how I still had in one of my drawers the police document I had kept for years and funked ever using, which contained the secret of Irene's past, known only to myself and the police, pure dynamite, which in my rage and anger I had once thought of showing to Freddie, when he himself was fed up with his wife, to expose her and destroy his marriage.

7 May 1949

Nancy went to May's [Buckingham] on Wednesday afternoon, and I joined her there with Queenie in the evening. I took Queenie by trolley to Hammersmith Broadway and then by train to Stamford Brook. Nancy seemed rather tired, but ate a huge dinner of cold tongue and salad. White wine. Later Morgan and Jack [Sprott] arrived, unexpected by us, but not by Bob [Buckingham] and May. Morgan was particularly kind to Nancy and walked with her and gave her his arm when we all left. She was very pleased with that and said how nice he was. He thought she looked an ill woman – and noticed the fluff of hair all over her face which I too noticed at Graylingwell and do not think was so conspicuous before she was taken ill. Morgan said 'glands'.

14 May 1949

What *does* she want? She does not like it here. She doesn't like the river. The walks are a bore. Queenie no fun. The shopping and household work are a drudgery. Yet all she has to do is shop for the evening meal, which is always a salad, and the cereals and bread for breakfast. I help her frequently in the washing up, and the shopping too. She has nothing to do at all, a few plates, a few vegetables, but she is bored and resentful. Dreadful. 'I have no friends, I haven't had time to make any.' (Geoffrey, who came one evening, has been written off again as a bore.) Diana [Petre] phoned me on Friday. I'd wondered what it really would be like to bring them together – feel a bit mischievous about it – and had already written to Diana to ask if she'd really like to. She said yes. I said I'd fix it. Nancy had already said she'd like to meet Diana (who had told me she had quantities of clothes she didn't want which might fit Nancy), but had later said, 'Diana isn't coming this week, is she?'

I said, 'No.'

'Let's not have her just yet.'

But yesterday, I said to Nancy, 'Diana phoned today.'

'Oh, what did she want?'

'She wants to come over and meet you.'

'What did you say?'

'I said sometime next week.' Silence. Then I added, to see what would happen, 'Of course we could have her this weekend. We haven't anyone coming.' Pause.

Then Nancy. 'No, don't let's have her this weekend. We've done enough entertaining this week.'

We! And this is the woman who accuses me today of neglecting her when she's got no one else to see! Of course Diana only wants to meet Nancy because she wants to see me, and fears she won't now Nancy is here unless she sees her too. And of course Nancy is jealous. I do feel mischievous, I must say. They'll soon tear each other to pieces – and perhaps me too!

In the evening she lectured me. She had had some gin and red wine, and no doubt this had the usual effect. I had been asking her what she would do if I went away for a weekend, and she said, 'Who to?' and I said, 'Jack,' and she said, 'Oh,' and I said would she get Bunny and Ann, for I didn't think she could have Bunny alone, and she said she didn't know quite, and then, 'Did Jack invite Queenie too to Nottingham?' and I said no, he couldn't, he had a bird, a cockatoo, but that Queenie had been invited for a weekend by a Miss [Elizabeth] Poston some months ago, who lived in Stevenage, and that I should want to take her there some time. Nancy said, '*I* should like to get away for a holiday into the country, too, but I don't suppose there'll be any chance of that.'

The discontented and jealous envy of these remarks struck a chill to my heart, and I saw in a flash that I should have the greatest difficulty in getting away for any sort of holiday or weekend with Queenie, it would be like trying to take her away from Wendy. I heard already as though it had been uttered: 'You might at least leave the dog with me. I think it's very selfish of you. You don't think of me at all or what I'm going to do here alone while you both go off enjoying yourselves.'

'But you can have Bunny and Ann with you.'

'I don't want Bunny and Ann. They don't like me – and I don't care about them' . . . and so on.

She then said, 'I hate towns as you know, and of all towns I hate Putney the most. I think it's the most horrible place I've ever seen. It seems to me to have nothing to recommend it at all. I'm sorry to seem to complain, but one may as well be frank about it.'

I was quite dumbfounded, not to say horrified by this. But I knew

I had to be careful. I said, 'Well, you know I'm sorry to hear that, and it does put me into rather a dilemma. You did after all want to come here – it was indeed the reason why you tried to 'bump yourself off', in your own phrase – and now if you hate it so much, what can we do for you?'

'I love the country,' said Nancy. 'I shall never be happy until I live there.'

I said, 'But you did live there, and were miserable and lonely and tried to kill yourself.'

'That wasn't the country.'

'But you had the offer of the country. I offered to buy you a cottage, only you couldn't find one. And in the end you didn't even want to. I'll still put you in the country if you like, but will you like it? You've always said you go to pieces by yourself. How could you live in a cottage alone? And certainly *I* can't join you there, if that's in your mind, and wouldn't if I could. I have my work in London, and anyway I like Putney.'

She said, 'Anyway I don't suppose I could go, could I, for what would you and Queenie do?'

Strange remark. I said I should get along all right no doubt on my own as I'd done for the last thirty years, and would invent some plan of self-help, though of course she was very useful to me.

'I am rather confused in my mind about it,' she said.

How right now everyone seemed about her, how foolish myself, to have taken her on again. Monstrous, surely, to assert herself again after all that had happened and the trouble she had given – but perhaps she no longer recollected that she had given trouble? Once I thought it a good thing she should have lost her memory. Now I wondered. And I hated her all over again. The bitch, I thought, destroyer of other people's lives, out of jealousy and envy and conceit. Interfering. Demanding. Niggling. Criticizing. What impertinence. And I remembered her remark in Worthing Hospital when she recovered: 'If I can help you just by taking Queenie out for you in the afternoon, it will be something to make up for all the trouble I've caused you.' But alas, that was not the note now. It was how awful and monotonous and toilsome and dreary her life was, how selfish I was, with my holiday plans and my morning walks, and how different everything was from what she'd expected. I tried to tell her about myself – how lonely-minded, self-absorbed writers were, not wanting company always, needing freedom and protection and so on, but I doubt if it registered. She is an aggrieved and a grievous woman. How can it all end?

15 May 1949

When she went to Dr Post at the Maudsley on Wednesday, she apparently said to him something about 'before I tried to bump myself off.'

He said, 'Do you remember why you did that?'

She said, 'No, I don't.' He said, 'Does it worry you?'

She said, 'No, except that I can't think why. I didn't think that it was in my character to do such a thing.'

21 May 1949

An uneventful week, dull, quiet; pleasant in its way. I have not attempted to take Queenie out by myself in the mornings, but have either taken Nancy with me or not gone at all. Nancy recovered herself over the resentment she displayed, and, the next day I think it was, when we were marching towards the Windmill together, she said, 'I'm sorry for what I said yesterday, Joe. I oughtn't to have said it, and I don't really feel like that. I want you to do just as you like.' That was handsome. That was nice.

What otherwise have I done? Social life: dinner with Jack Sprott on Tuesday, Kirkup and Nancy to a quite intolerably bad play (Michael Redgrave and Margaret Rawlings: a French comedy) at Wimbledon theatre: we walked out after Act II; saw Morgan off to America on Thursday evening – Benjamin Britten with us, very nice fellow; lunch Wyndham Lewis on Friday. An uncomfortable man, with such ugly horse-like teeth and a gaze which seems not to lift to one's own eyes, to be reluctant to rise quite up to them, a sort of curved glance which, instead of striking levelly at one, gives the impression of dropping as it leaves his own eyes and rising nearer one, unexpectedly, yet never quite to meet one's own. Like the handshakes of schizophrenics, I thought, who can't decide whether to or not, hold out their hands and then withdraw them from one's responsive action. He gave me an account of his row with the Sitwells, and of his friendship with Ezra Pound. More interesting still were his remarks about the slowness and difficulty of making a good portrait – he described in detail how he did it, building up the structure of the face, etc., putting in, making mistakes, painting out, and denied that one got quicker and more facile with practice. He said indeed that if one got quicker one was probably painting worse, and that it was all the same whether one was inventing a face or copying one. I instanced Tintoretto, whose immense opus I had been looking through in the Phaidon edition. 'Everyone instances him,' said W.L. at once – which pleased me rather, for a novice I felt I was on the mark. He said that Vollard had given Cézanne over 200 sittings. He himself had had only twelve (I think he said) from Eliot, a few of four hours in length.

4 June 1949

I make few notes now. Now that I scarcely ever go out alone, nothing happens to me. Trudging over Wimbledon with Nancy trailing behind, for I simply *cannot* walk her pace and even what seems to me the slowest stroll I can manage leaves her ten paces behind, I no longer take the interest in, have the feeling for, the woods that I used to have; my exact approach is barred and my sticks rot I suppose in their hiding places; the shrine is no longer visited.

I tried again this week to take a solitary morning walk with Queenie without repercussions, and going out at seven returned to the flat at 8.30. Nancy was again upset – clothed, and hurrying the breakfast onto the table. 'Where have you been? Did you go up on the heath?' – as though she hadn't some weeks previously said, 'I'm sorry I said what I did, Joe. You must do what you like.'

'I feel I must get out for a bit,' she said. This was simply another of her protest walks. It couldn't be anything else – a jealous and envious gesture. For if *I* don't go out – when, as lately, I've given up the idea and stayed in bed – she *never* goes out either, never appears to think of it. It is just that she doesn't want me to go up on the heath without her.

I said, 'I wish you would, and take Queenie, she's wet and it would be better for her to dry in the air.'

Nancy said, 'I don't suppose she'll want to come now.' However she took her. She didn't in the least need or want to go out; it was a protest. At breakfast she controlled what I could see to be her growing resentment and anger. The only thing she said was, 'I wake up so late now, I don't know why. I wake at 5.30, but that's too early to get up, so then I go to sleep again and then I oversleep. It's awfully annoying.'

I wondered if I could ask *why* it was annoying, and say that it suited me very well, for I didn't want her company, but I judged it better to remain silent.

But I must add in her favour that she has her cross to bear. She came into my room this morning after breakfast, and Queenie put up her usual jealous protest against the intrusion. Nancy paid no heed, except to say, 'Shut up, silly dog.' But Queenie paid no heed to that or to my shouts of silence, and when Nancy put out a hand, she bit it. She didn't draw blood, of course, but she gave Nancy a nip. Not very nice for poor Nancy, but she was quite good about it. 'Horrid dog to bite poor Nancy,' and appeared to forget it later when we went out. She ought to understand Queenie's jealousy after all, for she herself suffers from the same thing and has given her own 'nips' from time to time.

15 June 1949

Since Queenie was so wet, I did not hurry back, hoping the sun would dry her – indeed if there had been no Nancy at home I would have stayed out another hour or so in order to get Queenie dried out. When I did get in, at about 9.30, Nancy greeted me with 'Oh, why didn't you come back ten minutes earlier! Morgan has just rung up to say he'll be very pleased to come to dinner tomorrow evening.'

I said, 'Oh.' (The story of this is that I had invited John Morris to meet Jim Kirkup here tomorrow (Sunday) night for supper, thinking it might do K. a bit of good, for John might invite him to broadcast, and this would be useful to Jim who has given up his job in order to write. Later on I wrote and asked Forster too, who had said he would like to meet Nancy, but I hardly expected he would be able to accept, for he was in town last weekend on his return from the USA and I supposed he would be spending this one in Cambridge.)

She said, 'I thought you said you'd invited him in *after* supper.'

I said, 'I think I only indicated. It was difficult to be blunt about it, and he is an oldish man and I felt it might not be fair on him to ask him to come to far for so short a time.'

157

'Well, I can't stand all this,' said Nancy, re-entering her room. 'It's all too much for me, all this entertaining, it's getting me down.'

I didn't say any more for a bit. Then I asked, 'How are you feeling this morning?'

'Lousy,' was the reply.

'Did you have more stomach pains in the night?'

'No.'

'What is the matter then?'

'Oh, I don't know' (peevishly).

I made my coffee and sat down to breakfast. Soon she came out and joined me. I said, 'Why do you upset yourself about tomorrow evening? There is nothing to worry about.'

'It's nothing but entertaining,' she said. 'It makes me nervous. What are we going to give them to eat?'

I said, 'But we've done hardly any entertaining this week. And we have a large chicken already. And if more is wanted there is that tin of corned beef.'

She said, 'We've no room for such a large party. Where can we sit them?'

'Dear Nancy,' I said, 'they are easy simple people and don't come here for formal entertainment. They can sit on the floor if necessary and eat off their laps. They will not mind at all, they are not royalty. And you need not even make an elaborate salad. So long as we have drinks for them, which we have, and a bite of something, which we have, there is no need to be elaborate and particular. If you were not here, I should have them in, and as many more of my friends as I could get, and enjoy their company and put something together for them without fuss or bother. If there is any work to do I will do it all. There is nothing to bother about at all.

'Besides,' I added, seeing this as a good line as well as the truth, 'it is all for Jim's sake. It is a party to help him, and I know you would wish that. John may employ him, and of course it will be a great thing for him to meet Morgan. But for God's sake don't put yourself out over it.'

'We haven't any mayonnaise,' she said after a moment.

'I'll go and get some now if you like.'

Pause.

'I thought you were going to take me for a walk this morning,' she said pettishly. (I had told her yesterday that I was going for a swim and would take her for a walk later and for lunch in Wimbledon if she liked.)

'I meant this afternoon,' I said. 'I thought we could lunch in Wimbledon and walk back after it.'

'I don't want to walk in the afternoon when it's hot. I'm always doing that. I want to walk in the morning when it's cool.'

'So that is the real cause of all this,' I said. 'You're just annoyed because I've been out with Queenie, and it's nothing to do with tomorrow evening at all.'

'No, it's not,' she said, 'it's both. All this entertaining upsets me. And I *do* like a morning walk.'

I said, 'Well, we will give up entertaining if you wish. And as for the walk, I will take you out now if you like. We will give up the mayonnaise, for we can't have both, and walk up to Wimbledon and shop, and lunch there.' She said nothing. 'Would you like that?' I repeated after a time.

'All right,' she said, ungraciously.

So poor old Queenie and I, both rather tired after having just come in from a two-and-a-half-hour outing, had to turn out at once again, and re-embus, and walk back over the common again.

29 June 1949

She isn't really interested in people, and doesn't care for them. She makes use of them only. Yesterday I heard from Georges Duthuit that he could put me up if I went to Paris, so I have begun to arrange to spend a week of my holiday there with him. When I saw Nancy on Monday evening, I told her about it and said, 'Would you mind looking after Queenie for me for a week if I go?'

She seemed a bit taken aback (thinking I ought to take her with me? Making use of her?) and said, doubtfully, 'No', then, 'What about her meat?'

I said, 'I would show you the place in London and perhaps you could get some if you run short. Of course I would lay in ten pounds or so before I went, but in case it went off and you needed more, could you not go and get it?'

She made a sort of moue, and said nothing. Now should she not have said, 'Of course I'll go, Joe. I'll be only too glad to help you. I'm delighted you're going to Paris and will love to look after Queenie for you when you've gone'? But she made a moue.

I said, 'It's awfully easy. An easy bus ride to Piccadilly, five minutes' walk to the shop, no waiting, and then home.'

She said nothing, but smirked a little.

I said, 'Does the idea frighten you?'

She said, 'Yes.'

I said, 'Yet it's not much more difficult than going to Wimbledon to shop. It's only a slightly longer bus ride, that's all.'

She made no helpful remark.

I said, 'Never mind, I daresay I can get Jim Kirkup to get it for me.'

After a time she said, 'What will you do between going to Siegfried [Sassoon] and going to Paris? If Siegfried can't have you for so long? Will you come back here?'

I said, 'Yes, of course. Why, what are you thinking?'

'Oh, nothing. I just wondered.'

I said, 'Would that fit in with any plans you have in mind?'

She said, 'Oh, yes.'

I said, '*Have* you any plans in mind? What do you mean to do when I go?'

She said, 'Oh, I don't think I'll do anything. I've thought about the Benous Hotel (a vegetarian hotel she once stayed at in Brighton) but I don't think I'd like it much.'

I said, 'Will you ask Bunny and Ann along? It would be a nice change for them if you did.'

She said, 'I don't think so. I feel I need a rest.'

I said, 'Of course Ann could work for you here and do all the cooking, etc. I suppose you wouldn't like that?'

She said, 'No, I don't think that would work.'

I said, 'Won't you be lonely?'

She said, 'No. I'd sooner be alone. And of course I could always have company if I wanted – May [Buckingham] or Geoffrey or someone.'

I said, 'But you can't be sure of all that. May and Geoffrey may be engaged or on holiday themselves. Diana too. Of course Jim [Kirkup] will be here, and his mother. And perhaps John Morris might come along if you asked him for an evening. He likes you. I know, and though he'll do nothing himself – never ask you out or anything, for he's like that – I daresay he'd be pleased if you phoned him and said, "Do come and keep me company one evening, I'm alone here and want to be entertained." Then you could have Bunny and Ann over for the day, but if you do, I think it would be kind to let them stay the night, for they are old people and would find the double journey rather trying in one day.'

She said nothing to that, and I saw she didn't like it. She doesn't care for Bunny, or Ann, or think of them. She doesn't say to herself as I do, 'Poor old girl. Eighty-one years old and a good old sort. She's done lots of things for me in the past; and she's fond of us. Soon she will be dead, and I shan't be able to do anything for her then. I must do what I can now to make her last years happy, even though she is rather a bore.' I am continually 'ticking people off', as Morgan puts it – paying duty calls on Bunny, Lilian [Bowes-Lyon], May and others to give them pleasure and hear about their lives. Often I don't feel like it, but I go; whereas Nancy does none of these things.

If Bunny were here, she would not hesitate to get the old woman to mend her clothes, for she is useful with her needle while Nancy isn't; but out of sight, out of mind as far as Nancy is concerned – *until* circumstances such as being alone and lonely remind her of people, and then she may call them in – if they'll come – not because she really likes or feels for them, but because she is bored herself and wants company. But will she get them then? Why does she not phone people like May and Diana from time to time just for a chat? Why doesn't she go and visit them, and Bunny, and Geoffrey? Too much trouble. No interest. I doubt if Bunny would come now – 'sent for' at the last minute to keep Nancy from being bored. It would have been a very different matter if Nancy had written her weeks ago to say, 'Do come over and see me when Joe goes away. It will be a nice opportunity to have you and Ann here for a night.'

I shall be *extremely surprised* if I get off on this holiday of mine without Nancy doing or saying something to spoil it for me – she has already gone part of the way with her '*I* would like a holiday too.'

29 June 1949 (continued)

Diana gave her a lot of dresses when we visited her flat. Nancy never wrote to thank her for them. I don't think she ever tried them on for forty-eight hours; they were all nice things and fitted Nancy perfectly. But she never wrote to thank her. She never rings her up. I put it into her head that she should. But she didn't. She does nothing to make people feel interesting, important or happy, or to attach them to her. Strange, dim person. Not civilized really. 'Which of these two colours do you like?' she asked me the other day, handing me two bottles of nail paint. How odd women are. I chose one, and she spent the rest of the day painting her nails. And the previous day depilating her legs with Wax-away, an agonizing process. Why so much trouble over one's body? And for whom? I suppose that is just the woman's way.

Psychiatry and psychology: I was thinking of them this week, and do not get their functions straight. Is Nancy's trouble what's called illness, or bad character? Did something go wrong in her early life, or is she just to be written off (Morgan) as 'an awful woman'? Looking back at these last few notes, does psychology improve people who are just selfish, self-centred, envious, jealous, as it is expected to improve people who commit murders or imagine they are Queen Elizabeth? If that is so, then there are no bad characters, we are all fundamentally good, the same, so long, so to speak, as we undergo a course of treatment.

Yesterday morning, going off on my usual morning bathing expedition with Queenie, I had a guilty and sorry feeling for Nancy. The weather is so stifling; would it not be kind to give her a chance of a morning pre-breakfast walk too when it is comparatively cool? So I left a note on the table to say that if she liked to join me at the Windmill at nine after my bathe I would walk her back. I naturally hoped she wouldn't come, but would regard the kind thought as enough. But there she was, sitting on the grass; Queenie bounded towards her and lavished greetings upon her, and we returned to breakfast.

Last night Nancy said, 'Are you doing the same thing tomorrow. And if so can I meet you at the Windmill again?'

I said, 'Of course,' though I didn't want it.

She said, 'I'm not sure I'll come, but you could look for me there.' (She had some plan of shopping in Sloane Square, and wasn't sure she could manage both.)

I said, 'All right. Let's say between nine and nine fifteen.' For I have finished my Supplement, and wanted to stay by the pool till 'closing time', nine.

She said, 'Oh, I shouldn't be as late as that.'

She was up in the morning when I left. I said, 'Well, I'll look for you at the Windmill at nine. But I may be a bit late.'

'OK,' she said.

After my bathe, I didn't come up the main slope from the pool to the Windmill but circuitously in order to give Queenie more time to dry off, for she too had been in the water. Then I saw Nancy (it was 9.5) passing down the main avenue from the Windmill to the pool. She didn't see me. I was about to shout, but then I thought, Shall I have to be met *every* morning? I don't want that. She is making a convenient mistake by leaving our rendezvous place. I'll go home without her. Besides, why is she going down to the pool? She will only embarrass the bathers, who were still there when I left. So I let her disappear, and marched off home. On the way back Queenie went off into the woods and I heard her barking at a squirrel. Later I missed her, and realized I hadn't seen her for five to ten minutes. I got in my usual panic, and after calling in vain yelled and whistled. It was some minutes before she came, hurtling towards me with her ears back. People who are frightened are often angry; I had been afraid I had lost her, so I cursed her when she arrived. She looked abjectly at me, but I took the lead from my neck and gave her a cut with it. Then we went home.

I was shaving when Nancy arrived – very upset.

'*What* happened to you?' she cried. 'Why didn't you meet me?'

I was on safe ground, having been to the rendezvous at the agreed time, and explained this. It then appeared that she had heard Queenie barking at the squirrel, had recognized her bark, had called her and Queenie had found her. Hence Queenie's disappearance. Queenie, poor dear, had then hared back to me to tell me the news – and got a cut for her pains. I apologized to the little sweetheart with much love when I had her alone.

4 July 1949

Diana came to dinner last night, at Nancy's suggestion. She owed her an invite, since our last combined meeting was at Diana's flat, and I have been hoping they would get on together, though it would have pleased me better if Nancy had taken her out somewhere alone, especially since I took the girl to lunch myself only lately as a gesture of gratitude for her having given Nancy so many frocks.

However, I fell in with the scheme of inviting her, and Nancy bought and baked a chicken, made a salad, shelled peas, etc., and prepared a generally good meal.

Sweltering day and I felt dull and flat, and when Diana arrived at 6.30 would sooner not have had to entertain anyone but would rather have sat in my window reading a book. Nancy was lying on a blanket on the verandah sunbathing, with very little on, and did not rise when Diana appeared (I let her in) but said, 'Excuse me if I don't', and I said, 'Of course, don't get up.' Diana and I sat down and I hardly knew what to talk of. The sun boiled down, and Nancy lay some distance off. After about fifteen minutes I brought cocktails in, and Nancy got up and changed and came out and found us. Diana is a nervous, thin, highly strung girl, a woman with a way of fixing large blue eyes on one that makes it hard to evade her sociability. Writing a novel, and a great enthusiast over Henry James and other literary conversational gambits. I had to work hard to entertain her or to keep up with her breathless exclamatory manner. I felt pretty brainless most of the evening. Nancy did little to assist the conversation on, and I dare say was left behind by some of it. I didn't notice her particularly or anything else except the boredom and the heat. Dinner. And then it got cooler. And then Nancy began to collect the dishes, etc., and take them in.

I said, 'You're not going to wash up, are you?' She said she was. I didn't want to help, felt pleasantly cool for the first time that day and the river was nice to look at and listen to, with the little boys jumping and diving in down below – splash, splash. So I said, 'You don't want to do that. Mrs Thing is coming tomorrow.'

Nancy said something about her coming later, and she didn't want to leave things for her. So I struggled no more and thought, Well, if you want to be energetic, be energetic. So Diana and I remained on the verandah.

When Nancy eventually emerged, she was subdued and quiet, and, I thought, cross. Indeed it was evident something had displeased her, for Diana noticed it too and eventually decided to go. She was taking back a suitcase Nancy had brought the frocks in, so I offered to see her off to her bus – which I would have done anyway, being polite. I asked Nancy if she'd like to come too. No.

'Are you all right?' we both asked.

'I'm just tired.'

Goodbyes were said. I saw Diana off. There was a disturbance in the long weekend bus queue – someone trod on Queenie's toe, and she yelped and fell about among the people in her fright and a cross woman said, 'Your dog's dangerous and ought to be under control.'

And I said irritably, 'She's not dangerous at all. Someone hurt her.'

'Well, she nearly knocked my sister over. She shouldn't be in a queue.'

Fuck your sister, I thought but didn't say. Anyway, hot weather

164

crossness, and Diana said, 'Don't wait,' so I didn't but went irritably, and apprehensively, home. I knew Nancy was going to cause trouble of some sort, but didn't know exactly what.

I said, 'Are you tired, old girl?'

She said, 'No, only bored.'

I said, 'Oh.' Then I went in and kissed her goodnight quite affectionately.

When I was in my room getting undressed she called in to me, 'Why don't you have Diana to live with you, since you obviously like her better than me?' Maddening remark. As if I wanted either.

I said, 'Oh, jealousy, eh?'

'Not at all. And I must say I thought her extremely bad-mannered, the way she confined her conversation to you all evening. She hardly spoke to me at all.'

I didn't say anything. Went to bed. But that sort of scene irritates one's nerves, and it was a couple of hours before I slept. Got up early anyway and – the only part of my life I really love – took Queenie out alone, rambled about in Wimbledon woods, then bathed and talked to a nice young man I've seen there before – a medical student – and then home, Queenie catching and eating a rabbit on the way.

When I got back at 9.40 Nancy had had her breakfast and put mine ready and was sorting out the washing. My mind was still in a turmoil of annoyance and exasperation from her remark of the evening before. We exchanged a few remarks about nothing in particular, and then I sat to my breakfast.

She said, 'I'm so depressed. I feel sure I shall end up in Graylingwell or one of those places again. I didn't get to sleep last night till 5 a.m. I heard the clock strike every quarter. I put on my light and read a book at three.'

I did not say that I had not slept well either and that we should both no doubt have slept better if she hadn't prevented it, and that she deserved her self-induced sleepless night. I merely said that I hoped Queenie hadn't disturbed her.

She then went on, 'In spite of what you said about jealousy last night, Diana *was* very bad-mannered and you encouraged her. She only spoke to you, and you made it quite clear that you preferred speaking to her to speaking to me.'

How *can* people make such remarks? How can one live an adult life with such childishness?

I said, 'What on earth does all that matter? If you were bored you could have gone away quietly, or taken the dog for a walk. But it is nothing to lose your temper about. I fixed the evening entirely to please you, and did my best to entertain our guest. I don't know whether she spoke more to me than to you, I didn't notice. And as for manners, yours weren't any too good either.'

'What do you mean?'

'I mean the way you received her, lying there sunning yourself and stretching up a hand.'

'She didn't mind that. She said don't get up.'

'Of course she said don't get up, after you'd said excuse me not getting up. What else could she say? Not that it mattered particularly – only if you're talking of manners, yours weren't exactly right. And they had the added effect of throwing her from the outset into my company.'

'You can say what you like,' said Nancy, 'but it doesn't alter the fact that you both addressed all your remarks to each other as though I wasn't there, and you showed plainly enough that you enjoyed her society. The only person who ever treats me like a human being is Jim Kirkup.'

And so on. Maddening woman!

5 July 1949

No more was said that day, and no more has been said since. She washed my socks in the afternoon: repentance perhaps? and has been quiet and apparently without rancour since.

13 July 1949

Heytesbury. I came on Monday with Queenie to stay with Siegfried Sassoon. An earthly paradise surely – great yellow-grey stone manor house, early nineteenth-century restoration, stone or brick, in its own grounds, 180 acres of park and wood, much of the wood planted by Siegfried fifteen years ago. Wonderful immense trees round the house, a copper beech of elephantine trunk and proportions, 200 years old perhaps, the great branches of which have had to be chained to the main stem to support their heavy aged grey limbs. I thought, for some reason, of Nancy's fingernail with the brown bruise on it when she pinched it in her window in Winchester House

166

before trying to kill herself. Thereafter I watched one vast elm nearby which has put down its branches like a banyan, other larger trees growing out of them where they have thrust into the earth. Rabbits, squirrels – Queenie in heaven – foxes, stoats, badgers too, but these I haven't seen. Divine place. Fine weather. An extension of this long rainless June and July which has now become a drought.

Siegfried sweet, kind, loquacious, absent-minded, lonely, dreadfully self-centred and self-absorbed. I like him very much, there is something very touching about his aged, beautiful, worn face, the light in the eyes dimmed from constant looking inwards. He scarcely ever meets one's eye – he never has, I think – but talks, talks away from one, from side to side, or into his lap or over one's head, always about himself, his life, his past fame, his present neglect, his unhappy marriage, his passionate love for his son. It is all intensely subjective (he scarcely ever asks one about oneself – a flash or two of effortful interest, but always reminding him about himself) and threnodic, it is a man who has spent years and years of loneliness, talking his thoughts at last aloud to an ear. It is all delivered in a low, mumbling, self-absorbed, almost inaudible voice, a whisper sometimes, very refined, accompanied by gestures of pain or feeling – hand on heart, clasping his face. I don't mind all this – I listen and listen and try to help him with sympathetic attention – but why is he like this? His name and fame are assured. Though his poems and his memoirs and heroic exploits may be temporarily out of mind and a new kind of experimental poetry has superseded his, his work has a permanent place in our literature and his name an everlasting glory in the annals of war. Curious of him to fidget and worry about his present phase of obscurity. Desmond McCarthy once kindly wrote to me about my *Hindoo Holiday* that it would be rediscovered and rediscovered like *Eothen*. That is a remark which is far more applicable to the work of Sassoon whose poems and books contain the authentic passion that nothing can quench or stale. Dear Siegfried, he has taken a wrong turning somewhere. There is no happiness in self, self as a permanent diet is melancholic and poisonous, it kills, one dies, as he is dying, talking, talking away about his lost fame, his loneliness, his domestic affairs – his aged, worn, fine face turned sideways, sightless, towards the window. Look at Morgan, with his fine perceptions and interest in people and things, his sensitive understanding, his sympathy, his selflessness. Ten years Siegfried's senior, he is eternally young, eternally gay, cushioned in fat – the fat of secure love and personal esteem.

With little more than I, of a literary output, his fame extends and expands, to cover the globe, because his mind remains alert and responsive to the world about him, whereas Siegfried, with his short, selfish mind, sinks and sinks.

I wish I could help him. What happiness he could confer and receive. He is not beyond it: look at his kindness to me and to Kirkup. True it is a self-flattering or self-indulgent kindness – we minister to his needs of being sympathized with, befriended, respected; but that is something. He is not yet a permanent deaf recluse, as he might very well be. I must help him. Indeed, he is a lesson and a warning I must profit by, for I myself could easily become like him. He with his son George, I with my dog Queenie – we both of us run for a fall. All our eggs are in these baskets. He would go mad, I think, if anything happened to his son. And what will happen to me if Queenie dies! These are wrong roads, they lead only to disaster, to death. Even if George survives, the happiness and closeness, and present intensity of Siegfried's present relationship with him can't last, this schoolboy love. And Siegfried has nothing to put in its place – he is fixated upon the child. Alas, these passionate attachments, how little they are.

18 July 1949

Difficult to write. Why? The house routine is that I have breakfast by myself at nine in the library, and do not see Siegfried until lunch at one. After lunch he usually disappears, to rest or do odd jobs. Tea at about 4.30, and thence onwards I have his constant companionship and ceaseless reminiscing flow of talk until bedtime. A walk through the woods in the evening, after supper. So into the day from nine till 4.30, six hours at most, for lunch takes about two, I have to pack letter writing, exercising Queenie, reading and noticing. No time in life.

Dear Queenie is in heaven. Her journey down excited her so much, and finding herself in this bunnyland, that, on our first night here, she shit in the house. Not in my room, of course, but in the best bedroom that communicates with it. The door was open unfortunately. I should never have known about it if Miss Benn, Siegfried's housekeeper, not understanding whether I wanted breakfast in my room or downstairs, brought it up to this adjacent room and, setting the tray down on a table, stepped in Queenie's very loose shit which Queenie, I must praise her, such an intelligent dog, had deposited on a dark mat by this table instead of on the beautiful, thick, white pile carpet which covers the floors of most of the rooms in the house. However, her forethought was of no avail, for Miss Benn, having unwittingly stood in it, then walked over the white carpet of my room and wondered how she came to leave brown stains everywhere. Coming upstairs after breakfast I found the poor woman trying to clean up the mess with ammoniated water – and Queenie, outraged to find a stranger in her bedroom, menaced her and even nipped her ankle as a warning. But Miss B. has been a kennel maid luckily and understands dogs, and forgave Queenie both her shit and her nip, explaining, and quite rightly, both away as excitement and jealousy respectively. I debated whether or no to tell S. of this mishap. Was inclined to do so, then decided against, it seemed like sneaking on my dear doggie.

How happy Queenie is, to find herself living, as it were, in the middle of Wimbledon Common, with rabbits even in the shrubberies which surround the great house; yet so devoted is the dear bitch to me that even the love and excitement of going round the corner of the house to the rose garden, 200 yards away, where rabbits congregate, is insufficient to take her from my side. She bounds off with a flirt of her tail and legs, then stops to look back. 'Come! Come!' she clearly cries – and if I don't she at once abandons the project and goes back with me into the house. But she whines and natters a good deal indoors, and tries at night to prevent me going to bed by seizing my socks or slippers and hurrying downstairs with them. If she can only lure me in this way as far as the french windows downstairs, chasing her, will she not be able to attain her object, which is to drop them and lure me out into the grounds and round to the rose garden rabbitry?

Wonderful to be here. How happy I could be in such a place, during the lifetime of my dog, with no BBC, and no relatives, or relatives and friends coming for weekends. Or any arrangement whereby one had no one round one's neck. I could write a fascinating book, I know I could, a Siegfried book, only better, because it would be truly honest, no evasions, no deceptions at all. Shall I ever do it in my flat, with Nancy? I don't think so, though I must try.

She let me go very pleasantly. No jealous hindrance or trouble at all. Saw me and Queenie off at Putney station and did not embarrass me with any discontents or tears, consideration itself. Perhaps I shall manage the life I want when I get back, or anyway when the autumn and its fires come.

This lovely place, this immense private property: how much does Siegfried enjoy it? Does he write? Read? What does he do at those times of day when I don't see him? Perhaps he scribbles about me in his notebook, as I scribble about him? At any rate, he is engaged in nothing of any size. And he is dreadfully lonely, no one to talk to. Why not? He could invite and give pleasure to countless people. I suppose he does not want disturbers of the peace – or indeed anyone who likes to talk more than he does himself. He will easily develop into a kind of eccentric hermit. He goes about in the oldest and shabbiest clothes, and mends them himself. Never goes out of his domain, except in his car to see George or shop in Warminster. Takes luminal every night, half a tablet. (Did country gents in the old days ever leave their parks and seats? Perhaps not. Why should they? With all they wanted inside. I have done all my rambling so far within the walls of Heytesbury, although there are nicer walks outside. Perhaps that is why our ancestors knew and understood so little of the lives and grievances of the country labourers. They never met them, except as servants inside the walls of their parks.)

But thinking of bringing friends down here at some future date, William [Plomer] crossed my mind as a man who would enjoy these peaceful surroundings, and perhaps interest and amuse Siegfried and his loneliness. I share many of S.'s interests: Fitzgerald for instance, no doubt much else. But William would be bored surely. He is a great talker himself, and how would he put up with S.'s monologues, that rambling talk, which is scarcely conversation for he makes no real effort to send it across the table or the room, but is more a self-communing which, one feels, he is not concerned whether his audience hears or not? He really asks me nothing about myself at all, my whole life is untapped by him, though I have now been here some ten days. Occasionally he demands my opinion of a person, a book or a subject, but does he listen to the replies? I feel that it is really a pretext question to enable him to tell me something that has happened to himself.

Jim Kirkup came for the weekend. S. is really the man who put me on to Jim. I had corresponded with the latter for some time and accepted or rejected his poems, but never met him. Then he sent his poems to S. for his opinion. Though they are far from being S.'s kind of poem, S. was impressed by some quality in them, and communicated with me, asking me to help Kirkup. So I invited him out (he was then in great financial stress), got to like him and he became a friend. I was curious to see him. So he asked him down while I was here. A strange invitation! First, would he come for the day? By a careful selection of trains, he would be able to stay here six hours. Jim agreed to come, and I said I would pay his fare. But what a journey for so short a time. However, details were left to be arranged until I arrived here and discussed it with S. and when I did and saw the great house with all its rooms unoccupied and an adequate staff, I wondered why S. could not offer to put him up for the night. The same thought occurred to S., who is a kind man certainly, and he himself said it seemed unfair to expect the chap to come so far for a few hours and he could be asked to stay a night. This, as I knew, presented some little difficulty to Jim, whose mother is in London on a rare fortnight's visit, which I also knew, but he said he could manage, and came. When, however, he asked S. about his train on the following day, S. said why not stay another night and go back Sunday. I suppose he wished to see K. first before committing himself to too much, but it would obviously have been more convenient to Jim to have had the complete invitation in the beginning. Then if he stayed till Sunday, why not the whole weekend – but S. felt he had done enough no doubt, and George was due to come on Sunday for the afternoon. Still, he chose a train for K. which meant a 5 p.m. bus, so that he overlapped with George anyway.

Much rain on Sunday, a frustrating day; I wished he could have asked Jim to stay yet another night. And why not? Three nights are not more difficult than two; but although he clearly liked Jim and enjoyed his company and was much impressed by him ('He's such a *gentleman*. He never put a foot wrong.'), I suppose he felt he had done enough. So Jim went off on Sunday afternoon.

S. did him proud while he was here, his best sherry (which we did not drink; I bought some gin) and a bottle each night of his best burgundy. But although he praised Jim to me with the strongest and most emphatic and immediate and unqualified praise – 'But I think he's an absolutely splendid chap, so intelligent, so good-mannered and tolerant. He's read so much – how does he do it? – and knows so much, and is so sensitive and cultured. And such a *gentleman*, . . . etc.' – he must have gathered these impressions subconsciously for he spoke *at* Jim, not to him at all, and did all the talking himself. A spate, as with me, of mumbled, tumbled, inaudible reminiscences, with much sniffing and throat clearing, full of 'sort of' and muttered, swallowed whispers, more as though he were speaking to himself, and hardly looking at Jim at all, but always over his head or over his shoulder, when his own head was not absolutely turned away. Jim, actually, was much impressed, fascinated by it all, for twenty-four hours anyway, reminiscences of Hardy, Firbank, Edith Olivier, Miss Moberly, Ross and so on, and seemed to hear more than I did; but then he sat nearer to him, not, as I do, at the opposite end of the table. I cannot eat when he is talking, for the noise made by my own jaws, crunch or munch I ever so carefully and slowly, entirely obliterates the sound of Siegfried's whispered monologue. But towards the end, even Jim got a bit bored, I think, the strain of listening is so great. Indeed, excepting for this effort, it is a quite effortless place and holiday. I need not talk, think or even walk – to mooch into a neighbouring field with Queenie is enough.

But S.'s self-absorption was well exemplified just before Jim left. He had his five o'clock bus to catch, and S. started to make tea for him at about 4.15. I go through this every day. He likened himself once to the White Knight in a moment of self-knowledge, and indeed, unless I jogged his mind or took a hand, one would never get tea at all. When he once begins on a subject, he rambles on and on and cannot stop, and quite forgets what he is doing. The electric kettle has to be brought down from his bathroom and plugged into a point in the library where tea, if it ever comes, is dispensed. This first step is eventually accomplished, and the lights, which the switch has also turned on, extinguished. The kettle eventually boils, but Siegfried is talking and doesn't notice. At length his attention, if I do not draw it to this fact, wanders there of itself. The kettle is then unplugged, and the tea things fetched, the teapot brought and hot water poured in and into the cups. When all are warmed, the teapot is emptied and tea put in. Then the kettle has to be replugged to bring it back again to boiling point. Once more it is forgotten. I go to make it myself. The tea is made; again it is forgotten while S. rambles on. I pour it. The cake has been forgotten. I fetch it. I cut it. I offer it – to Jim, to myself. If I had not taken these steps myself, poor Jim, with his bus to catch, would never had had any tea at all. As it was, a cup was not put before him until 4.45. There was a pile of sandwiches on the table. For whom were they meant? Jim? Or George? George we supposed, for I had given instructions to Miss B. at lunch that sandwiches were to be made for George. But they were for Jim. How kind of S. – but he had forgotten all about them, and did not come back to earth and notice them until after Jim had eaten his cake and there was only ten minutes to go. Jim then crammed one into his mouth.

'I'm sure you'll miss your bus' (they only go once an hour), I said, as I walked him to the gate.

'Oh, I do hope I don't. I don't think I could face going back.'

It had been a very restless, wet unsatisfactory day for him, with George about, and S. distracted – but he enjoyed himself nevertheless, and was much impressed by S.'s conversation, especially about poetry, an important subject, to which it took him a very long time to come. Jim said, 'He has really opened my eyes to the virtues of traditional poetry.'

I have often noticed how very shallow and ineffective self-criticism is. S. knows he talks too much. In his letters to me he has twice said, 'If only I can manage not to talk too much.' And he interjects often, into his monologue, such phrases as 'If you'll forgive me meandering on,' etc. Yet he has often spoken to me of people, [Ralph] Hodgson for instance, and some servant he had 'who couldn't stop talking', and 'what a bore it was' this ceaseless chatter, without even adding 'just like me'. I remember how S.P.B. Mais once said, 'Americans are so loud and noisy and vulgar' – a description exactly applicable to himself.

21 July 1949

One could fade away here, of course, like a plant, flower and fade and never be seen. It is the enclosed eighteenth- and nineteenth-century world. In all the houses I was brought up in, when one walked out of the front door one walked smack into the life of the world, passers-by, tradesmen, cars, one jostled against life; here no, one walks into such a vast Garden of Eden of one's own, pre- or post-Eve, that one is entranced and has not the desire to go beyond, to go out of the great gates, for all one wants lies inside. No adventures, therefore, except the adventures of nature, the turn and fall of the leaves, song of birds, encounters with rabbits, squirrels and foxes – no adventures here.

I have taken one outside walk only, to Warminster on Tuesday with Queenie over Scratchbury and Battlebury Rings, which I wanted to see. A mistake to venture into life. The walk was toilsome and alarming. A strand of electrified wire the other side of Cotley

Hill; I did not know what effect it would have on Queenie if she came against it, and north of Battlebury the army was having some manoeuvres. Guns and rifles firing, rattle of machine guns. A distant noise but Queenie was frightened. She wanted to go back and turned to do so, standing and asking me not to go farther; but I went forward and, her love being greater than her fear, she slunk beside me with her tail down. All creatures had gone underground from the noise. There was nothing for her to chase. A melancholy walk over these fine hills in our threatening world. By Battlebury we came upon the battle, smoke drifted round the spur, rifles fired, small mechanized vehicles ploughed across the fields below.

In Warminster I could get no lunch. Neither the Bath Arms nor the Black Horse would admit Queenie to the dining room. No dogs allowed. I asked the proprietor of the former what he expected people who came walking into Warminster with a dog to do with it if they required lunch. He was irritable and offensive.

'I've made a rule. No dogs in the dining room.'

'May I ask why not?' I asked.

'Because they're a nuisance. Do you know I once had a dog there that howled all through lunch!'

I said, 'But you might also have had a human being that howled all through lunch. There are some troublesome members of all species. Why penalize the majority?'

No good. No lunch. I ate some cheese sandwiches at the Anchor. And found that Queenie had stepped in some tar somewhere and that two of her paws were clogged and clotted with it, grit and stones embedded in it between her pads. Tiresome and dirty stuff. How to get it off? I asked an ironmonger, and he said turps and sold me a bottle of 'substitute' turps, some kind of alcohol. Doubtful about it, but Miss Benn did not think it would hurt Queenie, so I applied it to all her pads. It was certainly successful in removing the tar, but the poor girl resisted after a time – I quite poured it over her feet – and then, when I released her, flew about on the grass like a wild thing. I thought she was just playing, but she wasn't, it must have burnt the poor old thing. For two hours afterwards she was greatly distressed, hid in my bedroom, or ran about all over the house and garden like a cat on hot bricks, lying down and getting up, unable to find comfort anywhere, and panting and sweating profusely. I put olive oil on her feet then, but it didn't seem to help much, then warm water. In course of time the sting wore off. A day of adventure outside of the peace of Heytesbury, yes, but unpleasant adventure in this unpleasant world. I shan't walk out again.

Yet even inside one isn't safe. Each morning since, a single large gun has fired, near Battlebury no doubt, sounding far away like an anvil being heavily struck by a giant hammer at intervals, and Queenie's never gone out once. No more interest in squirrels and rabbits and the woods. It is firing now as I write, and Queenie has slunk away and is hiding in a privet hedge nearby, in which she has taken refuge. She is sitting there on the ground in the shade, nervous creature, frightened away even from my side.

23 July 1949

Siegfried's wife Hester descends upon us almost every other day from her own home some miles away. She had been told by the doctors not to come and worry him, but won't leave him alone. He can't bear the sight of her any longer and treats her with no pretence of even politeness. When first she came (and I had had from him the whole history of her character and their relationship and her jealousy and emotional domination of him and George) I encountered her by accident in the hall. An unheralded visit as usual, unexpected, but this black-clothed youngish woman with her pale, lined, ravaged face, dark lines beneath her eyes, could be none other than Hester Sassoon.

'Oh, hello Geoff – oh, it isn't Geoff – it must be Joe Ackerley. I'm so sorry,' nervous, embarrassed, embarrassing. She had mistaken me in the half-light for Geoffrey Keynes. I made some polite rejoinder and Queenie helped me out – as a diversion for a moment.

'I've some important business matters to discuss with Siegfried. Do you know where he is?'

Poor Siegfried, I thought. Her usual business. I indicated the closed door of the library beside us and said I thought he must be there, it was where I had left him.

'Siggy, Siggy,' she cooed, as she opened it.

Poor Siegfried, I thought again.

But he wasn't there. Indeed he was descending the stairs behind us with a tray and made a distasteful moue at me as I turned and caught his eye when he saw to whom I was speaking – a moue which she, also turning, must have caught. When she did speak to him, he kept his face averted. He could not bear to look at her. I took Queenie off for a walk. But she was to have tea with us, I found on my return.

Siegfried said, 'You'd better come and do the polite teatable stuff. Besides it will be a help to me not to have her to myself.'

Awkward business. S. had already told me that Hester had alienated his friends from him – Blunden and Morgan, who took her side, Rex Whistler whom she fell for and would not leave alone – so it was clearly a question of 'camps' for visitors like myself: the battle, the fifteen years' battle, was still on; I belonged in S.'s camp, to S.'s side, and must not traffic with the enemy. Not that I had any wish to do so, constitutionally wary and critical of women, and with the Nancy troubles still upon me, it is hardly likely that a sex which has never attracted me and seemed to me an inferior and troublesome gender, should have produced a specimen in this particular situation which would have seduced my allegiance in this my fifty-fourth year. And Hester, even more than Nancy, seemed to me at once visible as the embodiment of all the emotional vices S. attributed to her. Nevertheless, I am a polite person by nature, and would not have known how to be rude to her nor cared to be rude to her if I had known. Nor was it suitable that I should be anything but polite, never having met the woman before and having nothing personal against her. Yet politeness must be formal and limited, I saw, overstepping no mark; a difficult situation. I confess I could not help feeling sorry for her, sorry without sympathy. She had alienated her husband and her son in the same way, according to S.'s account, that Nancy had alienated all the people who were fond of her, or of whom she was fond, and one could not help a sad feeling for this woman trying to hold on still to something she had lost through emotions beyond her control, making teatable conversation to a husband in whose face and manner aversion and distaste were only too plainly writ, and who made not the smallest effort to help her carry this social situation off, and to me, a visitor, whom she must slightly suspect of having already been put against her. Her manner was therefore nervous, ingratiating, squirming – a painful exhibition to watch. Any other onlooker might well have thought that S. behaved callously, rudely – abominably; but who am I to criticize the poor fellow whose life has been laid waste by another Nancy who, luckily for him, has not played the trump card of attempted suicide? Life has taught me never to interfere in, never even to criticize, the emotional affairs of others; the bonds of love and intimacy produce in us something quite different from our normal feelings and conduct in ordinary social life.

A couple of days later she came again, to upset S. with some story about a woman neighbour of hers who had come over and started talking in a pointed manner about S.'s affair with ————, sixteen years ago! She had already seen S. apparently but he had disappeared by the time – teatime – that I arrived. (It was my fatal Warminster-walk day). I had tea with H. S. did not·appear until 5.30. Then he passed rapidly through the room with his yellow pullover and billhook without a word to either of us. It all made me very uncomfortable, and when S. made his next appearance, I went off to feed Queenie and escaped.

Had I upset him? I made an apologetic explanation afterwards – awkward for me, could not very well be rude to his wife, felt I had been rude to her on the previous occasion – trying to explain that I was *his* friend, but in an embarrassing position. He quite understood, I think: 'You *can't* be rude to a woman like that. She's hide-bound. Water on a duck's back,' etc. He was much upset over the ———— business – out of all proportion, I think. I spoke to him sensibly and carefully – so bad for him to upset himself – and he soon recovered.

Why was he so upset? Blackmail of his good and famous name? An odd, muffled man.

He told me he had once found a soldier asleep in the ditch in front of his house. S. had been out riding, and his horse, when he returned, shied from the object. S. dismounted and went to see what it was.

'Wonderfully good-looking chap,' said S., 'most beautiful, mild gentle sort of boy, I almost asked him back to tea.' This was at a time when he was particularly lonely.

'What *did* you do?' I asked.

'Well, of course, I didn't say, "Now young fellow! What are you doing here? Don't you know this is private property and you're out of bounds? Come on, clear off" (imitating a sort of blimpish old colonel) – I just said, "You know you oughtn't to be here, this is private property. If you want a nap, another time go up into the woods – but not just in front of the house." '

Would *I* have said this? Would Morgan? The rich are very strange.

I felt that he was thinking that I was drinking too much of his wine. He began very graciously, taking me down to the well-stocked wine cellar and asking me to choose what I'd like. But then, as time went on, I sensed he felt I was drinking too much – a glass of wine at a meal, not half a bottle, which I am used to. He was slower in bringing bottles up. And they turned into half bottles instead of full ones.

I said at last, 'S. dear, I can't go on guzzling your drink like this. You've been immensely generous over it. I'm going to buy some *vin ordinaire* for myself instead.' He made no demur. So I've been buying cheap wine myself lately – 7s. 6d. a bottle – and he takes a glass or half glass. He doesn't drink much himself owing to his ulcer. He never offers me sherry now. The rich are very strange.

Last night, speaking of Roderick Meicklejohn he said he liked him, but he was such a bore, he really felt he couldn't ask him down here. 'Also he'd drink up my cellar in no time.' Then he added, thinking perhaps of me, 'Not that I'd mind that, of course.' But he would. The rich are very odd. But we all are no doubt. I expect a boy like Freddie thinks *me* very odd and mean too.

S. bought a picture this week – a Copley Fielding watercolour. Some £300 he paid for it, just like that. An investment, he said.

He craves for continual praise and recognition. All his conversation is on the lines of 'When I was writing *The Infantry Officer*', 'I had just finished *The Fox Hunting Man*', etc. What chances has he to be Poet Laureate when Masefield dies, he wonders. And would he accept? He thinks not – too many worries and responsibilities. But he would. Why do they never broadcast readings from his books? Morgan, William [Plomer] and my other friends do not talk end-lessly about their works in this way.

S. has never been into his local pub, the Angel. A charming fifteenth- or sixteenth-century pub, with such nice people and such nice beer. Last night I went down there, and drank some beer in the courtyard – benches, wooden tables – and a farm labourer, about thirty-five years old, who was talking to some mates nearby, and got into conversation with me over Queenie, said, 'Why don't you bring the Captain down here sometimes?'

I explained about his ulcer and drink.

'I know him very well' said the man. 'And he knows me. He's a decent old stick.'

I walked back with him, very nice man, a shepherd. 'Tell him you had a word with Tom. He'll know all right.'

I told S. He did know. 'Wonderful chap. Salt of the earth. Known him for fifteen years. Captain of my cricket team. I love him. He's a real dear, absolutely selfless. Real gentleman. Unmarried, lives with his sisters, etc.' But I don't think he relished the 'decent old stick' compliment! I wonder why S. won't have a chap like that to tea, mix with his local labourers like Jack [Sprott] does, who goes to tea with them and they with him. 'They aren't my mental stature,' said S. when I hinted as some such cure for loneliness.

He isn't really interested in people, I think. Like Nancy. He's intensely egotistical, subjective. Yet he's very kind and nice, and can be charming. Doesn't mind Caesar pissing against the furniture, or Queenie eating her bones on his mats.

George showed me his butterfly collection while Jim was here. Drawers and drawers of the creatures in a beautiful cabinet. He clearly had a wide knowledge of them, and their names.

In the pub there is a little boy, younger than George, named Robert, who made a set at me the moment he saw me, came and talked, and struck up a friendship with me: 'When shall I see you again?' pinning me down every day to another meeting. He is related, I think, to the people who keep the pub, and is not at school at present owing to his having had measles and then pneumonia. Quite well now. Not attractive. Rather boring. A lonely little boy. He too caught butterflies, between his hands he said, sometimes he squashed them, sometimes not.

'Shall I show you my butterflies?' he asked me the other day.

'Yes, please.'

He ran into the house and came out with a paper bag which he shook out onto the table. A dozen or so dilapidated greeny white cabbage butterflies fell out on the table, many in bits. He too was very proud of them – they were all the same butterfly – and collected them carefully back into the paper bag when I had admired them.

'I shan't be able to see you tomorrow or Sunday. Will you be coming down here again sometime? Will you promise to come and see me if you do?'

I buy him lemonade and ginger pop.

25 July 1949

A fête yesterday in Heytesbury Park, by the gates. The parson asked Mrs S. to open it much to S.'s surprise and indignation, and she accepted. 'How could she do such a thing? Can you understand it? Coming here, the place she has been turned out of, opening a village fête in the grounds of her husband from whom she is separated. Can you imagine anything so tactless or in such bad taste? So insensitive. It really beats me. But she doesn't seem to have the least inkling of the inappropriateness, the odiousness of the situation, or of how distasteful it must be to me' – and so on, with many a shrug of irritation and exasperation.

S. gave as little help to the organizers of the fête as he could. He had lent his grounds, and excepting for showing the old electrician vaguely where he could plug in his loudspeaker, he took no interest at all, except a sardonic one. Hester rolled up, pretending exhaustion, but got up on the platform created for her, and read her speech – written by the parson – in a firm carrying voice. S. watched the proceedings sardonically from his bedroom window. 'There she is, sitting with a bouquet! Can you beat it? Just as if she were still mistress of Heytesbury. Extraordinary' – slapping his leg and laughing. 'And do you know, she expects me to go out with her, as though nothing had happened. Happily married couple, husband and wife, drawing unitedly on their villagers! That's what it should have been, of course, if she hadn't thrown everything away by her behaviour. I would have opened the fête myself, with my wife beside me. But how can she suppose that I should show myself with her now – a woman I've got rid of?'

So the fête proceeded, from 2.30 to late in the evening. Children's dances, maypole, a band, children's sports, skittles, aunt sallies, stalls of things for sale, and in the evening, when the soldiers came down from their camp, a tug-of-war and so on. I wandered out two or three times. It was a pretty Hardyish sight under the great beeches and the high blue sky. A perfect cloudless day. Most of the village was there. But S. never crossed his bridge to it, never put in an appearance at all, even after Hester had gone. She came in and had tea with him. I didn't know whether to join them or not. The atmosphere was obviously so strained. No pleasure for me. But what did he want? At last after some hesitation I joined them. He behaved towards her with nothing but exasperation and impatience – whatever he said practically inaudible. Most of the day he spent hacking down nettles and thistles with his billhook. Every nettle or thistle was Hester, no doubt. The fête was still in full swing before dinner and after a cold bath I wandered out again. The tug-of-war was just beginning. Hester had gone.

'So good of you to lend us your grounds for this,' said a middle-aged man.

'Good heavens,' I exclaimed, 'I'm not Mr Sassoon.'

What could the villagers have thought, Siegfried never appearing at all? He was reclining in his deck chair out of sight when I returned.

'The soldiers are having a tug-of-war,' I said. 'Care to come and see it?'

'No, no, Hester might turn up again, you never know' – then (since he really knew she wouldn't come back at that hour), 'Besides I shall only have to speak to a lot of bores whom I ought to have invited to tea. Anyway, I don't want to. I'd sooner sit here. Rather nice having a band round the corner, isn't it?'

I went down to the Angel for a drink in the evening. Does S. like me doing this? I don't know. Or care. Tom was there. Same conversation.

'Have a drink?'

'No, thanks. I don't drink much. Just a couple of pints. I like to go home respectable. You don't mind do you?'

Talk about Queenie. 'She is my best friend. My "George",' I said smiling.

'You a bachelor?'

'Yes. Are you?'

'Yes. I looked after my old father and mother till they died. I did my duty by them. They were good to me. So I stayed by them. I owed them that, didn't I?'

I said I supposed so.

He said he lived with his sisters now. More talk of Queenie. I remarked that it was rather a job in London when she was on heat.

'That ought to be made a crime, I reckon.'

'What ought?' I asked mystified.

'Dogs together in public. That ought to be made a crime.'

'No, Tom, why?'

'It's not nice to see.'

'Nice? It's just nature. What d'you expect them to do?'

'Well, I reckon it oughter be made a crime.'

'No, Tom, that's because you're a bachelor.'

I don't think he liked that. But it upset me. I looked at his large red face, with its small very bright blue eyes, rather jutting chin. Mad? Sexually inhibited and frustrated? Sexually mad? I wondered. He didn't offer to walk back with me this time.

When I got back S., stretched full length as usual on his library settee (he never seems to read or write, just to sit about or lie on his back doing nothing), said, 'I've been looking up your trains on Monday. They're not very good. The 1.52 seems the best . . . ' Was he annoyed with me for going out and leaving him? Odd man. I'd listened to him for half an hour before dinner, during dinner and for about an hour's stroll after it. That was enough. Too much.

At dinner he had said, 'I don't know what you can do for Miss Benn before you go. She's not the sort of person you can give money to. But something should be done for her after the way she's looked after Queenie . . . ' Was it his place to prompt me over that? It was actually a question I had already considered and intended to ask him about. His opinion and advice should have waited upon that, I think.

I said to him at dinner, 'Well, Siegfried, my dear, I've never had a happier, more peaceful and carefree holiday in my life. I can't tell you how grateful I am to you. It's been lovely, and I'm only sorry it's over.'

Siegfried's reaction wasn't, 'It's been very nice to have you, Joe. Great thing for me. Do hope you'll come again.' Instead I got a muttered speech to say, Yes, I'd had a fortnight here and there was no doubt that had done me a lot of good, just sitting about in the park and woods and I would no doubt feel the benefit of it when I returned.

I said, 'It's been better than that, for I've had such a nice host too.'

He seemed to shrink a little from this, and mumbled something I couldn't hear.

If S. mumbles, George shouts. It is as if he could not quite control his excitable voice, which gets away from him in a hysterical shrieking way.

27 July 1949

Home again since Monday afternoon. A few retrospective notes. S. was very nice my last evening and day, more thoughtful for me and my affairs, less preoccupied with his own. I rather fancy he said he was sorry I was going, but I couldn't quite catch it. His audible advice to me was 'Count your blessings. You've had a fortnight's rest and peace down here. You must think of that.'

Our last evening we were speaking of his post-1920 diaries – I was trying to think of something he could do to beguile the coming winter evenings. We discussed them. He said, after a muffled preamble to excuse the remark, 'I do think I'm a man in whom posterity will be interested.' He then gave a resumé of the peculiarities of his character, life and work which, taken together and with his unpublished diaries, would probably have this far-reaching effect.

Bunny and Ann had stayed ten days with Nancy and enjoyed it. Nancy had enjoyed it too. Why did she show such reluctance to invite them in the beginning? She didn't want me to go, I expect.

6 August 1949

Train to Oxford to stay with Stuart [Hampshire]. I don't think Nancy cares for me going off and leaving her alone again – though this time she has the dog – 'leaving her to look after the dog' she might translate it to suit her mood. But she says nothing, except that she revives this business of wanting a holiday herself, a week or a fortnight, by the sea if possible. Does she really want this, I wonder. Or is it the workings of jealousy? I try to keep an attentive and open mind, but can't decide. She still wants vegetarian accommodation, she says, rooms would do. I am to write to Dr Latto and ask: a thing she could easily do herself. But if Latto suggested rooms somewhere, would she go to them? The whole of the past drama turned on this dislike of living alone; would she willingly go off to the seaside for a fortnight to stay in rooms by herself – or a hotel even or anything else? I find it hard to believe. So I am reluctant to trouble myself. What a bore repeating the boring past of hunting for places she really has no intention of occupying.

When I left today she said, 'Have a good time.' Nice, yes, she's very good really, but of course she doesn't understand. I go to Oxford, as I undertake any such expedition, for many and complicated reasons. Not just simply because I want to and am off for a good time. If asked to name the things I really want, what should I enumerate? First and foremost to be with Queenie and go walking with her. Then to have the time and right conditions to get on with my reading and writing. Then to have plenty of drink. What else? To see my friends? Of course – but conflict arises at this point. I would obviously prefer my friends to come to me, or to permit me to take Queenie to them. But I am very sensible of the obligations of friendship, and see that it can't flourish without give and take.

Jack [Sprott], Stuart and so on want to entertain me in their places, not just visit me. Their visits must be returned. They give pleasure. So I go – as I feel I ought to go; but I leave Queenie behind. I want to and don't want to, I am torn. But I go. I go to give pleasure – I shall receive it too – but at a sacrifice. And it is a sacrifice which, for another reason, I intellectually make, because I think I ought, I ought to leave my dog, break away from her, it is part of the hard schooling I must go through to accustom myself to separation from her, so that when she dies, as die she must – and I constantly think of this – I shall have prepared myself for this final separation to some extent – so far as it is possible, by such actions and by taking thought, for anyone to prepare themselves for the death of a loved one.

16 August 1949

After perhaps too much gin and wine last night, between dinner and going to the cinema, Nancy reverted to former sorrows. She wished she could have a dog herself, something to be fond of and fond of her.

I said, 'My dear, not *two* dogs, that's out of the question.'

'I suppose so,' said Nancy. 'But I've got no one to be fond of at all and no one to be fond of me. No husband, no son, no dog.'

I said that Queenie was all right at times and better than nothing, a walking companion anyway. Nancy said it was no fun to take her out. Tiring conversation. She said as often before that I had made Queenie possessive and jealous by paying too much attention to her. I asked if she wanted a dog to do the same thing with, and argued about it. Either one wanted dog love or human love; I had chosen, stupidly I thought, the former. Queenie took the place for me of human affection. Apart from her I was just as emotionally lonely as Nancy. And I knew it was a mistake, for Queenie's life was of such short duration. I hinted that Nancy would be more sensible to get herself human devotion, and Jim [Kirkup] had said he wondered she didn't 'for she was such an attractive woman'.

'No one's likely to want me,' said Nancy, getting up and going into the kitchen.

My dog. Also my room. When I came back from Oxford where I'd stayed the weekend before last with Stuart, Nancy said she'd slept in my room, and how much nicer it was than hers. And this morning she said, 'I had breakfast in your room. It's so nice in there. So much cooler and airier than mine.' This kind of remark also seems to me insensitive. It makes me feel embarrassed and guilty – selfish to have the best room. Why not use it when I am not there and say nothing? That is what I should do.

My dog, my room, my holiday. Nancy still goes on about hers. How much she would like to go away. Folkestone is the present idea. But does she really want to go, or is it envy because I have friends who invite me? Leaning over the balcony last night for a moment after supper, she beside me, she said, looking at the beautiful calm river, radiant and beautiful under the warm blue evening sky, she said, 'What a waste of a beautiful summer to have spent it here in Putney!'

'You mean you would have preferred the sea?' I asked.

'Of course I would, or the country.'

What a curious remark for a woman to make who tried to kill herself in Worthing, a few months ago! She then went on to say how much she wished we'd had a bungalow somewhere by the sea, where Bunny and Ann could stay with her and I could come for weekends. Wendy again!

I said, 'But they wouldn't like it, you know. Bunny anyway. What use would the sea be to her? She can't bathe or walk. She would be bored stiff. Indeed, I don't believe she'd go. She is an old woman, and all her interest now, at the end of her life, is on seeing her friends and enjoying herself with them.'

Nancy argued about this: they would like it when they got there, it would be good for them, etc. Strange girl. Does she really think that *I* shall go darting down to the coast for weekends again, either separating myself from Queenie to leave her there, or taking her with me? And where does she think the money is coming from?

19 August 1949

Train for Sheringham. I told Nancy that if I were to keep my engagement with Jack [Sprott] and his mother, whom I have not seen for many years, I must go this weekend or the one after next, Jack's last in Norfolk. Nancy said: 'Then you'd better go this one, I should think.'

But how little one knows what is going on in people's minds, and how shocking it is suddenly to be shown the seething mass of

185

jealousy, envy, discontent and, yes, hatred that is damped down in Nancy's. I knew it was there, as this journal shows, from previous signs and hints, but she had managed to keep it in. Last night after two gins and a glass of red wine she decided to speak her mind.

'And you can tell Jack from me,' she said, 'that he should have asked me too.'

I was quite shocked. 'I don't think I'll tell him that, old girl,' I said after a pause.

She then said, 'And Siegfried should have asked me too.'

I said, 'But he doesn't even know you.'

'He didn't know Jim but he asked him.'

'But he did know Jim in a sort of way. Jim had been in correspondence with him. Why on earth should he have asked you?'

'I'm your sister.'

'But he hates women,' I said. 'He's going through torments over his own woman already. He's a sort of hermit. He would never have had you in the house.'

She took no notice of this. 'Then you should have suggested taking me away for a holiday yourself. You never thought of this. You never think of me at all.'

These remarks quite shatter me. 'Never think of her at all'! – and I begin to shake inside and feel like saying, 'You bitch!'

I said, 'Well dear, there are a number of reasons for that. One is that to go away with you doesn't seem to me a holiday. My idea of a holiday is a complete change, to get away from everything, you too.'

She said, 'It's all right for you, you go away and get a holiday and a change, but I never get away at all.'

I said, 'Well, I'm sorry about that, old girl. I don't have much of a change. My fortnight with Siegfried was the first break I've had for years. Usually I can never get away, owing to my work and my dog; excepting for my ten days in Italy and my fortnight with S., I haven't been out of London for more than a few days at a time since the war began. After all, your own life has been constant change really, even if you didn't care for it. I don't particularly want to take this long journey tomorrow. I only go because I think I should. And I hate leaving Queenie.'

'You, all you think of is the dog. You don't care about me. I've no friends, nothing.' She said, 'Well I suppose I shall have to go to Folkestone by myself, and I don't expect I shall be able to stand them any more than I did before. You seem to forget that I've only just come out of hospital – then to have to cope with all the chores here. It's pulled me down already. I'm nothing like as well as when I came.'

'But everyone thinks you look so much better.'

'Who's everyone?'

'Well, Jim, Bunny, John Morris, Mrs D.'

'Well, I'm not and I can't stand this life any more.'

'Do you find it awfully hard?'

'I hate it. Boring, dull, same old thing every day. What is there to like about it?'

'Well, you're looking after Queenie and me.'

'Great fun! Dr Post warned me that I shouldn't see anything of you.' (Warned? she took it as a sort of criticism of me, not as a caution not to interfere!) 'And he was right. You were quite different to me when you came to the hospital. I really thought you were fond of me and wanted me. You take no interest in me at all, and I've got nobody and nothing to be fond of. My life's absolutely empty.'

'You have Queenie and me.'

'Great fun!'

(This week I took her to a film on Monday, and another on Tuesday, and Jim was invited to dinner on Wednesday.) I said, 'I'm sorry, old girl, if it's so dull. I find it a bit dull sometimes myself and, if I could, I'd give up my job and retire, I'm so dreadfully tired of it. But I can't, you see. I have you and Bunny to keep as well as myself, so I have to go on. And, of course, my salary's not enough to do all this, and though I don't worry about it at the moment, a time is bound to come when I shall be awfully broke. That's why I really must write this book if I can, dull though it is for you. I hope it will make some money for me.'

I also said somewhere, 'I do the best I can for you, old girl. I give you money, roof, and occupation. And all my friends. I can't do more than that. You must have patience and courage. That's all life is. You must wait for things to grow. You've already attached one of my friends, Jim, to yourself, and there's that Mrs Campbell you like. Isn't that a good beginning? Things may grow from those. Other things will come along. You came here with nothing. It takes time to build a new life. But as for myself, I can't give you more than I can give. I must have my freedom and independence to work and write.'

'If Paul sends me that money he spoke of, would you mind if I went to live somewhere else?'

'No, Nancy, if you are unhappy here I should want you to go. I should hate to think you were miserable here. I could always look after myself. I always have.'

'I think it's an awful place and an awful flat – I hate this air, it's enervating – and as for that room of mine, I think it's absolutely awful, and how you expect me to get through a winter in it, I'm sure I don't know. I shall have another nervous breakdown, I expect. Yours is the only nice room in the flat. I hate this middle room too, it's always either cold or draughty.'

'You can shut the door.'

'It has to be left open for Queenie.'

'Nonsense, dear. Are you cold now? Shall I shut it?'

'No, there's no wind today. Anyway I don't like it. Yours is the only decent room in the place, it's the only one that gets the morning sun and it's absurd to say that mine's warmer. How you expect me to survive a winter in it, I don't know.'

'But it's warmer than mine in winter.'

'Of course it's not, yours gets the morning sun.'

'Yours gets it all afternoon. And faces west; mine faces east.'

'What's that got to do with it?'

'Well, quite a lot, you know. But anyway there's very little winter sun, and it doesn't warm one much at that. I was thinking of the gas fires. Yours is much warmer than mine.' (I forgot till afterwards that the last time she stayed, some years ago, in winter, she envied my (now her) room as 'the only warm room in the house'!)

'Well, I think it's a horrible place.'

'Well, dear, unluckily for you, not so for me for I like it, I've got to live here. You see it's awfully cheap – thirty shillings a week – and I haven't much money and one could never now find a place so cheap. Also it's near my work, I have to work, tired though I am of it, and couldn't afford the time or expense of living in the country or by the sea, even if a place could be found.'

I was so upset by this conversation that I couldn't get to sleep. Before going to bed I thought I would go out for some air – for our conversation had ended, and after a long, silent pause during which Queenie became playful and I played with her under Nancy's, I suppose, jealous and hateful eye, she cleared the table. I didn't help with the washing up. In an agitated way I packed my bag. Then I went and stood out on the verandah alone. I thought she might come out and say she was sorry. But no. She then prepared herself for bed and went into her room.

I said, 'Do you want to come for a stroll down the front with Queenie and me?'

She was doing her hair. She turned and looked at me through it. 'No, I don't think I will.'

I went alone. When I returned her light was out. I got to sleep at about 12.30.

What an awful woman! I thought as, feeling very cheap, I took Queenie out this morning and had a swim with her. Horrible, horrible woman. Poisonous. Corroded with jealousy and envy. What a pity she did not die. What a pity. What an idiot I had been to feel remorse over her before. But never again. If I had fallen into any doubts about her character before, they had vanished now. A bad woman. Useless, uneducated, with all her hatreds festering in her mind, wrecking everyone's lives, earning nothing but fear and dislike – Mother, even Dad, Mary, her husband, probably her son, me – not to mention the lost army of lovers, friends and acquaintances, how I wished she had died, how I hoped she would have a relapse soon and go back to her mental homes. She has made me feel guilty about all my interests, guilty to have my writing to work at, guilty to have my river room, guilty to be fond of my dog, guilty over my morning walks with her, guilty to have my friends' affection, guilty for taking a few weeks off. With fear and hatred in my heart, fear and hatred of this grievous woman whose 'love' was seeking to destroy me, I walked the common saying aloud to myself, 'The wicked woman. Horrible. Horrible.'

When I returned she was calm and mild. I had a feeling she was sorry. What is the use of being sorry when, over and over again, one indulges one's latent spites and jealousies and envies, and plants in the minds of others these stubborn everlasting seeds of fear and dislike? I could think of little to say to her. Luckily Mrs D. was working then. Nancy asked sympathetic questions about my journey – would I get lunch on the train, etc.? – and remembered to provide nuts for Mary Sprott. I tried to think whom I could turn on to her to enliven her lonely weekend – and later asked Myles to call. Queenie with a sweet, sad, understanding expression watched me pack my sack. Then with a sigh, put her head down on her paws. I kissed Nancy goodbye – far more affectionately than I felt, but then how does one behave to a schizophrenic? 'I hope you won't be too lonely' was all I could think of to reply.

25 August 1949

Nancy went to tea with an old, neglected friend of hers, Thora Hummel, today. I remember Thora during the war calling on Nancy at Lichfield Court, and Nancy making plans to avoid her. This handsome and troubled girl, working in Eliz. Arden's, obviously had a liking for Nancy and did her utmost to make friends with her – but to no purpose. Now, twelve years later she writes and tries again. Nancy didn't want to go – such a bore. I said Thora had taken so much trouble that she really should. Nancy suspected an *arrière pensée* – Mrs Hummel perhaps had a room to let: in fact there was no *arrière pensée* at all. Mrs Hummel was there and a Danish woman friend.

Nancy, telling me of it, said, 'I told them of my indiscretion.'

I did not understand. 'What was that?'

She hesitated a moment – I will say that for her. 'That I tried to kill myself.'

I said, 'Were they shocked?'

'Well, I made a kind of joke of it.'

'Were they shocked?'

'Well, I think Mrs Hummel was. Thora said it reminded her of a film called *Obsession*.'

How very odd. I remembered all the trouble, the worry and misery I had had. An 'indiscretion'.

'I made a kind of joke of it.'

I said nothing more. What does one say? What does it all mean?

11 September 1949

Last night after dinner, Nancy said, 'Oh, I do miss Jim [Kirkup]. Every time I think of him I have a pang. He was the only friend I had in this godforsaken place.'

The bitch! What does she mean by remarks like that? They are aggressive. Frustration and aggression. '*You*'re no bloody good' is implied.

As she came out of her room later while I was reading in mine, Queenie, who was lying inside my door, growled at her.

'Don't you come in here,' Queenie said, '*my* room.'

Anxiety for me: my dog's love, my friends' love, my holidays, my

room, my work – these are now all full of worry and guilt for me
– something *I* have and she hasn't and envies.

'Go on, why don't you bite me?' said Nancy sourly.

'Shut up, Queenie,' I murmured, but she wouldn't shut up.

Queenie not only menaces Nancy when she tries to enter my
room, but, if she herself is outside when Nancy goes in, hurries in
ahead of her, nipping her ankles on the way, to get in front of her
and obstruct her progress. These jealous ladies!

19 September 1949

I see there is a correspondence between tapeworms and my sister
– perhaps women generally. Tapeworms are two or three yards long
and composed of segments. A well-grown worm may consist of 800–
900 segments. Each of these segments is hermaphrodite, and though
it is not certain how fertilization occurs, it must sometimes be
incestuous. A ripe segment, ready to fall off the end of the worm,
contains 30,000–40,000 eggs, each already developed into a little
six-hooked embryo and protected by a shell.

To the worm's monstrous body is attached a blind and mouthless
head no bigger than a pin's, by a neck as thin as sewing cotton. But
how aggressive it is, grappling itself to the wall of its host's gut by
four strong muscular suckers, and a circle of rose-thorn hooks to
make doubly sure. What chance has one to get rid of a thing like
that? As it lives a long time – probably its length of life is only
limited by the death of the host. One man was known to keep the
same tapeworm for thirty-five years. It is stubborn, resisting all
attempts to get rid of it; even if you manage to get rid of the main
body, the head remains and soon grows a new one, inch by inch.
However, it takes no holidays, and Nancy is going off for one on
Wednesday for three weeks. Bunny comes to take her place.

28 January 1950

My dear tree, or part of it, my shrine on Wimbledon Common, has
been cut down. Walking there with Queenie on Tuesday, I suddenly
came upon it, my lovely tree, with one of its great legs lopped off.
I was dreadfully upset. I had thought of it as a possibility, though
not seriously enough, for owing to the fires on the common of last

191

summer which burnt large areas of bracken and some of the trees, some clearing of trees has been going on, trees felled, on the other side of the 'valley' from my shrine, and I thought once, looking over to where the woodsmen were working, I hope they won't hurt this tree, but it seemed so unlikely they would that I thought about it no more.

Then suddenly on Tuesday, I came upon it, this grand old birch, mutilated. I looked for the woodsmen to try to save the remaining leg, but they were nowhere to be seen, then or on the following day. And anyway, what does the other leg now matter, for the attraction of the tree was the leave it gave to walk through it, the way it opened its arms or legs to receive one. I am so very sorry – and the common has now lost one of its main interests for me. How could they have mutilated it, that grand old tree, the largest and finest in the woods. Unfortunately, partly owing to Morgan's illness, I did not go on the common last weekend, when the deed must have been done. Too late now.

Morgan was operated on for prostate a fortnight ago yesterday (the first cut) and the second and severest op. on Tuesday last. I see him almost daily. He is going on very well. Morgan and my tree, both were cut together.

4 February 1950

Called to see Leonard Woolf in his nursing home yesterday. Prostate, like Morgan. But he'd had his out in one go, Dr Millin. He went in on a Saturday, had the operation on Monday, was sitting up on Thursday, goes out following Monday, or midweek at latest. This all according to schedule, Dr Millin using all the surgical improvements for this particular op., of which Kenneth Walker told me. Leonard seemed very comfortable, was working – reading a ms. – though there had been a slight setback, for the catheter was taken out on Wednesday, but Leonard then peed through his tube, and so the catheter had to be put back.

Morgan went into his home on Monday, 9 January. Had first part of op. – old method, Dr Roche does not use the new technique – 13 January, second part of op. 24 January, and does not expect to leave the home for another three or four weeks from today. And he too was having a setback when I went on Thursday. His urine, which had come clear, had gone pink again, showing that the internal wound had not healed. Twenty guineas a week – or eighteen? – his nursing home fees will cost. Some 120 guineas before he is through, as against Leonard's forty at most.

Surely it is extremely reprehensible for a surgeon *not* to adopt technical improvements when they are available, proved and in use? I was quite shocked when I first heard, from Morgan himself, that Roche disdained them. Morgan said, laughingly, that the nursing home staff were – what was the word? – contemptuous of Dr Roche for doing the prostate op. in the old way. Leonard said he had made the most careful inquiries in his own case and had been told by his doctor that it would be simply idiotic not to have the prostate out, by the new technique, in one. Dr Millin says he has only three per cent of failures. I wonder what Roche's percentage is.

12 February 1950

I said to Nancy this morning, 'I'm wondering whether to ask John Morris over today.'

'Oh no, don't let's have him,' was her reply. This is her usual reaction to social engagements. She likes John, and there is plenty of food in the house, but she 'isn't in the mood'. Yesterday she wasn't well, she said, and stayed in, a slight temperature (cold) in the morning, which disappeared during the day. I asked her how she was this morning and she said Oh, much better: no reason at all why John shouldn't come.

A little later she said to Bunny, 'I put the joint in at quarter past ten this morning. It weighed over five pounds so it will take three hours.'

Bunny said, 'Twenty minutes to the pound, isn't it?'

'Yes,' said Nancy.

Overhearing this, I said, 'Then how do you get three hours?'

'Well, three pounds would be two hours,' said Nancy, 'at twenty minutes to the pound . . . '

She did not know that there were sixty minutes in an hour, so it took her some time to see her error. We shall have to have lunch at about twelve.

4 March 1950

Never a dull moment, I think to myself when I look back over four years with Queenie. What a rare thing to be able to say of any relationship.

That is why one is never free from anxiety and fear. Life is so insecure. Happiness is so insecure. At any moment, some disaster. Now, travelling to Notts., I look at my watch and say, 'She's having a fine walk on Wimbledon Common with Nancy.' Then I think, Perhaps at this very moment she has been run over and is screaming in her death agony.

Georges [Duthuit] said of dogs: 'How sad and frustrating for them: never quite able to say, to convey, what they wish and try to convey.'

Georges also said, about women: 'Each one believes herself to be the centre of the cosmos.'

12 March 1950

Nancy asked the time the other day. I didn't know and told her to ask on the phone. She said she never could understand what the voice said. I said, but it keeps repeating it. But she said she didn't understand. Unbelievable! But I see now that it's true. For *I* rang TIM in front of her yesterday since our watches were at variance, and said to Nancy, it is six and thirty seconds. Nancy, after a pause, said, 'What is that? Three minutes past six?' I suddenly realized that she did not know what a second was, or that there were sixty to a minute. Her ignorance is formidable.

On Thursday night I took Diana out to dinner. I know that Nancy was jealous of her, so I postponed telling her of the engagement until Wednesday, although it had been fixed some time before. I was taking Nancy to a cinema on Wednesday afternoon, and she said something about having bought a sheep's heart from the butchers. I said, 'By the way, I'm going out to dinner with Diana tomorrow.'

'Oh, are you?' she said. A little later she said, 'Well I wish you'd told me earlier you were going out. I wouldn't have bought the heart.'

I said, 'Can't you eat it yourself?'

'I never eat such things when I'm alone,' she said.

I said, 'Well you can stew it anyway, it will keep.'

Later she said, 'I see it's no good my going to the butcher's for offal like you asked me, if you're not going to be here when I get it.'

I said, 'The weather isn't sultry, the meat can keep. You could ask Jim Kirkup to come and eat it with you.'

She said nothing. All this about a sheep's heart, which doesn't cost 1s. I think.

I said, 'There are nicer things than hearts, anyway. They're difficult to cook. I've never managed to make one tender.'

Later she said, 'It's about time Diana asked me out, too.'

I said, 'She didn't ask me, I asked her.'

She said, 'I didn't know she'd rung up. I thought she was away.'

I said, 'She was away and she didn't ring up. I've been corresponding with her.'

She said, 'Well, it's about time she did something about me.'

I said, 'But she asked you out last, and you put her off.'

'She didn't,' said Nancy – but by this time we had reached the cinema, and I did not feel inclined to take up the conversation again afterwards.

Jealousy. Nothing else. And all mixed up with this feminine deceit and illogicality which I hate so much.

The broken glass: I have devised a number of exquisite tortures for little boys who break bottles, such as circumcising them with the jagged fragments, if they have not been circumcised already, or even if they have; but psychology is so tiresome that one simply doesn't know whether hurting people does not in fact give them pleasure and induce them to repeat the offence in order to get hurt again.

6 June 1950 (Sunday)

At Bob's [Buckingham] today the copy of the *Listener* with Morgan's portrait on the cover turned up, and we talked of it for a moment. I asked if it had yet been hung in King's and Morgan said, 'Oh yes, it was there at the end of the hall, with Roger [Fry] and Goldie [Goldsworthy Lowes Dickinson]' – 'Flimsy Corner,' he suddenly added and then burst out into peals of laughter as indeed did we all.

'Flimsy Corner,' I repeated, amused.

'Yes, I suddenly thought of the word,' said he.

It is indeed where he belongs, this strange, and wonderful man, not among the famous, the bishops and generals – elder statesmen and learned – the big guns, the big wigs – but in Flimsy Corner, with Goldie and Roger, greater than either, not of their calibre.

Take a grey dog, the colour of birch bark. Fashion her a jacket of black satin.

Then, owing to the brevity, the brevity and the indefinability, of the chance moment, there is a dreadful sense of urgency about it, of something to be caught, soon to be lost, the irretrievable moment – the moment one gets also in human relationships, the feeling that someone had at a certain moment something to say, something to give, something to hear, that at that moment one could have done something to alter the course of life or to understand something one had failed to understand before, but that for some reason, out of timidity or imperception, one let the moment go. So with this animal's heats, so brief, so strong, so transient, they leave behind a sense of remorse, of regret, of failure, of loss, of death – and this is enhanced by the change in her own behaviour, the softness and appeal in her eyes, the acute physical discomfort, and the passion of her panting assaults upon me – her dew claws. Then suddenly this wonderful flowering is over, the bud has closed, something has been lost – and now it is forgotten by her – but not by me.

A dreadful sense of opportunities lost, of the waste and passing of time, of growing old, of death, of *jeunes filles en fleur*, of *temps perdu*.

20 May 1950

When I told Nancy about Mrs Sassoon phoning up S. every night from Mull, with nothing but trumped-up things to say, and knowing that he could not bear her and hated the telephone, but unable to accept defeat of her marriage, Nancy said, 'I don't know how women can behave like that, forcing themselves where they aren't wanted; it's so undignified.'

20 December 1950

'How's your sister? All right?' asked the young lady (a fluffy, blonde, hardboiled little piece, I always think) in the tobacconist's the other

196

day. Something in her tone of voice seemed to make this question sound like a serious inquiry.

'Yes, thank you. Did you think she wasn't?' I asked.

'Oh no. I didn't think so. But things seem to happen so quickly these days. One day you're all right, and the next you're . . . ' she seemed to hesitate.

'Dead?' I supplied, but simultaneously she brought out, 'Not so well.'

The conversation seemed to me worth recording.

11 October 1950

'Are you lost or eternally saved?' This was on a sandwich board being carried out in Regent Street by a young man. I frowned at it, because it isn't really right to ask such intimate questions in public. The young man smiled.

'It's all right,' he said. 'It ain't meant for you.'

Be kind to dogs, dear reader; they deserve your sympathy and even gratitude. For they are the universal consoler. The love which was once lavished upon you or which you once so ardently sought and then found insufferable and escaped from, it is all now lavished on them. They have taken your place, and enable you to live in carefree independence and freedom elsewhere. But for them there is no escape. To extricate yourself from the possessive, jealous and interfering clutches of wife, mummy, sister or mistress, a number of courses were open to you – the army, the colonies, murder, the divorce court, or simply the train and desertion. But poor doggie, the univeral consoler *malgré lui*, has no such means. He mops up for you, in the slobber on his coat, the eternal tears of the world, tears of frustrated love, of grief, of rage, which you have caused to flow. That love from which you fled with a shudder, he is the substitute victim of it now. Anything you revolted against – loss of freedom, nagging, jealousy, emotional scenes and so on – the whole bag of tricks is your legacy to him. Do not hate or despise him: he is your saviour; he earns your pity and gratitude.

So when you see a lady dragging a little dog along on a string, think to yourself, 'There, but for the grace of God, go I.'

Oh, for the joy of coming back to an absolutely empty flat for a week or a weekend. But no. In spite of my every endeavour, *I* am the object of interest, and at every turn I am confronted with the one thing I most hate: permanent family life. They want to look after me; and I cannot bear being looked after. It is hell. They wash and iron my clothes, cook, make cakes and bread, darn and sew – and never leave the flat. Nancy has no friends – not a single one – and wants none. Bunny has a few, but can't or won't ask them because Nancy is always here, and Nancy has constituted herself Mistress of the House and wouldn't perhaps like the extra work.

Whenever I pass Leader's Garden of an evening, I think, Oh England! Oh civilization! This small square green retreat, conferred upon the citizens of Putney by that Mr Leader who once lived on Putney Hill, is closed every evening at four in winter, at 8.30 in summer. Enclosing it are tall railings surmounted with thin spikes for wounding anyone who tries to enter it. Oh England! Oh civilization! On a hot summer's night, or a mild winter evening, it would often be pleasant to go and sit there on the benches under the trees beside the river, or to take one's dog for a lark on the grass. But these things are not permitted. This, the only asylum in the district, is closed. I complain – and I know the answer by heart: people would steal the flowers, perhaps even the benches. Oh England! Oh civilization! They might even make love on the benches – a consideration I fancy, more important to our rule-makers than any other, though of course it is not named.

25 May 1952

Queenie's birthday today. Her seventh. How beautiful she still is – and still how young looking and active. Everyone remarks on her beauty and then they say, 'She's very young, isn't she?'

'How young do you think?' I ask.

No one guesses more than two years. Most people think she is under a year. And she has caught a rabbit every day this week, except Monday. How I wish it had been I who took her out. It is what I most enjoy. But this week I have had my Book Supplement, and have had to let my sister take her. My idle-minded sister has precisely the life that *I* would like to lead – and even could lead if I did not have to keep her. She takes out my dog, and sits all day upon my terrace sunning herself. So I could not take Queenie out

198

today, on her birthday, though I should have liked to. If I had, she could have eaten her rabbits – my sister takes them away. Women are bitches. But I took Queenie out along the embankment – at 5.30. There was much of the usual flotsam and jetsam on the ramps, driftwood and rubbish washed up by the tide, together with identifiable and unidentifiable dead creatures – dead fish, a fowl, a seagull, and some curious cheesy, or chalky lumps which had once been cats and dogs. Queenie peed on them all. There was also a human corpse, but farther down by the water's edge. Whether it was man or woman, or how it came there I don't know; it was a stiff shape covered in a brown tarpaulin, and a policewoman and river policeman stood beside it chatting together. I suppose they were waiting for the ambulance to come and take it away. A few curious onlookers stood staring hypnotically at it; I too stood and looked, wondering what lay beneath the shrouding cloth, and what once eager and hopeful life had come to this stiff, strange, lonely, waterside end. Queenie did not notice it or approach it. What would she have made of it, I wondered, if she had. Would she have pissed on it as she had pissed on sundry other dead things? Possibly. Indeed, the strange doughy or cheesy objects which I took to be dogs might, for all I knew, be portions of human anatomy instead. Then a sudden uproar arose, bawling and shouting, and round the river bend came two boats rowing a race, accompanied by the usual tug and mad people hurtling along on bicycles. All these extraordinary lunatics flew past us, past the dead fowl, the corpse, Queenie and everything else, shattering the silence and making the dead seem immensely dignified and wise.

Indeed, the animal is dumb. And what a good thing! This divine gift of speech! *How* people talk! And *what* they talk about! It might well be said that the less they have in their heads the more comes out of their mouths. Impossible to escape it. Wherever one goes talk talk talk, jabber jabber, and all about nothing. And when they have no one to talk to, they whistle. Read? Never, except newspapers and the digests, taking over as their own the ready-made opinions they have culled from such sources they yap yap yap about them from the cradle to the grave and say that they cannot endure dogs, because they are such noisy creatures.

3 November 1952

Victor and I took little Bernard, aged ten?, for a walk rabbiting. He is the son of an embezzler, serving some years in prison, a curious child with enormous blue eyes, rather uncanny. He begged to be taken. He was in war-like attire – Indian trousers made of sacking, gum boots and a metal rod which he said was a gun. We had not gone far when Tripp, the hotel dog, located a rabbit in a bramble clump and killed it. He took some time to kill it, owing to the thickness of the undergrowth in which they both were, so that he could not get at the rabbit properly. He is said not to be good at killing things anyway. Quick though he is to catch them. So the rabbit squealed and squealed.

The effect on Bernard was most interesting. He almost had hysterics. He was quite overwrought. 'No. No. Oh, look, look. Let me. Let me. There it is. Oh, stop it, stop it' – all that kind of exclamation; he tried to rush into the bush, jumped about, began to cry, pulled himself together, and every now and then looked into my face, gave a sort of smile, and then darted back to the bush again. All within a minute. Victor was very good with him. He commanded him firmly to behave, said he would send him home if he misbehaved, and pulling the still-alive though bleeding rabbit out of the bush, dispatched it with a single blow of his hand. Then he told Bernard that he must not be so silly, rabbits were vermin and had to be killed and that if he wanted to come hunting he must get used to it. Bernard recovered and wanted and was allowed to carry the corpse, but every now and then as we walked he remarked, 'I heard it squeal. I heard it squeal.' Later on, since it was awkward for him to carry it by its legs in his hand, we decided to tie my dog's lead to it so that he could sling it over his shoulder. Before doing this, Victor held the rabbit by its ears and shook it, so that the contents of its bowels and bladder fell out. Then he tied my lead round its legs. He pulled the knot tight. 'Not so tight! Not so tight!' cried poor little Bernard, thinking for a moment still that the rabbit was being hurt. Then he appeared to forget and became a mighty hunter, pretending to shoot more rabbits and birds with his metal rod.

Of course it was disgusting, say what one may about vermin, and *I* disliked it too, but life has inured me to its horrors. The episode will obviously be remembered by Bernard all his life. (Though he had wanted to come out hunting rabbits, he has always wanted a pet rabbit for his own.) Whether it will affect his life, and if so for good or ill, who can tell. It was certainly a frightful shock to him.

And vermin! How arrogant people are. Does the earth belong to them? Do not the rabbits think *them* vermin too, so to speak. And are they, in fact, not a greater menace to the whole living world than the rabbits themselves?

19 December 1952

I hire a dinner jacket suit to dine at Oxford. My women very excited at the prospect of seeing me once more, a rare sight, in such clothes. I explain that they will not have that pleasure, since the suit has to be returned next day. Bunny says, 'When I was in the concert world I often used to think how different evening dress looked on different men. You could always tell the men who were "of the people", they never seemed to carry it well.'

22 December 1952

The Movietone News this week had a Christmas feature. A large number of flustered turkeys were driven towards the camera, and the commentator remarked that the Christmas rush was on, or words to that effect. Next they were seen crowded about their feeding trough, making their gobbling turkey fuss, and the commentator observed, with dry humour (again I do not remember his exact words), that it was no use their holding a protest meeting, for they were for it in the morning. Similar facetious jokes followed them wherever they went, hurrying and trampling about in their silly way; for to make them look as silly as possible was no doubt part of the joke and easy to achieve: turkeys, like hens, like all animals, are beautiful in themselves, and have even a kind of dignity when they are leading their own lives, but the fowls, in particular, look foolish when they are being frightened.

These jolly, lip-licking sallies, delivered in the rich, cultivated, self-confident voice of one who has no sort of doubt of his own superiority to the animal kingdom, raised no laugh from the considerable audience, I was pleased to note. I took it from the silence that many other people besides myself would have been glad to be spared jeers and jibes at these creatures who, parting unwillingly with their lives, were to afford us pleasure at our Christmas tables. It reminded me of a shop window I noticed in Marylebone High Street, not many weeks ago. A whole calf's head was displayed upon a dish, and the tongue of the dead thing had been dragged out and twisted round into the side of its mouth so that it appeared, idiotically, to be licking its own lips over the taste of its own dead flesh. In order to make it more foolish still, a tomato had been balanced on top of its head. How arrogant people are in their behaviour to the domestic beasts at least. Indeed, yes, we feed upon them and enjoy their flesh; but does that permit us to make fun of them before they die or after they are dead? If it were possible, without disordering one's whole life, to be a vegetarian, I would be one; nothing could have been more disgusting and degrading than the insensitiveness displayed by these two exhibitions I have described.

Nancy to Bunny: 'Do you have to get up so late in the morning?'
    Bunny: 'Yes, I do. I'm old and get tired.'
    Nancy: 'Do you wish to be regarded as an invalid?'
    Bunny: 'Yes, I do.'
    Nancy: 'You are not much help to me.'
Bunny calls her the Sergeant Major.

'My kitchen maid has arrived,' Nancy said to the people serving in the local dairy, when Bunny walked in.

Nancy never suffers from remorse. I do.

Nancy to Bunny when Bunny is grieving over the sudden death of an old friend: 'He'd had a good innings, so snap out of it.'

22 March 1953

I said to Bunny this morning, 'What a lot you have been coughing dear; I have heard you often in the night and all this morning.'
    'Yes,' she said, 'I think it is a degenerative condition of the throat and chest,' and went on to say that she thought she would apply to Dr S. for some more vitamin pills. 'Degenerative condition': admirable old lady, to have applied the phrase so detachedly to herself, even to have known it at all. The right words – her generation was better brought up than mine.

Bunny said, 'How long are you going away for?'

'Two or three weeks,' I said.

'Then I shall be left with Sunny Jim,' said she.

'Who's that?'

'Nancy.'

'Is that what you think?'

After a pause she said, 'Joe, she's the most boring woman in the whole world.' After another moment she added, 'And I'm absolutely convinced she doesn't have the smallest feeling for me.'

28 July 1953

Lunch with Edith Sitwell at the Sesame Club. Osbert [Sitwell], Rose Macaulay, Rebecca West, Rosamund Lehmann, John Hayward, Geoffrey Gorer and Angus Wilson were also present. Afterwards Rose said that, for the second time, Rebecca West had remarked to her that it was extraordinary how like Angus Wilson was to Jane Eyre.

I love WCs as much as Queenie does. She reacts instantly to their odours and with her ears and tail high investigates their urinal runnels with such an intensity of emotion that I feel that at any moment she might roll in them. She is always on the verge, swaying towards them with delight and her shoulder down, but since the configurations of the floor are not really satisfactory for turning upon one's back, she usually contents herself with rubbing herself ecstatically against the porcelain partitions. She is in her element here, and I understand and love to see her amusing herself.

I enjoy them for other and more intellectual reasons. I like to see humanity demeaning and humbling itself. I like to think that in the shut-up shit-house boxes respectable persons are behaving in a way of which they are slightly ashamed. At Waterloo Station for instance I am often fascinated by the sight of the lines and lines of cubicles all full with the shadows of the shitters' coats hanging up against the glass panels from pegs, while some embarrassed young man, who is bursting for a shit, hurries self-consciously up and down the line, with his cricket bag in his hands, trying in vain to get in. Who are occupying all those shit-houses? I think to myself gleefully, and populate them, in my imagination, with all the people I most despise, the eminently respectable and blimpish, the black-coated high-ups, let us say, of the BBC.

Possibly Sir John Reith is shitting there, I think to myself, and Sir Basil Nicolls, and Sir Ian Jacob. I like to think of them all with their black-striped trousers down, sitting with their pale legs apart, having a GOOD SHIT, and I like this because I know that they would not like me to think it. It is the people who put up the greatest show of not having any cocks or arseholes, who regard such interesting objects as rude and shameful, that I like to think of as having to admit to them, the people who preach and moralize and censor, they are the people with whom I fill my WCs, the people who religiously wash their hands, even if they have only taken out their penises, as though they had done some disgustingly defiling act.

7 May 1954

When Nancy heard that her mother-in-law was dead she said, 'The old battle-axe is dead.' It was the name she had called her – the woman who, according to Nancy, had ruined her marriage – for twenty years. No human feeling. No thought of the awfulness of death, which she herself, in her fifty-fourth year, is approaching. Bunny would never have said a thing like that. She wrote to her doctor some weeks ago for some specific for the palpitations she sometimes gets. And received no answer. She said a fortnight later, 'I do hope poor Dr Sinclair is not ill!' To excuse, to be sorry for, people who may appear to inconvenience or neglect or be discourteous to her, would not occur to Nancy; she thinks instantly the worst of everyone. Bunny thinks the best.

Bunny remembers: Mother said about Nancy – 'One day when she makes someone happy.' Dad replied: 'She will never make anyone happy.'

Mother (quoted by Bunny): 'Don't let that woman come in. Don't let her near me. I can't bear her.'

'I don't want you to speak to Darny like that,' little Paul would say, weeping, when Nancy, at meal times, was being particularly offensive to Mother. (Bunny remembers this.) The child was very fond of Mother and Bunny.

Bunny was talking of Herne Bay last night – the life she led there with Mother and Granny and us three children, all very young then. Nancy, indeed, was born there. Rosemead the name of the house, on the seafront. What fun they had there, Bunny said, and

204

how nice and sweet Mother was, and how happy, before Dad put her into larger and larger horrors with maids and butlers. Rosemead was small, Dad was away all week (he had a bachelor flat in London), only coming down at weekends. Randolph (Bunny's husband) was also usually absent. They did not mind their husbands being away, and had all sorts of parties. One was a 'Servants'' party, with Granny dressed as a housekeeper, Mother as the maid, and Bunny as a seamstress. Guests were only admitted by the back door – the local people, doctors, etc. – and there were lots of cosy nooks to sit in, and decorations, and a cup, and a tipsy cake. We were all in bed of course. She spoke of Herne Bay with such happiness – a lovely life – with a pierrot troupe nearby and all sorts of amusements. When Nancy was ill with bronchitis, Bunny stayed up three whole nights, on strong tea, to relieve Granny, and sang Nancy to sleep. I asked her if she would have done that if she could have foreseen Wendy, and she laughed.

26 May 1955

Conversation at dinner about Paul Jr led to the discovery that Nancy could not remember the sequence of her English wanderings with him in the pre-war years. This unfortunately brought her to refer to her collapse and blame it for loss of memory.

Later when she and Bunny were washing up she said, 'I wish I hadn't been reminded of Graylingwell.'

Bunny said kindly, 'Oh, I shouldn't think about it, dear; it belongs to the past.'

'You'd think about it, I suppose, if it'd happened to you!'

Bunny said to me amusedly afterwards, 'Well, it did happen to me in a way, for I caught the brunt of it. Yet I don't think of it now much.' Then she added, 'She's always the person who has the grievance. A very comfortable state of mind to be in, I suppose.'

Bunny: 'Nancy called me a half-wit the other day. I said, "Well, half a loaf is better than no bread." '

Louis MacNeice told me that he once had an old-fashioned sheepdog who used to go to bathe and cool itself in a stagnant pool in the grounds which was full of dead leaves and other mouldering things. Dirty and with its heavy coat choked up with all this flotsam, his wife (his first wife) would not at last allow it into the house and made it lie in a kennel outside instead – a roomy, old-fashioned kennel of the Victorian kind. Louis was so sorry for the dog, to whom he was devoted, and himself so crushed and persecuted by his wife, that he would slip out of the house and, crawling into the kennel with the dog, spend the evening sitting there beside it.

8 August 1956

Upon the concrete verandah the bars of my cage are cast, cast by the sun as it sinks below the balustrades. How pretty the pattern they make, the bars of my cage. They lie beside me, bars of shadow, bars of brightness, on the concrete ground, they lie upon my body as I sit in my deck chair and upon the body of my dog beside me. We are within our cage together, the cage we have chosen, as happy as it is possible to be with death drawing closer.

9 July 1957

Symbionts are creatures (of different kinds?) that live together to their mutual advantage. Commensals are creatures that live together without injury and may or may not benefit from the association (*mensa* = table). Inquilines are creatures that live in the abodes of others and are not parasites. Parasites are creatures that live at the expense of their host and harm it.

Notes

p. 25 *my mother*: Gianetta (Netta) Ackerley, *née* Aylward. 1869–1946.

p. 25 *Queenie*: his Alsatian bitch, b. 1945, who appears as Tulip in 'My Dog Tulip' (1956) and as Evie in *We Think the World of You* (1960). With extreme reluctance, Ackerley had her destroyed in 1961, when she was so emaciated that she could hardly stand up and so incontinent that Ackerley was perpetually on his hands and knees clearing up and scrubbing.

p. 27 *Kingsmere*: a lake on Putney Heath, to which Ackerley frequently walked with Queenie.

p. 28 *my old aunt*: Bunny, d. 1961. Younger sister of Ackerley's mother, whom she outlived by fifteen years. She had early success as a mezzo soprano in concert hall and opera, but later was reduced to singing, usually on tour, in musical comedy. Married (1) a gambler, Randolph Payne, and (2) an inebriate doctor, Hodgson Chappell Fowler, whom Ackerley greatly disliked. She would often say, 'I'm afraid I've been unlucky with my men. But I've had a marvellous time.'

p. 28 *Bertorelli's*: a small restaurant, little more than a café, in Fulham Palace Road.

p. 29 *my father*: the story is told in *My Father and Myself* (1968).

p. 35 *General Charlton*: L.E.O. Charlton, 1879–1958. Chief Staff Officer, Iraq Command. Resigned in 1925 in protest against the British bombing of unprotected villages. Three years later he was forcibly retired. He wrote two volumes of autobiography and a number of books for boys. He once remarked of his sex life, 'One is always dreading the sound of parental hooves up the garden path.'

p. 35 *Freddie*: the former guardsman, whom Ackerley had befriended and then 'shopped' during the Second World War, and from whom be bought Queenie. The story is told in *We Think the World of You*. After a life of petty crime in his youth, Freddie settled down to respectability after marriage.

207

p. 38 *Siegfried Sassoon*: CBE, MC, 1886–1967. Poet and autobiographer. Married Hester Gatty, 1933. One son, George. Lived in Heytesbury House, Wiltshire.

p. 40 *Goldie*: Goldsworthy Lowes Dickinson, 1862–1932. Historian and philosopher. Elected Fellow of King's College, Cambridge, 1887; lecturer in political science there, 1896–1920. (See E.M. Forster, *Goldsworthy Lowes Dickinson*, 1934.)

p. 40 *Enrico*: an Italian sailor, met on the boat that took Ackerley out to India in 1923, and re-encountered in Turin in 1924. (See *My Father and Myself*, pp. 145–7, for an account of how Ackerley's deception was revealed when, on his visit to Turin, he told his parents that he was going, not there, but to Weybridge to stay with E.M. Forster.)

p. 40 *Demetrios*: Demetrios Capetanakis, 1912–44. Greek poet, who reviewed for Ackerley in the *Listener* and published poems (in English) in *New Writing and Daylight* and other periodicals in Britain. He died of leukaemia, aged thirty-two, much to Ackerley's shock and grief.

p. 44 *William [Plomer]*: 1903–73. South African poet, novelist and biographer. For many years literary adviser to Jonathan Cape. Having been extremely sociable, he became something of a recluse – a change that both Ackerley and Forster ascribed to 'glands', since he also underwent a physical transformation.

p. 44 *Henry Reed*: 1914– . Poet and reviewer.

p. 44 *John Morris*: 1895–1920. Officer in the Gurkhas. Controller, Third Programme, BBC, 1952–58. Author of various books of travel and reminiscence, the most famous being *Traveller from Tokyo* (1943).

p. 45 *Jack*: Walter John Herbert Sprott, 1897–1971. Called first 'Sebastian', then 'Jack'. Became lecturer in psychology at University of Nottingham, later professor. One-time lover of Maynard Keynes and intimate of Lady Ottoline Morell.

p. 49 *Lilian Bowes-Lyon*: 1895–1949. Poet, whose work Ackerley greatly admired and published in the *Listener*. Immune to pain-killing drugs, she spent several years in agony before her death.

p. 49 *Rose Macaulay*: DBE, 1881–1951. Poet and novelist.

p. 49 *Richard Jefferies*: 1848–87. Author of *The Gamekeeper at Home* (1878), *Wild Life in a Southern County* (1879), and *The Story of My Heart* (1883).

p. 49 *the Sprotts*: Jack Sprott lived with his sister Velda, who bred dogs.

p. 50 *Bob Buckingham*: Robert Buckingham, 1904–76. Ackerley was introduced to him in October 1929 by Harry Daley, when both Buckingham and Daley were members of the Metropolitan Police Force. Forster met Buckingham after Ackerley had done so – though he liked to maintain that it had been before – and the two men then became the closest of friends until Forster's death. Buckingham used to declare that he had never realized that Forster was homosexual until he made a confession near the end of his life; but it is unlikely that he could have been so ingenuous. He also professed to have been deeply shocked by *My Father and Myself*.

He married May Hockey, a hospital nurse, in 1931. He subsequently became a probation officer. The Buckinghams had one son, Robin, born in 1932, who died of Hodgkin's disease in 1962.

p. 53 *Wendy*: a bungalow, rented by Nancy West, in Beehive Lane, Ferring.

p. 68 *Miss Elizabeth Poston*: 1905– . Composer. The Poston family lived in Rooksnest (Stevenage), the house in which E.M. Forster spent the major part of his childhood and which he depicted in *Howards End*.

p. 68 *Georges*: Georges Duthuit, 1891– . French critic. He had been Nancy's lover for a brief period. One of the few heterosexuals to whom Ackerley was deeply attached.

p. 75 *my editor*: Alan Thomas, 1896–1969. Second editor of the *Listener* (1939–58). 'The best of editors' was how Ackerley often described him. He wrote a number of sober, even dull novels, and himself often struck strangers as being sober, even dull. But he was a man of quick sympathies, alert mind and wide tolerance. He would often sigh and shake his head over Ackerley's unconventional behaviour, but he was always loyal to him and would support him in any disagreement with the BBC.

p. 90 *'In tragic life . . . is false within'*: George Meredith, *Modern Love*, xliii.

p. 91 *Colon*: in Panama.

p. 92 *Harry Daley*: 1901–71. Joined the Metropolitan Police, 1925. The following year, while on duty in Covent Garden, he recognized Ackerley as the author of *The Prisoners of War*, then running in the West End, and spoke to him. A life-long friendship followed. Daley wrote an autobiography; but since, greatly to his credit, he refused to capitalize on his intimacy with people like Forster and Ackerley, no publisher was interested.

p. 114 *Morgan's story*: 'The Road from Colonus' (1903).

p. 123 *James Kirkup*: 1923– . Poet. Ackerley and Nancy were both closely attached to him.

p. 127 *Francis Bennett*: E.K. Bennett, 1887–1958. Fellow of Caius College,

Cambridge. Friend of E.M. Forster, who wrote an obituary tribute to him in the *Caian* (Michaelmas Term, 1958), after he had committed suicide.

p. 132 *Kenneth Walker*: 1882–1966. Surgeon and author of books on medicine, psychology, mysticism, etc. Reviewed for the *Listener*.

p. 132 *Dr Ed Glover*: Edward Glover, well-known psychoanalyst.

p. 136 *V.*: the Maharajah Vishnwarath Singh, Bahadur of Chhatarpur (1866–1932), the original of 'the Maharajah of Chhokrapur' in Ackerley's *Hindoo Holiday*.

p. 136 *Forrest Reid*: 1876–1947. Belfast novelist of boyhood. A close friend of E.M. Forster, through whom Ackerley met him.

p. 143 *Edwin*: Edwin Muir, 1887–1959. Poet and author of a splendid autobiography, *The Story and The Fable* (1940).

p. 144 *Cecil Day-Lewis*: 1904–72. Poet Laureate. Author of some highly successful detective stories.

p. 144 *Elizabeth Bowen*: CBE, 1899–1973. Novelist and short-story writer.

p. 147 *Diana*: Diana Petre, 1912– . Ackerley's half-sister. Her *The Secret Orchard of Roger Ackerley* perfectly balances Ackerley's *My Father and Myself*, to make a diptych representing their father's divided life.

p. 151 *the passions that had rent us all*: the story is told, with each of the characters ascribed a fictional name, in *We Think the World of You* (1960). Molly was Freddie's mother, Bob his father.

p. 152 *Geoffrey*: a man with whom Nancy had had an affair and whom she still saw occasionally.

p. 155 *Wyndham Lewis*: 1884–1957. Painter, novelist, poet and critic. Reviewed art for the *Listener*. Ackerley found many of his political views abhorrent, and his appearance and personality unattractive. But he had an enormous admiration for the power of his intellect and for his courage during the years of his increasing and eventually total blindness, the result of a pituitary tumour.

p. 167 *Desmond McCarthy*: 1878–1952. One of the first critics to recognize the value of Ackerley's work. Ackerley once remarked to F.K.: 'I may have been lazy about producing books. But at least I haven't been as lazy as Desmond McCarthy.'

p. 167 *Eothen*: (1844) by Alexander William Kinglake, 1809–91. A travel book that has eclipsed the vast bulk of the same author's *History of the Crimean War*.

p. 170 *Fitzgerald*: Edward Fitzgerald, 1809–83. Translator of *The Rubaiyat of Omar Khayyam*.

p. 172 *Hardy*: Thomas Hardy, 1840–1928. Novelist and poet.

p. 172 *Firbank*: Ronald Firbank, 1886–1926. Novelist.

p. 172 *Edith Olivier*: 1879–1948. Author of *The Love Child, Without Mr Walkley*, and *Wiltshire* in the County Book series.

p. 172 *Miss Moberly*: Charlotte Moberly, 1846–1937. With her friend Emily Jourdain, she wrote *An Adventure*, a now discredited account of psychic phenomena in Versailles.

p. 172 *Ross*: Robert Ross, 1869–1918. Writer on art, literature and drama. Loyal friend of Oscar Wilde. When he died of a heart attack, Sassoon remarked, 'It was the only time that his heart had ever failed him.'

p. 173 *[Ralph] Hodgson*: 1871–1962. Poet. Author of 'The Bull' and 'A Song of Honour'.

p. 173 *S.P.B. Mais*: 1885– . Critic and travel writer.

p. 175 *Geoffrey Keynes*: (Sir), 1887– . Surgeon and writer. Built up an unrivalled collection of Blake drawings and paintings.

p. 178 *Roderick Meicklejohn*: (Sir), 1876–1962. A highly cultivated civil servant. Private Secretary to Herbert Asquith, 1905–11. First Civil Service Commissioner, 1918–39. A clandestine homosexual, he disapproved of Ackerley's frankness on the subject – as he did of his tendency to dispense with a tie and carry a rucksack around with him.

p. 183 *Stuart [Hampshire]*: Sir Stuart Hampshire, 1914– . Philosopher. Warden of Wadham College since 1970. Ackerley often declared that the success of *We Think the World of You* could largely be ascribed to his having given it 'an enthusiastic shove' in a review in *Encounter*.

p. 192 *Leonard Woolf*: 1880–1969. Writer; husband of Virginia Woolf. Ackerley shared his hatred of religiosity and admired him for his critical acumen. It was largely Woolf who persuaded Ackerley to delete from *We Think the World of You* an explicit scene in which the hero goes to bed with his working-class lover. Woolf said that the passage was 'sexually naive'; but Ackerley wondered to F.K. if it were not Woolf himself of whom that judgement would be made. Later, however, Ackerley acknowledged that the excision had been artistically right.

p. 195 *Roger [Fry]*: 1866–1934. Art critic. Member of the Bloomsbury group.

p. 201 *to dine at Oxford*: with Stuart Hampshire.

p. 203 *Edith Sitwell*: 1887–1964. Poet. Ackerley cared less and less for her poetry as he grew older.

p. 203 *Osbert [Sitwell]*: 1892–1969. Poet and autobiographer. One of the few people with whom Ackerley never felt at ease.

p. 203 *Rebecca West*: 1892– . Novelist, critic and journalist. Ackerley admired her journalism; but he always suspected that she disapproved of his homosexuality.

p. 203 *Rosamund Lehmann*: 1901– . Novelist. She was one of the few women whom Ackerley admitted to finding sexually attractive.

p. 203 *John Hayward*: 1905–1960. Editor, anthologist and critic. Long confined to a wheelchair with muscular dystrophy. Shared a flat for many years with T.S. Eliot, until Eliot's second marriage broke up the ménage.

p. 203 *Geoffrey Gorer*: 1905– . Anthropologist and journalist. One of Ackerley's closest friends, whom he generally consulted about his work.

p. 203 *Angus Wilson*: 1913– . Novelist and critic.

p. 204 *Sir John Reith . . . Sir Basil Nicolls . . . Sir Ian Jacob:* Reith and Jacobs were directors-general of the BBC, Nicolls acting director-general, during Ackerley's period of employment.

p. 205 *Louis MacNeice*: 1907–63. Poet and BBC playwright and producer. Contributed to the *Listener*.

Index

Ackerley, Gianetta (Netta; J.R.A.'s
    mother)
  relationship with J.R.A., 25–6, 43–4
  Nancy's jealousy of, 55–6, 204
  Nancy lives with, 90, 92–4
  marriage, 95
  death, 98
Ackerley, J.R. (Joe)
  family background, 10–11
  love for Queenie, 11, 25, 26–7, 42
  relationship with Nancy, 12–14, 22,
    29, 94–9, 102–9
  character, 19–21
  relationship with his mother, 25–6,
    43–4
  holiday in Worthing, 31–3
  on death, 40
  and Bunny, 41–3, 46, 134–5
  on the working classes, 48
  Christmas 1948, 50–59
  and Nancy's loneliness in
    Worthing, 50–51, 52–68, 69–73
  and Nancy's suicide attempt,
    73–89, 109–13
  life at Wendy, 99, 102–7
  Bunny lives with, 107
  visits Nancy at Graylingwell, 113–
    16, 117–18, 130–33, 140–42
  suggests Nancy should live with
    him, 116–18
  and Nancy's relapse, 120–25
  feelings of guilt over Nancy, 125–
    30, 133–40, 189
  self-dislike, 135–7

Nancy lives with, 144–66, 184–98
plans holiday in Paris, 159–61
stays with Sassoon, 166–83, 186
goes to Oxford, 183–4
Nancy's jealousy of his visits to
  friends, 185–6
death, 7–8, 14–15
Ackerley, Peter, 10
Ackerley, Roger (J.R.A.'s father)
  marriage, 10, 11, 95
  second family, 11, 29–30
  and Nancy, 90–91
  in Herne Bay, 205
Allison, Miss, 65, 145
Ann (Bunny's friend), 60, 64, 118,
  136, 160–61
  stays with Bunny in Putney, 50, 52,
    58, 62
  and Nancy's suicide attempt, 74,
    76, 81
  Bunny goes to stay with, 98, 119–
    20, 144

Bachardy, Don, 12
Barnes Common, 29–30
Battlebury Rings, 173–4, 175
BBC, 107, 203–4
Benn, Miss, 168–9, 174, 182
Bennett, Francis, 127
Benous Hotel, Brighton, 160
Bernard (child), 200–201
Bertorelli's, 28–9, 100
Blunden, Edmund, 176
Bowen, Elizabeth, 144

Bowes-Lyon, Lilian, 49, 68–9, 161
Brighton, 13–14, 18, 98
Britten, Benjamin, 155
Brodie, Dr, 110, 111, 114, 121, 123,
    132, 139–40
Buchanan, Jack, 45
Buckingham, Bob, 18, 50, 51, 152,
    195
Buckingham, May, 50, 51, 152, 160,
    161
Buckingham, Robin, 51–2
Bunny (J.R.A's aunt), 34–5, 95, 160–
    61, 185, 201
    character, 11, 100–101, 102
    visit to Bertorelli's, 28–9
    Nancy's jealousy of, 31, 53–6, 59–
        62, 66, 101–2, 105, 202
    J.R.A.'s opinion of, 41–3, 46
    dislike of Freddie, 49
    Christmas 1948, 50
    and Nancy's suicide attempt, 75–6,
        81, 116
    goes to live with J.R.A., 98, 107
    life at Wendy, 99–103, 105–6
    goes to stay in Thornton Heath,
        119–20, 114
    relationship with J.R.A., 134–5
    visits Nancy at Graylingwell, 142
    ill-health, 202–3, 204
    in Herne Bay, 204–5

Cambridge University, 10, 195–6
Campbell, Mrs, 187
Cézanne, Paul, 156
Charlton, General Leo, 35, 92, 126,
    127
Chichester, 142
Christie, Agatha, 89
Clark, Kenneth, 15
Clark, Miss, 98

Daley, David, 18
Daley, Harry, 18, 92
Day-Lewis, Cecil, 144
Dickinson, Goldsworthy Lowes, 40,
    195
Drummond, John, 13
Duthuit, Georges, 68, 70, 85, 89, 126,
    159, 194

Eliot, T.S., 156

Evershed, Joan, 51
Evershed, Raymond, 51

Ferring, 99, 100
Fielding, A.V. Copley, 178
Firbank, Ronald, 172
First World War, 10
Fitzgerald, Edward, 170
Folkestone, 185
Forster, E.M., 114, 119, 114, 152,
    161, 178
    letters to J.R.A., 9, 15–16
    friendship with J.R.A., 10, 19
    on Queenie, 11
    on Nancy, 13, 126, 127, 129, 138,
        148, 162
    and Bob Buckingham, 18
    and Siegfried Sassoon, 39
    seventieth birthday party, 45, 67,
        68, 69
    Christmas 1948, 50
    advises J.R.A. how to cope with
        Nancy, 63–4, 75
    goes to America, 155
    dinner with J.R.A., 157–9
    character, 167–8
    and Hester Sassoon, 176
    prostate operation, 192–3
    Listener cover portrait, 195–6
Fowler, Doc, 49, 63
Freddie, 20, 35–8, 46–9, 76, 126, 147,
    150–52, 178
Fry, Roger, 195, 196
Furbank, P.N., 16

Geoffrey, 152, 160
Glover, Dr Edward, 132, 139
Gorer, Geoffrey, 203
Grant, Duncan, 10
Gray, Mrs, 70, 72, 74, 78, 84, 86–9,
    109–10, 111–12, 139, 141
Graylingwell, 110, 111, 112–16, 117–
    18, 120–25, 130–33, 140–42, 205
Greece, 16
Guy's Hospital, London, 132

Hampshire, Sir Stuart, 183–4
Hardy, Thomas, 172
Hayward, John, 203
Haywards Heath, 51, 52–9, 60, 62,
    128–9

214

Herne Bay, 204–5
Hextable, 145
Heytesbury, 166–83
Higham, David, 16
Hindoo Holiday, 10, 167
Hodgson, Ralph, 173
Hove, 98
Hummel, Mrs, 190
Hummel, Thora, 190

Irene (Freddie's wife), 136, 137, 147, 150–52
Isherwood, Christopher, 12
Italy, 99

Jacob, Sir Ian, 204
James, Henry, 164
Japan, 13, 16
Jefferies, Richard, 49

Keynes, Geoffrey, 175
King's College, Cambridge, 195–6
Kirkup, James, 17, 123, 143–4, 155, 157, 158, 160, 166, 168
Nancy's friendship with, 12, 187, 190
in Japan, 13
and J.R.A.'s death, 14
stays at Heytesbury, 170–73, 186
Kitchin, Clifford, 14, 15
Kyoto, 13

Latto, Dr, 98, 123, 183
Leader's Garden, Putney, 198
Lehmann, Rosamund, 203
Lewis, Wyndham, 155–6
Listener, 9, 10, 12, 14, 22, 144, 148, 195
London Magazine, 14

Macaulay, Rose, 49, 69, 144, 203
McCarthy, Desmond, 167
McKelvie, Ian, 18
MacNeice, Louis, 205–6
Mais, S.P.B., 173
Masefield, John, 178
May, Derwent, 14
Meicklejohn, Roderick, 178
Millin, Dr, 192, 193
Moberly, Charlotte, 172

Morris, John, 8, 10–11, 44, 127, 157, 160, 193
Movietone News, 201
Muir, Edwin, 143
My Father and Myself, 10–11, 15
Myles, 189

News of the World, 41
Nicolls, Sir Basil, 204

Olivier, Edith, 172
Orwell, Sonia, 7, 14, 16, 17
Oxford, 183–4, 201

Paris, 159
Payne, Randolph, 205
Petre, Diana (J.R.A.'s half-sister), 18, 147, 149
The Secret Orchard of Roger Ackerley, 11
and publication of *My Father and Myself*, 15
proposed meeting with Nancy, 152–3
gives dresses to Nancy, 161
dines with Nancy and J.R.A., 163–4
Nancy's jealousy of, 165–6, 194–5
Plomer, William, 44–5, 67, 92, 127, 137, 170, 178
Post, Dr, 147, 155, 187
Poston, Elizabeth, 68, 153
Pound, Ezra, 155
The Prisoners of War, 10
Putney Heath, 146
Putney Hospital, 98

Queenie (J.R.A.'s dog), 9, 10, 13, 36–7
J.R.A.'s love for, 11, 25, 26–7, 42
bites J.R.A., 26
daughter, 38
life at Wendy, 102, 103
on heat, 146, 147
Nancy's dislike of, 146, 147, 149–50
at Heytesbury, 167, 168–9, 173–5
seventh birthday, 198–9
death, 20–21
et passim

Raven, Simon, 17
Rawlings, Margaret, 155

Redgrave, Michael, 155
Reed, Henry, 17, 44
Reid, Forrest, 136
Reith, Sir John, 204
Richmond Theatre, 35
Robert (boy at Heytesbury), 179
Roche, Dr, 192–3
Ross, Robert, 172
Rota, Bertram, 15
Royal Academy, 147–8, 149

St Mary's Hospital, 127
Sally (J.R.A.'s half-sister), 15
Sassoon, George, 168, 170, 171, 172–3, 175, 179, 182
Sassoon, Hester, 39, 175–7, 179–81, 196
Sassoon, Siegfried, 41, 160
  character, 21, 167–8
  marriage, 38–9, 175–7, 179–80, 196
  J.R.A. stays with, 166–8, 170–73, 175–83, 186
  and James Kirkup, 170–73
Second World War, 10, 95, 96
Sendai, 13
Sesame Club, 203
Sheringham, 185
Sinclair, Dr, 204
Sitwell, Edith, 155, 203
Sitwell, Osbert, 155, 203
Sprott, Jack, 45, 49, 126, 145, 152, 155, 179, 183–4
  J.R.A. visits, 50, 185–6
  on Nancy, 127, 138
  and Irene, 136, 137
Sprott, Mary, 189
Sprott, Velda, 145
Sylvester, David, 17

Thomas, Alan, 22, 75
Thornton Heath, 98, 119–20, 144
Thwaite, Anthony, 14
The Times, 44
Tintoretto, 156
Tom (Heytesbury shepherd), 178–9, 181

Victor, 200
Vollard, Ambroise, 156

Walker, Kenneth, 41, 132, 139, 192

Warminster, 173, 174
We Think the World of You, 9, 10
Wendy (bungalow at Ferring), 53, 54, 56, 63, 66, 99–107
West, Jane, 92
West, Nancy (J.R.A.'s sister)
  birth, 10
  relationship with J.R.A., 12–14, 22, 29, 94–9, 102–9
  friendship with Kirkup, 12, 187, 190
  agoraphobia, 18
  character, 18–19, 89–91
  jealousy of Bunny, 31, 53–6, 59–62, 66, 101–2, 105, 202
  holiday in Worthing, 31–3
  financial problems, 32–4, 49–50, 93
  marriage fails, 32, 33–4, 91–2
  resents J.R.A.'s love for Queenie, 42, 146, 147, 149–50
  loneliness, 50–51, 52–68, 69–73, 128
  relationship with her mother, 55–6, 204
  suicide attempt, 73–89, 104, 109–13, 114–15, 129, 190
  life with her mother, 90, 92–4
  and her son, 94–5, 96–8
  lack of interests, 95–6
  ill-health, 97–8
  life at Wendy, 99–107
  at Graylingwell, 113–16, 117–18, 120–25, 130–35, 140–42, 205
  J.R.A. suggests she should live with him, 116–18
  J.R.A.'s feelings of guilt over, 125–30, 133–40, 189
  lives with J.R.A., 144–66, 184–98
  J.R.A. plans holiday in Paris, 159–61
  jealousy of Diana Petre, 165–6, 194–5
  jealousy of J.R.A.'s visits to friends, 169–70, 185–6
  and her mother-in-law's death, 204
  and J.R.A.'s death, 7–8, 14, 16–19
  death, 21
West, Paul (Nancy's husband), 32, 33–4, 68, 91–2, 97, 138
West, Paul (Nancy's son), 18–19, 68, 91, 92, 94–5, 96–8, 136, 138, 150, 204, 205

West, Rebecca, 203
Whistler, Rex, 176
Wilson, Angus, 203
Wilson, Mrs, 63, 106, 127
Wimbledon Common, 39–41, 46, 68, 114, 118, 122, 133, 137, 141–2, 191–2

Woolf, Leonard, 192, 193
Worthing, 31–3, 50, 65, 68, 69–73, 77–82, 109–13
Worthing Hospital, 75, 80–82, 85–7, 112–13, 141

Young, Mrs, 31

OXFORD

MORE OXFORD PAPERBACKS

Details of a selection of other Oxford Paperbacks follow. A complete list of Oxford Paperbacks, including The World's Classics, Twentieth-Century Classics, OPUS, Past Masters, Oxford Authors, Oxford Shakespeare, and Oxford Paperback Reference, is available in the UK from the General Publicity Department, Oxford University Press (RS), Walton Street, Oxford, OX2 6DP.

In the USA, complete lists are available from the Paperbacks Marketing Manager, Oxford University Press, 200 Madison Avenue, New York, NY 10016.

Oxford Paperbacks are available from all good bookshops. In case of difficulty, customers in the UK can order direct from Oxford University Press Bookshop, 116 High Street, Oxford, Freepost, OX1 4BR, enclosing full payment. Please add 10 per cent of the published price for postage and packing.

MY LIFE

Marc Chagall

Translated by Dorothy Williams

Chagall's *My Life* has established itself as a modern classic since it first appeared in English translation in 1965. The book is a lyrical and evocative account of the artist's early life; his childhood in provincial Russia, his first meeting with Bella, who was later to become his wife, and his struggles and later fruitful years as an artist in Paris. It also offers a fascinating insight into the shaping of the creative genius of one of the greatest of all twentieth-century painters.

'this unusual book has an idiosyncratic charm and suggests fresh interpretations of his art' *Sunday Times*

Oxford Letters & Memoirs

PAGES FROM THE GONCOURT JOURNAL

Jules de Goncourt and Edmond de Goncourt

Edited and translated by Robert Baldick

The brothers wittily describe many of the major French literary figures of the 19th century, including Flaubert, Gautier, George Sand, Victor Hugo, Rodin, Degas, Baudelaire, and Sainte-Beuve in this frequently racy read—Jules and Emond de Goncourt are always gossipy and often slanderous.

'It surely ranks as the most entertaining work of literary gossip of the nineteenth century.' *Spectator*

'The literary liveliness of the belle époque is exactly caught. Plushy, sleazy-sexy, cocottish, with the pox and the clap always waiting to pounce—yes; but the accompaniment to all this is a passionate and unqualified concern for good writing, and an abundance of power.' *Punch*

Oxford Letters & Memoirs

PACK MY BAG

Henry Green

Just prior to the Second World War, Henry Yorke (*nom de plume* Henry Green), at that time author of three novels, *Blindness*, *Living*, and *Party Going*, began to write his autobiography in the belief that he would not survive the war years. These evocative and sensitive memoirs capture that sense of urgency as Green turns his thoughts to his boyhood and early manhood. In particular he recalls on his Oxford years: the Hunt Balls, the libraries, the parties, the dons, the flappers, the solitary afternoon drinking or idle visits to the cinema. It is a world of aspirations and disappointments, hilarity and melancholy, sensitively described by one of this century's most talented authors.

Oxford Letters & Memoirs

LEAVES OF THE TULIP TREE:

Autobiography

Juliette Huxley

It was as a governess at Garsington, Lady Ottoline Morrell's mansion outside Oxford, that Juliette Huxley met the glittering Bloomsbury set, and among them her future husband Julian Huxley. She recalls the excitement and occasional chaotic moments of their courtship, and their later life together in London. She also describes with affectionate humour friendships with D. H. Lawrence and Frieda von Richthofen, Aldous and Maria Huxley, and H. G. Wells.

'This is the story of a real-life Jane Eyre, her romantic courtship and stormy marriage to a brilliant, masterful and ruthless Mr Rochester.' *Observer*

'Against a background of two World wars and enormous social change, Juliette Huxley's autobiography has a fascinating and at times sad immediacy.' *Times Educational Supplement*

Oxford Letters & Memoirs

MEMOIR OF A THINKING RADISH

Peter Medawar

Sir Peter Medawar is one of the greatest scientists of our day (recipient of the Nobel Prize in 1960 and the Order of Merit in 1981) and a brilliant, engaging writer on science for the general reader, famous for his series of essays now collected as *Pluto's Republic*, and two books, *Advice to a Young Scientist* and *The Limits of Science*.

Incisive and witty as ever, Sir Peter describes his life and times in richly anecdotal style, conducting us from Rio de Janeiro to the Rockefeller Institute, via Oxford and Birmingham, and introducing us to such characters as his extraordinary brother Philip, luminaries like Karl Popper and J. S. B. Haldane, and his wife Jean and their family.

'extremely funny . . . Peter Medawar was always one of the most humanly likeable scientific personalities.' Alex Comfort, *Guardian*

Oxford Letters & Memoirs

SELECTED LETTERS

Wilfred Owen

Owen's letters, almost all to his mother, constitute a self-portrait from childhood to the eve of his death.

'Moving and compelling.' *The Literary Review*

Oxford Letters & Memoirs

BLUE REMEMBERED HILLS

A Recollection

Rosemary Sutcliff

Rosemary Sutcliff is one of our most widely acclaimed novelists for children (and she has many adult admirers too). In *Blue Remembered Hills* she gives a moving account of the influences and the people that helped in her personal development as a writer.

'It is a remarkable book, not only for the clarity of her memory and for her determination to be honest, however painful the revelation, but also for her considerable powers of description.'
Caroline Moorehead, *The Times*

Oxford Letters & Memoirs

AN ENGLISHWOMAN IN INDIA

Harriet Tytler

Edited by Anthony Sattin
With an Introduction by Philip Mason

On 11 May 1857, mutiny broke out in Delhi and Harriet Tytler, eight months pregnant, with two children to look after, was forced to flee from the city. Yet when her husband, Captain Robert Tytler, returned to Delhi, she went with him, and for the next three months was the 'only lady' present at the so-called Siege of Delhi, sharing the dangers faced by the soldiers.

This is her story, not just the Siege of Delhi, but also of her childhood and travels in India and England: the record of a courageous, endearing, remarkable woman.

'extraordinarily vivid . . . should appeal to every type of reader'
British Book News

Oxford Letters & Memoirs